The First Book of

Windows® 3.1

The First Book of

Windows® 3.1

Jack Nimersheim

A Division of Prentice Hall Computer Publishing

11711 North College, Carmel, Indiana 46032 USA

For De, my oldest and dearest friend. (Somewhere along the way, De was converted into a Mac zealot. Hope springs eternal, however, and there's a good chance Windows 3.0 will compel him back to our side of the PC fence.)

Printed in the United States of America

Screen reproductions in this book were created by means of the program Collage Plus from Inner Media, Inc., Hollis, NH.

Publisher
Richard K. Swadley

Publishing Manager
Joseph B. Wikert

Managing Editor
Neweleen A. Trebnik

Acquisitions Editor
Linda Sanning

Development Editor
Jennifer Flynn

Production Editor
Katherine Stuart Ewing

Editors
Becky Freeman, Erik Dafforn, Bryan Gambrel

Technical Reviewers
Greg Schultz, Rob Caserotti, Sky Caserotti

Editorial Assistant
Rosemarie Graham

Production Analyst
Mary Beth Wakefield

Book Design
Michele Laseau

Cover Artist
Held & Diedrich Design

Indexer
Johnna VanHoose

Production Team
*Claudia Bell, Brad Chinn, Michelle Cleary, Mark Enochs, Denny Hager,
Audra Hershman, Betty Kish, Anne Owen, Juli Pavey, Cindy Phipps,
Joe Ramon, Dennis Sheehan, Louise Shinault, Kevin Spear, Bruce Steed,
Lisa Wilson, Allan Wimmer, Phil Worthington, Christine Young*

Contents

ix

X

xi

xii

Introduction

Everyday, millions of people struggle with their personal computers, trying to make sense of MS-DOS. DOS, arguably the most widely used operating system in the short history of computers, is about as much fun to use as a lug wrench. Start your typical IBM-compatible personal computer, and you're greeted by the infamous DOS system prompt, a marvelously obscure C> symbol, which doesn't provide a lot of information for a novice user.

Instead, imagine seeing true graphic icons on your DOS display. Imagine being able to load and run any DOS program—or alternately, Windows application—by double-clicking its corresponding icon. Imagine being able to organize all the programs and data files relating to a given project into a single, logical group and then assigning that group its own icon. Imagine being able to move a file around within a hard disk's directory structure by simply dragging its icon from one position on your computer monitor to another. Imagine being able to perform multiple tasks concurrently and even switch between them without interrupting what has gone before. Imagine being able to transfer data between different applications programs with a quick drag of an on-screen arrow and a couple of clicks on a mouse button. Imagine all this and more. Then you'll begin to comprehend the joys of working with Windows 3.1.

Now, imagine knowing what all those admittedly obscure buzzwords and procedural descriptions in the previous paragraph mean—even if you've never used Windows before. That's what this book, *The First Book of Windows 3.1,* is all about.

Over the course of the next 15 chapters, we'll examine what Windows 3.1 is, what it does, and what you need to do to take full advantage of this next phase in the ongoing evolution of personal computing. That's much ground to cover, to be sure, but we'll manage, and manage in a way that's comfortable and constructive for all readers, regardless of their level of PC expertise.

If you're a relative newcomer to personal computers or Windows, don't worry. I've designed this book to get you running and then gradually increase your understanding of how a graphical user interface (or GUI) like Windows can simplify most personal computer operations. Experienced Windows users, on the other hand, will find practical information in this book about the new features incorporated into Windows 3.1. Everyone, I hope, will find the journey from here to there educational, entertaining, and, who knows, maybe even enjoyable. After all, how much benefit is there in learning something new if an element of fun is not somehow incorporated into the learning process?

What's my overriding message about what Windows can help you accomplish on your PC? How's this: Windows is the wave of the future!

That sounds good to me.

Jack Nimersheim
Vevay, Indiana
January, 1992

Conventions Used in This Book

The First Book of Windows 3.1, second edition, uses some special conventions and features that make it easier for you to learn Windows. The following describes each special convention and feature.

To make your learning easier, we have incorporated certain typographic conventions. Text that you should type is shown in boldface monospace typeface, for example,

Type **SETUP** and press Enter.

When a term is mentioned the first time, it is displayed in *italics.*

In Windows, you see underlined letters in menus, commands, and dialog boxes. The underlined letter is the keyboard key that you press to activate a menu or command. In this book, the letter appears boldfaced rather than underscored: **F**ile. Note that to activate a menu, you must press Alt *and* the keyboard letter.

To help you learn about Windows and to emphasize important points, this book incorporates special features. Each feature has its own distinctive icon to help you identify it.

Quick Steps are step-by-step instructions summarizing the sequence of tasks needed to perform a common Windows procedure. The left column explains the actions you perform. The right column explains Windows' response.

 Tip: Helpful ideas and advice or shortcuts for a Windows command.

 Note: Practical, creative ways to use Windows to solve a business problem or perform a task.

 Caution: Potential pitfalls and problems.

XV

√ Check mark icons identify steps that accomplish a specific task.

Acknowledgments

How do you thank all the people who made completing a project like this one possible? That's the question every writer faces when the time comes to write acknowledgments. I'm always concerned that I'll overlook someone. If in this case, that someone is you, I apologize. Here, however, are those folks I haven't forgotten.

▶ Jennifer and Becky at SAMS. Guess what? We did it!

▶ All the good people at all the software companies and PR firms who sent me the various programs profiled in Chapter 13. There are simply too many of you to mention individually, so consider this a "group thanks."

> ► Doug Kilarski and Peter Otte, the editors of Vulcan's *Computer Monthly* and *Portable Computing,* respectively. These two guys financed my trip to Fall COMDEX, which is where I made initial contact with many of those good people mentioned in the previous acknowledgment.

> ► Finally, and as always, Susan and Jason, my wife and son. Living with any writer is no easy task. Living with this particular writer is no exception to this general rule. They take it all in stride and in the process, make my life wonderful. (For these two, I don't mind getting maudlin.)

Trademarks

All terms mentioned in this book that are known to be trademarks or service marks are included in the following listing. In addition, terms suspected of being trademarks or service marks have been appropriately capitalized. SAMS cannot attest to the accuracy of this information. Use of a term in this book should not be regarded as affecting the validity of any trademark or service mark.

Crosstalk is a registered trademark of Digital Communications Associates, Inc.

dBASE is a registered trademark of Ashton-Tate Corporation.

Etch-A-Sketch is a registered trademark of Ohio Art.

IBM is a registered trademark of International Business Machines Corporation.

Lotus and 1-2-3 are registered trademarks of Lotus Development Corporation.

MS-DOS, Microsoft, Microsoft Windows, Microsoft Windows Paint, Microsoft Windows Write, Microsoft Word, and Microsoft Paintbrush are registered trademarks of Microsoft Corporation.

Novell is a registered trademark of Novell, Inc.

PC Paintbrush is a registered trademark of ZSoft Corporation.

PostScript is a registered trademark of Adobe Systems Incorporated.

WordPerfect is a registered trademark of WordPerfect Corporation.

Part One

Getting Started

The three chapters comprising Part One describe what you could call Windows Itself—that is, the graphical user interface Windows positions between you and your computer's operating system. Individual chapters in Part One contain information on what Windows is and how you can use it to simplify many of your personal computer operations. You also learn how to install Windows on your computer. Finally, Part One contains information on the procedures used to initiate specific activities during a Windows session.

Welcome to Windows

In This Chapter

- ▶ *An explanation of Windows*
- ▶ *The contents of the basic Windows package*
- ▶ *The features added to Windows 3.1*
- ▶ *The hardware you need to run Windows*

What Is Windows?

Let's start by discussing the most obvious answer to this question. Specifically, Windows is a program designed to run on personal computers that use the MS-DOS operating system—or to use the terminology commonly applied to such computers, an IBM or IBM-compatible PC. As is true of any computer program, Windows consists of a series of coded instructions. These instructions, in turn, make the computer that Windows is running perform a special operation, using precise and predetermined procedures. In this respect, Windows is much like other computer programs that also run on MS-DOS systems (for example, Lotus 1-2-3 or dBASE, to name but two popular application programs). Beyond this simple comparison, however, Windows is more than either Lotus 1-2-3 or dBASE. This is true, not because of what Windows is—a program designed to run on an MS-DOS personal computer—but because of what Windows includes, how Windows works, and what Windows is designed to accomplish.

Have you ever heard of a Chinese puzzle box? This is an intriguing little brain twister that consists of one small box inserted into a slightly larger, second box, which then fits within a third box (only slightly larger still), which then fits within a fourth box, and so on. Windows incorporated a similar structure in that it is, in actuality, several programs sold as a single package—programs within a program or a "Chinese puzzle program," if you please.

For example, the basic Windows package includes its own word processor, Write. Although it is not as powerful as a stand-alone word processor such as WordPerfect, Write can be used to compose and edit fairly complex documents.

Windows also includes a telecommunications program, a module that it refers to as Terminal. Again, you won't be able to do all the things with Terminal that are possible with a more advanced (and more expensive) program such as CrossTalk. Still, Terminal is surprisingly flexible and might surprise you with what it can accomplish. Perhaps even more important, Terminal is always available and only a few keystrokes away whenever you're in Windows. The basic Windows package includes other application modules as well, all of which I get into more completely in Part Two, "The Windows Accessories."

"Okay," you might be thinking, "So Windows is a bunch of different applications sold in a single box. Big deal! How does that make Windows any different from any other integrated package?" In truth, it doesn't. Now, however, let me tell you something that differentiates Windows from every other stand-alone PC program or integrated package. Let me tell you about the "real" Windows.

Will the "Real" Windows Please Stand Up?

All the attributes I've described to this point are icing on the electronics cake compared to Windows' most important feature. For beneath its bundled application modules, beneath several additional utilities I've not yet mentioned (but will, as this book progresses), beneath everything else that makes Windows special, Windows is, first and foremost, a *graphics-based operating environment.*

Exactly what does this strange buzz-phrase mean? I'm glad you asked. In essence, it means that Windows (the Windows environment, as opposed to the bundled applications, utilities, and accessories also included in the Windows package) is capable of managing other PC programs—not just those bundled with the basic Windows package. It also manages any additional applications you use regularly on your IBM or IBM-compatible PC. Windows manages these other programs by presenting a visual interface that you use to communicate with your PC. This is what truly makes Windows a *graphical* user interface.

Figure 1.1 shows a typical MS-DOS display screen. Not very impressive, is it? In fact, it's downright dreary. To tell the truth, DOS is a boring operating system. Even the most dedicated DOS advocates—a group within which I hold a charter membership—find it difficult to argue that DOS, a utilitarian but admittedly ambiguous operating system, offers much in the way of assistance for the inexperienced PC user. Let's face it, the information contained in Figure 1.1 does not indicate what you are expected to do next if you expect to accomplish something concrete with your PC.

5

> **Note:** DOS is one of those generic terms used to describe several variations on the same theme. There's MS-DOS, Microsoft's version of its venerable operating system, and PC DOS, IBM's "official" version of MS-DOS, and DR DOS, an MS-DOS like operating environment from Digital Research. Windows runs under all these operating systems. To avoid clutter, I'll refer to either MS-DOS or use the generic term DOS throughout this book to indicate DR DOS, MS-DOS or the latter's electronic sibling, PC DOS.

Now, feast your eyes on Figure 1.2. A pretty impressive display, isn't it? It also happens to be a display that's fairly typical of what you see when you get Windows 3.1 running. To put it bluntly, Windows looks good—especially when compared with the uninspired appearance of Figure 1.1 or what I refer to as "naked DOS."

```
(C:\) dir /w

 Volume in drive C is MS-DOS_5
 Volume Serial Number is 1749-6011
 Directory of C:\

[AOL]          [BATCH]        [CAPTURE]      [COLLAGE]      [CONFIGS]
[DOS]          [DOWNLOAD]     [DV]           [HIJAAK]       [MSDIAGS]
[PCPLUS]       [QEMM]         [WIN31]        [WS]           PRINT
PRINT2         WINA20.386     MIRROR.BAK     AOL.BAT        AUTOEXEC.BAT
COMMAND.COM    TREEINFO.DT    SETCOM.EXE     MIRROR.FIL     BOOKEXER.GRP
AUTOEXEC.HLD   CONFIG.HLD     NWINAUTO.HLD   NWINCONF.HLD   NORTON.INI
BOOT.LAY       TREEINFO.NCD   BOOKEXER.QAG   CONFIG.SYS     HIMEM.HLD
[HOLD]         CONFIG.OLD     AUTOEXEC.OLD   CONFIG.000     AUTOEXEC.000
[DOCS]         HIMEM.SYS
        42 file(s)      187725 bytes
                       2648064 bytes free

(C:\)
```

Figure 1.1. Dreary DOS.

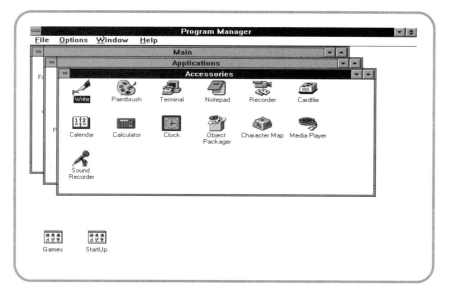

Figure 1.2. Wonderful Windows.

Most experts agree that graphics-based environments are the wave of the future for PC operations. People want more information about what goes on inside that black box called a personal computer than tired, antiquated, boring DOS provides. Windows, on the other hand, puts a whole new face on your PC to provide this higher level of information. As a rule, Windows offers assistance in the form of prompts and dialog boxes to help you accomplish something with your PC. Consequently, Windows is easy to learn and intuitive to use. In fact, working in Windows can actually be fun. Throughout this book, you'll discover how fun Windows is as we examine some of the various Windows features. For now, we still have some fundamental ground to cover, beginning with an explanation of why Windows might be the ideal graphics-based operating environment for people who already own an IBM or compatible PC that uses MS-DOS.

Windows Does DOS

For all its inherent shortcomings, MS-DOS excels at one thing. It supports more, and more varied, types of hardware and software than any other operating system that has appeared since the dawn of the so-called computer age. Either DOS has something of value to offer, or 60 million people have been bamboozled by one of the most successful scams in human history. It would be a shame if all this time and money ended up being wasted because someone decided the only way to put a new face on our PCs was to replace DOS with an entirely new operating system.

The good news is that Windows doesn't demand this sacrifice. Because Windows itself runs under DOS, it's capable of peacefully coexisting with the rest of the DOS world. Chances are that the IBM-compatible hardware sitting on the table in front of you runs Windows fine, just as it is. See all those MS-DOS application programs lining your bookshelf? They also have a few good years left in them. That's because Windows was designed to supplement rather than supplant DOS.

Windows places itself between you and the admittedly minimalist design of MS-DOS. Consequently, you no longer need to memorize a series of complex commands to get something done. Rather, as I demonstrate shortly, with Windows you can accomplish many tasks by managing and manipulating visual elements on your PC's display screen. Stated simply, Windows makes DOS look good. As a wise person pointed out, however, looks aren't everything. To be truly helpful, Windows must do more than merely spruce up the appearance of DOS with pretty pictures. Don't worry. It does.

More Than Pretty Pictures

Did you notice all those stylized illustrations in Figure 1.2? There's that two-drawer file cabinet near the upper-left corner, located in a partially obscured box marked "Main." One of my favorites is the artist's palette and paintbrush, which can be found in that portion of the screen labeled "Accessories" in Figure 1.2. These are but two examples of *icons*, pictures that represent actual programs.

As potentially useful as icons are, however, they represent only one of many enhancements Windows brings to DOS. There are other enhancements. Perhaps the most impressive is the manner in which Windows transforms usually cryptic DOS into a truly interactive operating environment, one in which information on the exact steps required to perform a specific operation is always at your fingertips.

Let's Get GUI

The computer industry thrives on acronyms—those cute, little nonwords generally derived from a technical and totally obscure phrase someone, somewhere, came up with to identify his or her latest digital brainstorm. (In fact, MS-DOS itself is an acronym, one that stands for the Microsoft Disk Operating System.) It shouldn't surprise you, therefore, to discover that there's an acronym used to describe what a program like Windows is and what it does. That acronym is GUI or "gooey," for those of you into phonetics.

GUI stands for *graphical user interface.* Stated simply, a GUI is a graphics-based program that can be used to organize and manage other PC operations. As a rule, working in a GUI such as Windows offers the added attraction of simplifying these operations by converting the procedures required to perform them into a series of interactive steps rather than a list of commands typed at a system prompt. Let me give you an example of what I mean.

Suppose that you wanted to relocate a file in one directory on drive C (or hard disk) to a different directory on a second hard disk, drive D. The series of commands required to perform this operation on a DOS machine without Windows would resemble the following:

```
COPY C:\DOS\ANSI.SYS D:\WINDOWS

DEL C:\DOS\ANSI.SYS
```

The first command line in this sequence makes a duplicate copy of the specified file on your drive D hard disk, placing it in a directory called \WINDOWS. Because DOS doesn't have a MOVE command, the DEL command is required to remove the original file from its initial location—that is, the \DOS subdirectory of drive C. Admittedly, the procedure I've outlined here is not terribly complex to someone familiar with DOS. For those of you just learning how to use your PC, however, DOS provides no assistance in determining the exact steps required to perform even this simple move (or more correctly, COPY/DEL) operation. With Windows running on your PC, however, the situation is quite different.

9

Figure 1.3 shows a Windows *pull-down menu*—specifically, the File menu from File Manager, a Windows utility represented by the two-drawer file cabinet icon shown in Figure 1.2. Pull-down menus are only one way in which Windows simplifies using your PC. Instead of forcing you to type the precise DOS command required to initiate an activity, you use pull-down menus to tell Windows what type of operation you want to perform. Windows simplifies many operations even more through its use of *dialog boxes,* interactive display prompts that you use to verify or where necessary, modify information Windows presents about the activity you are performing. A pull-down menu gets its name from the fact that the user "pulls it down" with the mouse, and then selects an option from that menu.

Figure 1.4 contains the dialog box that appears when you select the **M**ove command from the pull-down menu shown in Figure 1.3. (Unlike DOS, with Windows, you can move a file directly from one location to another without the required two-step procedure outlined earlier.) Notice that Windows itself is aware already of most of the information it needs to complete the requested **M**ove command. For example, Windows already knows what file you want to move and where that file is currently located. (You'll learn how Windows determined this information in a later chapter; for now, take my word for it.) All you need to do to complete the **M**ove command, therefore, is supply Windows with the information specifically requested by the dialog box shown in Figure 1.4—that is, the location you want this file moved to. Thanks to this interactive design, where selecting one option causes Windows to request any subsequent information it needs to perform the specified operation, Windows might be the ideal operating environment for beginning PC users.

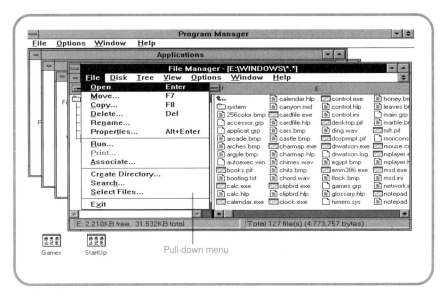

Figure 1.3. Windows provides pull-down menus to simplify operations.

Experienced users, too, can profit from incorporating Windows into their daily PC operations. As the Move option outlined in the previous example demonstrates, Windows supports some procedures that can't be performed directly in DOS. For this introductory tour of the Windows environment, I purposely selected a relatively simple example. The deeper we delve into Windows 3.1, the more you power users will realize how flexible and powerful the new and improved Windows GUI can be.

In other words, we've barely scratched the surface when it comes to demonstrating what Windows can do. Please have patience. After all, we're only halfway through Chapter 1. Besides, before I get down to the details of how to install and use Windows 3.1, we need to cover some general ground.

10

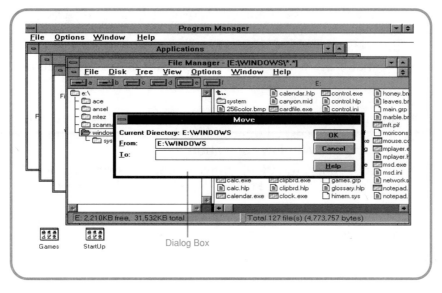

Figure 1.4. Windows dialog boxes request needed information.

The Windows Advantage

Windows 3.1 provides a number of advantages over working in what I earlier referred to as "naked DOS." These include

▶ A special setup program that automates most aspects of Windows installation.

▶ A graphics-based user interface that includes true graphical icons. These icons can be used to initiate most Windows operations with simple "point-and-click" mouse procedures.

▶ The capability of modifying your Windows environment as you add new equipment and programs to your PC.

▶ The capability of organizing program and data files into logical groups, regardless of their physical location on your system disk drives.

▶ The capability of performing file-related operations—copying, moving, deleting, and the like—using on-screen icons.

▶ True multitasking of both Windows and standard DOS applications when Windows is installed on a system with as little as 2 megabytes of RAM.

▶ Compatibility with a number of popular networks, including Novell, Microsoft LAN Manager, LANtastic, and IBM PC LAN, among others.

▶ A built-in macro recorder, so you can record keyboard and mouse sequences, which can later be used to automate virtually any Windows operation.

▶ Printer support for a wide range of popular printers, including Hewlett-Packard, PostScript, or compatible laser printers.

(Don't panic if you're confused by some of the "technobabble." Everything will be explained as you read along.)

As I stated earlier, Windows is more than just a visually attractive enhancement for standard DOS. The basic Windows package also includes a number of useful application programs and utilities, designed so that you can begin working immediately in the Windows graphical environment. These include

Write	The Windows text editor.
Paintbrush	A graphics program based on the popular PC Paintbrush program from Z-Soft.
Terminal	A telecommunications program, so that you can communicate with other personal computers, electronic bulletin boards, and commercial information services from within Windows.
Calendar	A monthly calendar and daily electronic appointment book you can use to organize your time more efficiently.
Cardfile	A flat-file database for organizing and managing information on your PC.
Program Manager	The "main" Windows program. Program manager helps you switch between programs and customize the way you work with your programs.

| File Manager | A program that helps you manage file tasks such as copying, moving, renaming, and deleting files. |
| Print Manger | A program that helps you manage your printing tasks. |

Windows 3.1 also has a number of utility programs that we cover briefly, including a calculator, a notepad, and a macro recorder. For more courageous users, Windows 3.1 has included an object packager (for linking data objects to icons), and a sound recorder and media player (for playing sound and video on your personal computer).

You'll examine each of these, and many others, as you learn more about the Windows environment and the applications it is designed to run. Before getting into the specific steps involved in using this impressive graphics-based operating environment, however, it might be a good idea to take a look at the equipment you need if you want to use Windows effectively on your PC.

13

What You'll Need to Run Windows

I alluded earlier to the diversity that exists in the MS-DOS community. This is not mere hyperbole. If you need to get something done, chances are that someone, somewhere, produces a piece of hardware or software capable of doing it. More often than not, this piece of equipment was designed to run on an MS-DOS computer. As is often the case, however, this convenience carries with it an accompanying curse: As more (and more varied) products enter the DOS marketplace, you need to be especially careful to purchase only those PC tools that work properly on your PC.

You do not have the same problem with Windows, however. About the only prerequisite for running Windows 3.1 is that, due to Windows emphasis on icons and other visual elements, your PC must include a graphics display.

Beyond this single caveat, the type of system on which you choose to run Windows is precisely that, your choice. I don't mean to imply, however, that all PCs are created equal. They aren't. Consequently, the specific hardware installed in a given system influences how well it handles Windows.

We'll look at some specific examples of how certain hardware components influence the Windows operating environment in a moment. First, let's list the basic equipment you need to run Windows 3.1.

The minimum hardware requirements for Windows 3.1 include:

▶ An 80286, 80386, 80486, or higher IBM or IBM-compatible personal computer.
▶ 640K of random-access memory (RAM).
▶ The MS-DOS operating system, version 3.1 or higher.
▶ A hard disk with 6 to 9 megabytes of free space.
▶ One 3 1/2- or 5 1/4-inch high density disk drive (needed to install Windows on a hard disk from its distribution diskettes).
▶ A graphics monitor.

14

To get the most out of Windows, however, you probably want to install it on a system that exceeds these minimum requirements. In some cases, you might choose to equip your system with a more powerful variation of one of the components listed previously, as would be the case if you installed a VGA (Video Graphics Array) rather than a CGA (Color Graphics Adapter) monitor on your system. The best way to enhance Windows' performance is to add a few "extras" to this basic system, additional hardware components that make Windows easier to use or to increase its capabilities. Let's look at some of these variations of the basic Windows theme and examine the different ways in which they can improve how well Windows performs on your PC.

PCs, a Potpourri of Power and Price

Personal computers come in all shapes and sizes. An 8088-based PC/XT system like the original IBM PC is now considered almost an anachronism—the Model-T of modern PC technology. Newer, faster, and more advanced systems have been introduced at a breakneck pace since the PC/XT's initial introduction in 1981. Today's so-called "fourth-generation" systems (that is, personal computers based on Intel's 80486 microprocessor) are capable of running over 50 times faster than the original PC/XT.

Of course, the type of PC on which you run Windows is your decision—a decision that probably is based on how much power you need and even more important, how much money you can afford to spend. The critical point to realize here is that Windows runs on any DOS-based personal computer with at least a 286 microprocessor. Although Windows runs on an 80286-based with 1M of memory, most "experts" agree that a 16-MHz 386 5K system with at least 2M of RAM represents the minimum platform on which Windows performs acceptably.

Display Options

As pointed out in the previous list of Windows' "bare-bones" system requirements, Windows runs on any monitor capable of generating graphics. Unfortunately, the PC marketplace is overflowing with graphic alternatives, which makes picking the right display for your Windows operations anything but a simple task. Over on the color side, you can choose from the CGA, EGA (Enhanced Graphics Adapter), or VGA "standards." For people who don't feel the need for color, a Hercules-compatible video card and monitor should suffice. In fact, a Hercules-compatible display might represent the most logical choice for a number of reasons.

15

First, aside from the "golly gee" factor of being able to generate pretty tints and hues, a color monitor does not contribute that much to your overall PC productivity. Second, the resolution of a Hercules display—and, therefore, its image quality—is actually higher than either the CGA or EGA standard. Finally, a Hercules-compatible display card and accompanying monitor can be purchased for under $100. Unless color is mandatory for your Windows operations, I strongly recommend you go the Hercules route. If you are looking for quality but can't afford color, try a monochrome VGA monitor.

Of Mice and Menus

If you allow yourself one luxury item when gathering the hardware for your Windows system, make it a mouse. Although it is possible to run Windows exclusively from your computer's keyboard, doing so is comparable to reaching for the hand brake each time you want to stop a car. Sure, this technique works and might even be required in an emergency, but who wants to go through all that hassle when a better and more convenient alternative is readily available.

A GUI like Windows is suited ideally for the kinds of "point and click" operations at which a mouse excels. Selecting menu items and initiating operations from the Windows display is simplified greatly when a mouse is available. Furthermore, if you plan to work extensively with graphics applications like Windows' Paintbrush accessory or other similar programs, a mouse crosses over the line from being a luxury item to becoming a real necessity. A mouse's capability of emulating paper and pencil simplifies using such programs.

Windows can use virtually any PC mouse designed to be compatible with MS-DOS systems. The type of mouse you own is one of the items you specify during Windows installation, as explained in the next chapter, "Getting Started."

 Caution: If you own an IBM PS/2, you will need to use a PS/2 brand mouse.

Printer Power

You also will need a printer if you wish to generate a permanent record of any work you perform in the Windows environment. The quality of those printouts will be determined by what type of printer you choose.

Given Windows' reliance on graphics, one of two types of printers seem a logical choice for a Windows-based PC: a dot-matrix or a laser printer. Because Windows includes a driver capable of supporting over 150 popular printers in these two categories, the actual brand of printer you buy is up to you.

Modem Madness

A modem puts your PC in touch with the rest of the world. One of the built-in Windows accessories, Terminal, requires a modem to run properly. You also will need a modem if you plan to install any other communication packages in your Windows environment.

Modems come in two basic types: internal and external models. An internal modem plugs directly into one of the expansion slots located inside your PC's system unit. External modems communicate with your PC through a standard serial port; these modems sit outside your PC. Keep in mind, however, that should your system include a serial mouse, you will need two serial ports in order to install both a mouse and a modem. Windows 3.1 supports modem communications on COM (serial) PORTS 1 through 4.

A second consideration when selecting a modem for your system is the maximum data transfer rate that a modem supports. Commonly referred to as a modem's *baud rate,* this specification determines the speed with which your system is able to exchange data with another PC. Common transfer rates for PC communications include 1200, 2400, 4800, and 9600 baud, with the first two being the most widely used. Windows supports modem communications anywhere within this range.

Additional Hardware

17

Personal computers are extremely flexible. Given their modular nature, you can customize a DOS-based PC to include a wide variety of hardware options—called *peripherals,* in the PC vernacular. The items outlined previously represent merely the most common hardware components that can be found on many PC systems. They are by no means the only ones you can attach to a personal computer. Although none of the following additional peripherals are addressed in this book, you should know that they exist and are compatible with Windows.

Other peripherals you might want to incorporate into your total Windows environment include

- ► Alternate "mouse input" devices (for example, a joystick or a trackball).
- ► An A/B switch, so you can use a single serial port for multiple purposes.
- ► A printer buffer.
- ► A network board.

Windows can recognize several popular PC networks, including any networks that adhere to the Novell, 3Com, LANtastic and IBM PC LAN STANDARDS.

During installation, Windows itself assumes responsibility for determining much of what it needs to know about the hardware comprising the system on which it is being installed. In other cases, the person installing Windows needs to provide this information. One good place to go from here, therefore, would seem to be installing Windows on your PC. That's what we do in the next chapter.

What You Have Learned

► Windows is a collection of programs designed to be used with IBM and IBM-compatible personal computers. Beyond this, however, Windows also is the graphical user interface under which all these programs run.

► Windows includes a number of applications you use to perform specific tasks on your PC. Write, for example, is the Windows application used for word processing. Other Windows applications include Paintbrush, Calendar, Terminal, and Cardfile.

► Windows runs on any personal computer that uses the MS-DOS or PC DOS operating system, version 3.1 or later, so long as that computer has at least a 286 microprocessor, 640K of memory, and a graphics display. Windows also is compatible with a variety of additional hardware peripherals that can be installed on an IBM or IBM-compatible personal computer.

Installing Windows

In This Chapter

- ► *How to run the Windows Setup program*
- ► *How to access the Windows on-line help feature*
- ► *How to modify the system configuration Setup uses to install Windows*

Getting Ready

Now that you have a basic idea of what Windows is, it's time to begin transferring the various programs included on the Windows distribution diskettes to your hard disk. During installation, you are asked to provide or in some cases verify, certain information about how Windows should be configured to run properly on your system.

Installing Windows isn't as difficult as you might think. Microsoft provides a special installation program, *Setup*, that walks you through each step required to get Windows running on your PC. Part of Setup's job is to configure Windows to take full advantage of the hardware and software previously installed on your PC. Setup also converts several Windows files compressed for distribution back into usable programs. Consequently, Windows will not run properly if you copy the files contained on its distribution diskettes to your hard disk, as you can do with some other PC applications. You must run the Setup program to install Windows.

Depending on how you run Setup, it might request information on some or all of the following topics:

► The disk drive and directory on which you want Windows installed

► The type of computer you have

► The kind of monitor you use

► Whether you own a mouse and what kind you have

► The type of keyboard connected to your PC

► The language Windows should use in its screen messages and displays

► Whether your PC is connected to a network and what kind of network it is

► Whether you own a printer, what kind of printer it is, and to what port of your PC that printer is connected

► What application programs on your hard disk you want installed as icons within your Windows environment

You find the Setup program on Disk 1 of the Windows distribution disks. During installation, Setup also needs to access files stored on several other disks shipped with Windows. Make certain that you have all the Windows distribution disks (or copies of these disks, as explained in the next section) available before beginning the installation procedures outlined in this chapter.

Protecting Your Programs

Most programs today, including Windows, are shipped on several distribution disks. These are the disks included in the original packaging for a given program. Although disks (both the 5 1/4- and 3 1/2-inch varieties) are durable, no one has yet invented the perfect diskette—one that is invulnerable to accidental damage or inadvertent erasing. For this reason, it's always a good idea to make copies of a program's distribution disks before installing the program. This way, you always have your original disks should something go awry (as George Bernard Shaw tells us "oft times" will for mice and men) later.

The easiest way to protect your Windows software against accidental damage is to use the DOS DISKCOPY command to create an exact copy of each distribution diskette. After duplicating your distribution disks, place the originals in a safe place and install Windows from this second set of disks.

 Note: Your DOS manual includes complete instructions on how to perform a DISKCOPY operation.

Express Setup Versus Custom Setup

21

Beginning with Windows 3.1, Microsoft provides two different procedures for installing Windows on your system.

> Express Setup
> Custom Setup

Selecting the Express Setup option fully automates the process of transferring Windows 3.1 from the distribution disks to your computer's hard disk. During Express Setup, Setup relies on the results of its own analysis of your PC to determine how to configure Windows for your system. This is the best option to choose if you are not familiar with how your PC is set up.

To modify the default values for certain aspects of your Windows environment, use the Custom Setup option. I follow the Custom Setup procedure in this chapter so that you have complete information if you choose to use this option.

The Setup program consists of two parts.

1. DOS-related operations.
2. Windows-related operations.

The actual installation of Windows begins in the DOS portion of Setup, from which several important operations are performed.

▶ If you use the Custom Setup option, Setup asks you to specify a directory in which to copy those files required to install Windows on your system.

▶ Setup then analyzes your hardware and asks you to verify that the results of this analysis, on which it bases your Windows configuration, are correct.

▶ After verifying your system configuration, Setup copies several essential files to the specified directory. When these files exist, Setup actually starts Windows and completes the installation process.

Setup then launches Windows and continues. Several important operations happen:

22

▶ If you allow it, Windows modifies your system files.

▶ You specify which printer you want installed to use with Windows.

▶ You specify which of your applications should be installed so that you can run them from Windows.

You can run Setup from any floppy disk drive. The drive you use is determined by the type of disks included in your Windows package. On my system, for example, I had to run Setup from drive B, my 3 1/2-inch disk drive, because Windows was shipped to me on 3 1/2-inch diskettes. If you are installing Windows from drive B, remember to substitute that drive letter when drive A is specified in the following exercise.

Starting Setup

√ To Begin Setup

▶ Place Windows Disk 1 into the appropriate disk drive for your system.

▶ Type **A:** and press Enter.

▶ Type **SETUP** and press Enter.

> ![icon] **Caution:** Remember, you might need to specify a different drive letter here, corresponding to the floppy disk drive on which you are running Setup.

After a few seconds, Setup displays its opening message, shown in Figure 2.1. In addition to welcoming you to Windows (Setup's a congenial little program, isn't it?), the opening message screen in Figure 2.1 contains information about what Setup does and how it works. Notice also, that the bottom line of this screen lists the options available to you at this point in your Windows installation.

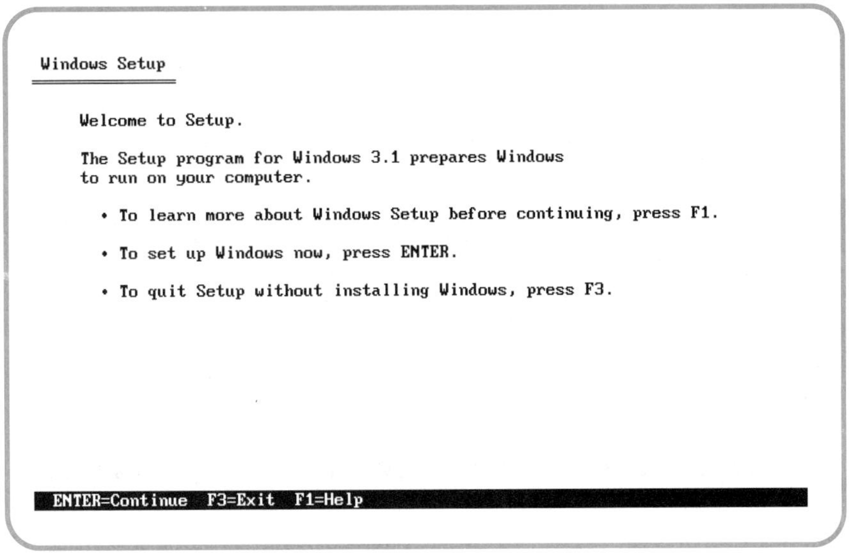

```
 Windows Setup
 ══════════════

     Welcome to Setup.

     The Setup program for Windows 3.1 prepares Windows
     to run on your computer.

       • To learn more about Windows Setup before continuing, press F1.

       • To set up Windows now, press ENTER.

       • To quit Setup without installing Windows, press F3.




    ENTER=Continue  F3=Exit  F1=Help
```

Figure 2.1. Use the Setup program to install Windows.

23

Before telling Setup to continue installing Windows, let's take a short detour to examine an extremely helpful Windows' feature, its on-line Help system.

Getting Help

As intuitive as Windows is, there might be times when you could use a little more information about the steps required to perform a specific operation. Thanks to Windows on-line Help system, such information is always a mere keystroke away. On the bottom line of the screen in Figure 2.1, for example, one of the listed options is Help, which you access by pressing F1. Let's do this now just to see what happens.

√ To Access the On-Line Help System

Press F1.

Pressing F1 displays the first screen of a multiscreen Setup Help message, as shown in Figure 2.2.

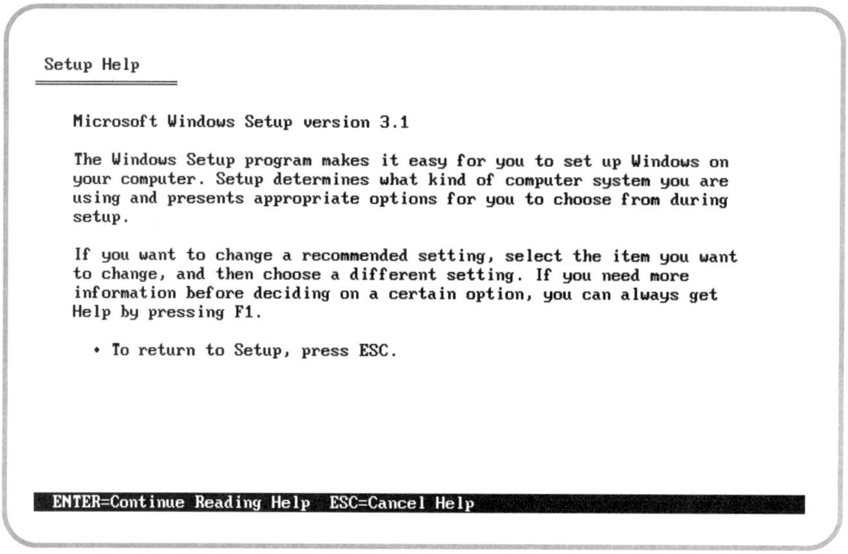

```
Setup Help
━━━━━━━━━━

  Microsoft Windows Setup version 3.1

  The Windows Setup program makes it easy for you to set up Windows on
  your computer. Setup determines what kind of computer system you are
  using and presents appropriate options for you to choose from during
  setup.

  If you want to change a recommended setting, select the item you want
  to change, and then choose a different setting. If you need more
  information before deciding on a certain option, you can always get
  Help by pressing F1.

    • To return to Setup, press ESC.




 ENTER=Continue Reading Help   ESC=Cancel Help
```

Figure 2.2. On-line help is available at almost any time during a Windows session.

Notice the bottom line of Figure 2.2 contains additional options available in Setup Help. Pressing Enter, for example, shows the second screen of the current Help message. This is another example of how Windows provides information about its use.

Press Enter to view subsequent Setup Help messages. Now, you're ready to exit Help and continue installing Windows.

✓ To Exit Setup Help

Press Esc.

> **Note:** The next chapter, "Navigating Windows," contains additional information on using the Windows on-line Help feature.

Pressing Esc returns you to the opening Setup screen shown in Figure 2.1. From here, you can inform Setup that you're ready to install Windows on your computer. Again, notice that the option line at the bottom of your display includes instructions on how to tell Setup you're ready to continue installing Windows on your computer.

✓ To Continue Installing Windows on Your PC

Press Enter.

25

This displays the screen shown in Figure 2.3.

```
Windows Setup
═══════════════

    Windows provides two Setup methods:

    Express Setup (Recommended)
    Express Setup relies on Setup to make decisions,
    so setting up Windows is quick and easy.

        To use Express Setup, press ENTER.


    Custom Setup
    Custom Setup is for experienced computer users who
    want or need control over how Windows is set up.

        To use Custom Setup, press C.


    For details about both Setup methods, press F1.



 ENTER=Express Setup  C=Custom Setup  F1=Help  F3=Exit
```

Figure 2.3. You can choose between Windows' Express or Custom Setup.

Choosing Between Express and Custom Setup

As I mentioned earlier, Windows 3.1 provides you with two installation options: Express Setup and Custom Setup

At this point in the Setup program you are asked to make a choice between these installation options.

The only thing you are asked to do during Express Setup is insert specific Windows distribution disks in your floppy drive at the appropriate times. Setup assumes responsibility for all other aspects of your Windows installation.

With the Custom Setup option, you have the flexibility of changing the Windows default selections. The rest of this chapter covers the details of a Custom Setup installation.

26

 Tip: Express Setup is the logical choice for new users or anyone unfamiliar with how personal computers work.

 Installing Windows Using Express Setup

1. Boot your computer so the DOS prompt (usually C:\>) appears.

2. Place Windows distribution Disk 1 in the floppy disk drive you want to use to install Windows.

3. Type the name of the drive from which you are installing Windows (**A:** or **B:**) and press Enter.

    The DOS prompt changes to the active floppy disk drive.

4. Type **SETUP** and press Enter

    This starts the Windows Setup program, which uses a series of interactive prompt screens to walk you through the Windows installation.

5. When Setup is completed, click the appropriate icon indicating how you want to proceed.

As Setup's final option, you can either return to the DOS prompt, immediately begin working in the Windows environment, or reboot. ☐

To run the Express Setup procedure from this point:

Press Enter.

Caution: Do not perform this exercise unless you want to have Setup execute an Express Setup at this time. To use the more interactive Custom Install procedure, see the next section.

√ To select Custom Setup

Press C.

27

After a few seconds, you see the prompt screen shown in Figure 2.4. During Custom Setup, several screens similar to the one shown in Figure 2.4 prompt you for information regarding your system configuration. Answering these questions correctly ensures the proper installation of Windows.

Specifying a Disk and Directory for Windows

You can tell Setup to copy the Windows files to any directory on your hard disk—or for that matter, to any hard disk installed on your PC. During installation, Setup takes all necessary steps to ensure that Windows can find these files later, when needed. The default location Setup uses for Windows' installation is a directory called WINDOWS on drive C, as shown in Figure 2.4.

To accept this default directory, you simply press Enter. As I said earlier, however, where to install Windows is up to you. To illustrate how easy it is to change a default value in Setup, specify a directory other than C:\WINDOWS for this installation.

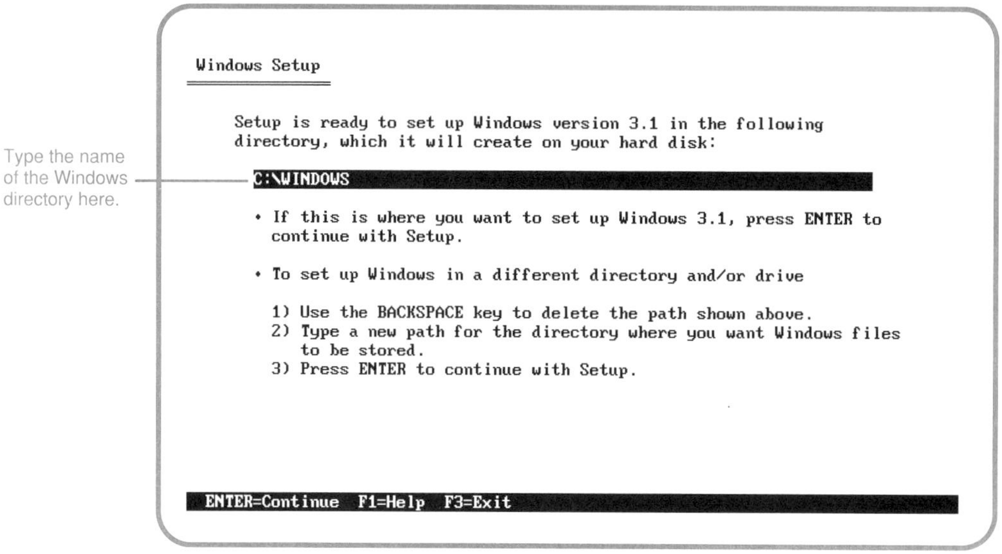

```
Windows Setup
═════════════

    Setup is ready to set up Windows version 3.1 in the following
    directory, which it will create on your hard disk:

    ▌C:\WINDOWS                                                    ▐

    • If this is where you want to set up Windows 3.1, press ENTER to
      continue with Setup.

    • To set up Windows in a different directory and/or drive

      1) Use the BACKSPACE key to delete the path shown above.
      2) Type a new path for the directory where you want Windows files
         to be stored.
      3) Press ENTER to continue with Setup.




  ENTER=Continue  F1=Help  F3=Exit
```

Type the name
of the Windows ———
directory here.

28

*Figure 2.4. Setup asks you to specify the directory in which
Windows should be installed on your system.*

✓ To Specify a Different Windows Directory

▶ Press Backspace four times to position the cursor after the N
  in C:\WINDOWS.

▶ Type **31** and press Enter.

This tells Setup you want to install Windows in a directory on
drive C called \WIN31. Don't worry if this directory does not exist.
Setup creates the directory before moving to the next stage of the
Windows installation.

Modifying Setup's Analysis of Your System Components

After recording the specified Windows directory (and creating this
directory, if necessary), Setup displays a screen similar to the one in
Figure 2.5. This screen represents Setup's "best guess" as to the type
of hardware and software installed on your PC—information needed
to configure Windows to run properly on your system.

```
 Windows Setup
 ════════════

       Setup has determined that your system includes the following hardware
       and software components. If your computer or network appears on the
       Hardware Compatibility List with an asterisk, press F1 for Help.

              Computer:          MS-DOS System
              Display:           VGA
              Mouse:             No mouse or other pointing device
              Keyboard:          Enhanced 101 or 102 key US and Non US keyboards
              Keyboard Layout:   US
              Language:          English (American)
              Network:           No Network Installed

              No Changes:        The above list matches my computer.

       If all the items in the list are correct, press ENTER to indicate
       "No Changes." If you want to change any item in the list, press the
       UP or DOWN ARROW key to move the highlight to the item you want to
       change. Then press ENTER to see alternatives for that item.


    ENTER=Continue  F1=Help  F3=Exit
```

Figure 2.5. Setup automatically analyzes the hardware and software installed on your PC.

 Note: The individual items displayed on your screen probably differ from those shown here. Figure 2.5 represents the hardware and software Setup on my system.

If the system configuration that Setup displays is correct, you can press Enter to specify "No Changes" and have Setup continue installing Windows. What if Setup did not correctly analyze your system components? That's no problem. As a quick glance at the instructions in Figure 2.5 reveals, you can modify the results of Setup's system analysis easily.

✓ To Modify Setup's System Analysis

▶ Use the arrow keys to highlight the field containing the information you need to change.

▶ Press Enter.

For example, because I did not load a mouse driver into memory prior to installing Windows, Figure 2.5 indicates that Setup discovered "No mouse or other pointing device" on my system. If I want

Windows configured to recognize a mouse, I would need to change this field. Highlighting the mouse field and pressing Enter displays the screen shown in Figure 2.6, which I could then use to tell Setup what kind of mouse is installed on my PC.

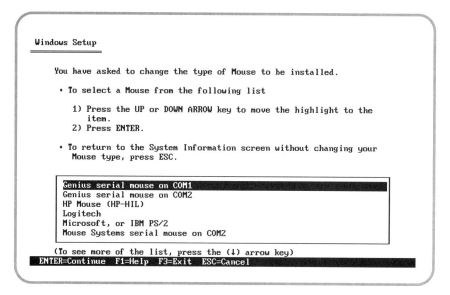

Figure 2.6. You can modify the results of Setup's system analysis.

> **Tip:** Pay special attention to the value Setup lists in the Display field of its system analysis. Given Windows' reliance on a graphics-based interface, you want to make sure that Windows is configured to take full advantage of your monitor. In addition, pay close attention to Resolution and Colors. For example, do you have an 800 x 600 monitor that displays 256 colors?

When all the system components listed on Setup's analysis screen are correct, press Enter to continue your Windows installation.

✓ To Continue Installing Windows on Your System

Press Enter.

At this point, Setup begins copying files from the Windows distribution diskettes to the \WIN31 directory you specified earlier. During the initial stage of installation, Setup needs to access files from a distribution diskette other than Disk 1. When this happens, Setup pauses, displays the information pertaining to the diskette it needs, and then instructs you to press Enter to continue installation.

At some point in this process, your monitor goes blank for a few seconds. When Setup resumes, you see the screen shown in Figure 2.7. Congratulations! Setup has advanced to the Windows portion of its installation procedures, and you are looking at your first Windows graphics-based display.

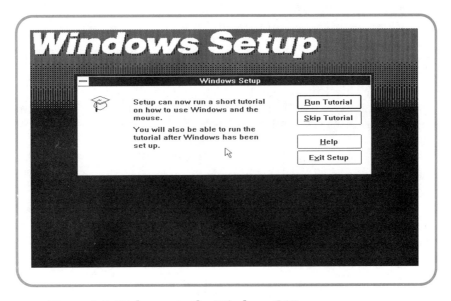

Figure 2.7. Welcome to the Windows GUI.

At this time, Setup has switched to the Windows portion of its installation procedures, as I mentioned earlier. From now on, you actually are using Windows to finish installing Windows on your PC. (Pretty nifty, huh?)

The Windows Tutorial

Setup includes a short tutorial that introduces basic concepts relating to working within the Windows environment. If you want to run this tutorial, you can choose the Run Tutorial option in Figure 2.7. In truth though, using Windows is what this book is all about.

Everything covered in Setup's tutorial is discussed in greater detail throughout the following chapters. For now, therefore, let's skip Setup's tutorial and move on.

✓ To Skip the Windows Tutorial

Press S to select Skip Tutorial.

Next, Setup asks you to enter information about the person who will be using this copy of Windows. At this screen

▶ Type your name and press Enter.
▶ Type your company and press Enter.
▶ When Setup asks you to verify this information, press o.

During Custom Setup, you can choose to install only specific elements of Windows. The next screen Setup displays offers this option. For this initial installation, we'll install all the Windows components. To install the entire Windows package, using the default Windows configuration:

▶ Press w to set up all Windows components.
▶ Press o to continue installation.
▶ At the Virtual Memory prompt, press Enter.

Setup returns to transferring files from the Windows distribution diskettes to your hard disk. Once again, Setup walks you through the required procedures. Setup even sounds a distinctive beep and displays an on-screen message to inform you when you need to place a new distribution diskette in your floppy disk drive and which disk it needs. Follow these instructions, and you soon have all the Windows files installed on your hard disk. This process takes some time because Windows consists of many files.

> **Note:** Exactly what disks you'll use, and the order in which you'll use them, is determined by the various hardware and software components installed on your PC. To try to cover all the possible permutations of the Setup procedures would be impossible. The best advice I can give you is read. Read. READ! Specifically, read any instructions Setup displays and then follow those instructions carefully. If you read and follow the instructions, you should have no trouble transferring the remaining Windows files onto your hard disk.

Modifying Your CONFIG.SYS and AUTOEXEC.BAT Files

When Setup has transferred all the necessary files from the Windows distribution diskettes to your hard disk, it displays the message shown in Figure 2.8. This message requests information on whether and how Setup should modify two critical DOS files on your hard disk: CONFIG.SYS and AUTOEXEC.BAT. I'm going to assume that, if you understand this message, you'll know which option is best for you. If you don't understand, let Setup make any changes that are required in these two files.

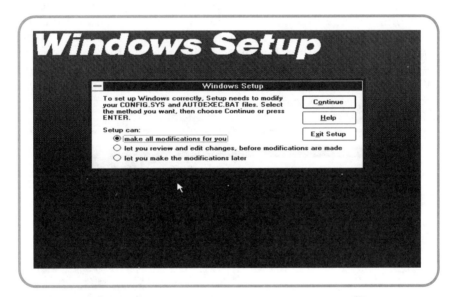

Figure 2.8. With Setup, you can specify whether your CONFIG.SYS and AUTOEXEC.BAT files should be modified for Windows.

✓ To Have Setup Automatically Modify CONFIG.SYS and AUTOEXEC.BAT

Press Enter.

> **Note:** If these files did not previously exist, Setup creates them. If your system had a CONFIG.SYS and AUTOEXEC.BAT file, Setup makes the required modifications but saves the earlier versions under the names CONFIG.OLD and AUTOEXEC.OLD, respectively. See how considerate Windows is?

Specifying a Printer

Next, Setup asks you to install a *printer driver* for your Windows environment, as shown in Figure 2.9. Basically, a printer driver is a file containing the specific instructions Windows needs to control a given printer. Installing the correct printer driver in your Windows environment is important because any programs you run under Windows that are "Windows-aware" use the specified printer driver for all their print operations.

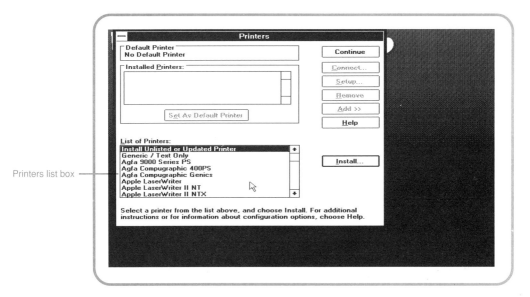

Printers list box

Figure 2.9. Setup requests that you identify what type of printer you are using with Windows.

Though important, all is not lost if you do not select the correct driver for your printer. With Windows 3.1, you can modify your system setup without completely reinstalling Windows, a process we'll look at more closely in Chapter 4, "Customizing Windows." For now,

▶ Use the arrow keys to highlight the type of printer you have in the Printers list box.

▶ Press Enter.

▶ Insert the disk Setup requests in Drive A.

▶ Press Enter.

▶ When your printer's name appears in the Installed Printers box, press Enter.

▶ At the Connect prompt, use the arrow keys to highlight the port the printer is attached to and press Enter.

▶ Press Shift+Tab to highlight the Continue button and press Enter.

Setting Up Applications

As its final step in Windows installation, Setup offers to scan your hard disks and automatically install into your Windows environment any applications programs it recognizes, as shown in Figure 2.10. Once again, unless you understand this option, it's best to let Setup automatically handle everything for you. If Setup misses some of your favorite programs (it's not infallible), you learn to add new programs to your Windows environment in Chapter 5, "Managing a Windows Session."

35

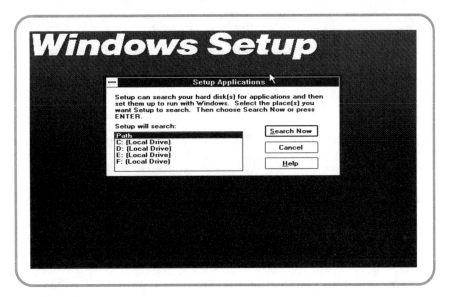

Figure 2.10. Setup automatically can install applications in your Windows environment.

✓ **To Have Setup Automatically Install Programs into Your Windows Environment**

Press Enter.

After scanning the files on your hard disks, Setup displays a screen similar to Figure 2.11, giving you one more opportunity to specify which programs it should install in your Windows environment. This is a different screen than you've seen previously, but the same principle: If you don't understand what this is all about, let Setup take care of things.

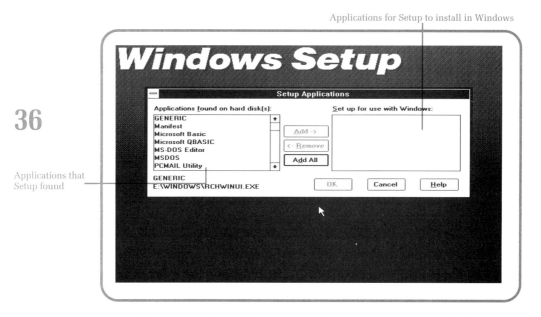

Figure 2.11. Setup lists any application programs it finds.

✓ **To Automatically Add All Applications Setup Finds to Your Windows Environment**

▶ Press Enter to select **A**dd All.
▶ Press Enter to select OK.

Ending Setup and Starting Windows

You are almost finished with your Windows installation. At last! All that remains is to decide what should happen when you exit Setup. As illustrated in Figure 2.12, you have three options:

▶ Reboot your computer to put into effect any changes Setup made to your CONFIG.SYS and AUTOEXEC.BAT files.

▶ Automatically start Windows, so you can begin using this impressive GUI.

▶ Return to DOS and take no further steps.

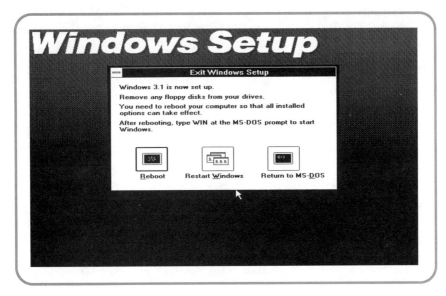

Figure 2.12. The final step in Setup is to specify what should happen when Setup ends.

√ To End Setup and Reboot Your Computer

▶ Remove any Windows distribution disks from your floppy disk drive.

▶ Press R to select reboot.

Guess what? Windows is completely installed on your system. There's still much to do, as we get down to the nitty-gritty of learning how to work within the Windows environment.

What You Have Learned

▶ Windows includes a special program, Setup, that simplifies the process of installing Windows on your PC.

37

▶ Setup automatically analyzes the hardware and software installed on your PC and uses this information to determine the most appropriate configuration for Windows. You can, however, override individual settings Setup selects, as needed, to ensure that Windows runs properly on your system.

▶ Windows includes an on-line Help feature that you can access by pressing F1. Help messages contain specific information about a wide range of Windows procedures.

38

Navigating Windows

In This Chapter

▶ *How to use a mouse with Windows*

▶ *How to rearrange elements of your Windows display*

Windows Parts

You should now be at the DOS system prompt and I would hope, eager to load Windows. Before loading Windows, however, look at a generic Windows screen and identify the various Windows elements you'll be working with in this chapter.

First, I must explain the difference between Windows and a window. When I mention *Windows* (with a capital W), I mean the Windows program itself or in a more universal way, the total Windows GUI environment. A *window* (with a lowercase w) is a discrete portion of the complete Windows screen—generally, the outlined display box in which a given application, program, or utility is running. Big Windows versus little windows—that's not such a bad way of thinking about it.

Figure 3.1 shows a typical Windows screen—a relatively boring one, I will admit, but a Windows screen, nonetheless. Several elements have been pointed out on this screen; you need to be familiar with these elements as you begin navigating Windows.

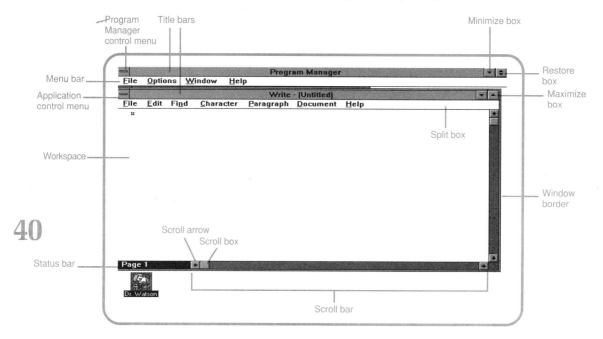

Figure 3.1. Elements of the Windows display.

Specifically, these items are

Control menu box (application)	Click this box to display the pull-down Control menu for an application window. The Control menu includes command options for sizing, moving, shrinking, enlarging, and restoring an application window.
Menu bar	This bar displays the Main menu options available in a window. Clicking a menu item displays a pull-down menu associated with the item that, in turn, lists additional command options. The specific options listed on the Main menu bar depend on the application running in a window.

Control menu box (file)	Click this box to display the pull-down Control menu for the file on which you are working. The Control menu includes command options for sizing, moving, shrinking, enlarging, and restoring the active window.
Workspace	This is the area in which your windows are displayed. You can, of course, have multiple windows open in the workspace at any given time.
Status bar	Use the status bar to display information and messages relating to a window's current status or a selected command. Each window open in the workspace has its own status bar. If you want, you can turn off the status of most Windows applications.
Window border	Each window has its own border. If your system includes a mouse, you can use a window's border to modify the size of that window.
Title bars	Each window in your workspace contains a title bar, which shows the name of the program, accessory, or utility running in that window. If your system includes a mouse, you can use a window's title bar to change the location of that window.
Minimize box	Clicking this box shrinks a window to icon size. If a window cannot be represented as an icon, that window does not contain a minimize box.
Maximize box	Clicking this box enlarges a window to its largest possible size, usually to where it occupies the entire screen.
Restore box	Clicking this box restores a window to the size it was before you performed a Minimize or Maximize operation on that window.

41

Split box	Dragging your mouse on this box splits a window horizontally. Certain Windows applications also have a vertically split box that, if available, is located to the left of the horizontal scroll bar.
Scroll box	Windows uses this box to indicate its position in a file, relative to the file's beginning and end. As you drag this box up and down the scroll bar, Windows automatically scrolls through the file's contents.
Scroll bar	Clicking this bar moves the cursor through a file too long or wide to be displayed completely in a single window. If you want, you can turn off the scroll bar in most Windows applications.
Scroll arrow	Clicking a scroll arrow moves you through a file in small increments, in the direction of the arrow.

Take a few moments to familiarize yourself with these various Window parts and how each is used within the Windows environment. I refer to them frequently in the remainder of this chapter—indeed, throughout the rest of this book.

Starting Windows

As part of its installation procedures, Setup appended the Windows directory—WIN3, if you followed the steps in the previous chapter—to a PATH statement in your AUTOEXEC.BAT file. Consequently, DOS can locate the program used to run Windows, WIN.COM, without requiring you to first change to the Windows directory. Now, let's begin a Windows session.

To Start Windows

Type **WIN** and press Enter.   This loads Windows and
                                  displays its opening screen.

After displaying a brief copyright message, Windows advances
to the opening screen shown in Figure 3.2.

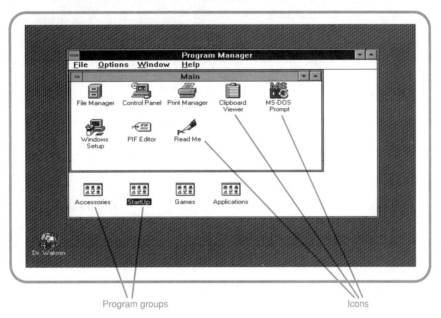

*Figure 3.2. Opening screen Windows shows the first time it's
started.*

43

Windows starts with a screen resembling Figure 3.2, the first
time it is run. Later in this chapter, you learn how to customize this
opening display to correspond with your usual work habits.

The window displayed in the workspace of Figure 3.2 contains
several Windows System Applications that Setup automatically
created and organized into a program group called Main during
installation. These include

File Manager   Performs file-related operations
                       such as COPY and DELETE
                       during a Windows session.

Control Panel	Changes how your system is configured during a Windows session.
Print Manager	Manages printing during a Windows session.
Clipboard Viewer	Transfers data between applications during a Windows session.
MS-DOS Prompt	You can enter commands directly from the DOS prompt during a Windows session by temporarily exiting the Windows GUI.
Windows Setup	Accesses Setup and modifies elements of your Windows environment during a Windows session.
PIF Editor	Used to customize the setting Windows uses to run application programs.
Readme	Accesses the On-line documents, which contain important Windows information that may not be included in the manuals.

Other icons across the bottom of the workspace represent additional program groups created when you installed Windows. These include

The Accessories Group	Contains the various applications mentioned in Chapter 1 that Microsoft includes in the basic Windows package (Write, Paintbrush, Terminal, Cardfile, and so on).
The Games Group	Contains two games also included with Windows, Minesweeper and Solitaire, that offer an ideal diversion from the more important work you'll soon be accomplishing with Windows.

	(After all, as the old adage states, all work and no play makes Jack a dull boy.)
The Applications Group	Contains any applications Setup found on your hard disk during installation
Startup	Special program group you can use to automatically run a certain application each time you start Windows.

You learn to access each of these groups and work with many of the applications they contain as we dig more deeply into Windows throughout the rest of this book. Our main goal in the remainder of this chapter, however, is to become comfortable navigating the Windows GUI, something we accomplish using the various elements contained in the opening Windows display.

Now that we're actually in Windows, it's time to begin taking advantage of the graphics-based interface it provides. We begin by examining how Windows uses a mouse to simplify the tasks that you perform on your PC.

45

Using a Mouse

As mentioned in Chapter 1, "Welcome to Windows," a GUI like Windows is suited ideally for mouse operations. Because any procedure you can perform is clearly shown on the Windows display, it's a simple matter to identify a given operation using the two-step "point and click" common to mouse operations:

1. Use the mouse to point at the procedure you want to initiate.
2. Click the left mouse button to get things underway.

That's really all there is to it.

Notice the small arrow located in the center of Figure 2.7. This is the Windows' mouse pointer. If this mouse pointer appears anywhere on your Windows display, Windows recognizes that an electronic rodent is attached to your PC and is configured to enable mouse operations. If you have a mouse and do not see this pointer, you need to use Setup, as described in Chapter 2, "Installing Windows," to install the appropriate driver for the mouse in your Windows environment.

> **Note:** No mouse pointer appears on your Windows display if you did not specify a mouse (or if you specified "No pointing device") during the DOS portion of the Setup program. Although it's technically possible to run Windows exclusively from the keyboard, keep in mind that doing so is extremely awkward and inefficient. I'm going to assume, therefore, that you have incorporated a mouse in your environment.
>
> Consequently, I'll mention only keyboard commands when I feel doing so is absolutely necessary or when an available keyboard command is more convenient to use than the corresponding mouse procedure.

46

When you work in Windows, use a mouse for a variety of operations including

- ▶ Selecting menu and dialog box options.
- ▶ Choosing and executing on-screen commands.
- ▶ Modifying the placement and appearance of elements in your Windows display.
- ▶ Selecting text and objects for additional processing.

Don't worry if the meaning of these various activities isn't clear to you right now. You perform and practice each of them as we move along. For now, I want to outline, in a general way, some of the activities for which you use a mouse while working in the Windows environment. Let's perform one of these activities.

Moving the Mouse Pointer

Are you ready to play with a mouse? Okay, begin by using the mouse to access the Windows on-line Help feature.

To Access On-Line Help with Your Mouse

1. Move the mouse until the tip of the mouse pointer is positioned over the Help button in the Program Manager menu bar.

2. Click the button located on the left side of your mouse.   The **Help** menu is displayed.

3. Point to the **C**ontents option in the subsequent pull-down menu.

4. Click the left mouse button.   The Help screen, shown in Figure 3.3, opens.   ☐

Your display should now resemble Figure 3.3, which shows an outline containing a partial listing of the various topics available under Help. If it does, congratulations! You just learned to use a mouse! Wasn't that easy? Point and click. That's all there is to it. Now are you beginning to understand why the PC community is excited about Windows?

47

Figure 3.3. Clicking the Help button accesses Windows On-Line Help feature.

While we're at this Setup Help screen, let's look at some additional attributes of using a mouse to navigate in Windows.

The Chameleon Cursor

It really is a misnomer to refer to a mouse pointer. Certainly, right now, that's what it is. The following exercise, however, points out how problems can arise with this little bit of PC jargon.

✓ To Move the Mouse Pointer

Move the mouse up and to the left until the mouse pointer is positioned over the Arrange Windows and Icons entry in the Setup Help outline.

Suddenly, you might find yourself saying, "What mouse pointer?" Now it's a mouse hand. As this exercise shows, the Windows mouse pointer can and does change shape, depending on what you're doing at the time. Want to see some more? Follow these steps:

1. Move the mouse to the left until the mouse pointer reaches the vertical line marking the left side of the Setup Help display window. (Now it's a double-headed, horizontal arrow.)
2. Move the mouse down, until the mouse pointer reaches the lower-left corner of the Help display window. (The pointer is still double-headed, but now it's diagonal.)

As these few examples illustrate, the mouse pointer is an adaptable little creature, indeed. Given this fact, I'll refer to it as the *mouse cursor* from now on. I also describe what these various mouse cursor shapes indicate as we encounter them within the Windows applications. For now, let's get back to the opening Windows display and begin using our mouse to perform some basic tasks. To exit the on-line Help:

▶ Point to File in the Program Manager Help menu bar.
▶ Click the left mouse button.
▶ Point to the Exit option in the subsequent menu.
▶ Click the left mouse button.

Working with Icons

After discussing icons several times, it's finally time to begin learning the manner in which icons are used within a Windows session. Put simply, icons provide a quick and convenient method for managing different elements of your overall Windows environment.

For example, instead of forcing you to type an exact filename and then press Enter to run a program, as is required in standard DOS, you can accomplish the same thing in Windows by simply clicking that program's icon. Previously convoluted operations like copying files to a new location also are simplified by Windows' use of on-screen icons. To pull a pathetic pun out of my bottomless bag of literary tricks: "If you can do it in DOS, 'icon' do it more easily in Windows."

Icons can be used to represent a variety of items on your Windows display, including

49

► Individual program and data files stored on your disks.
► Multiple files that have been organized into logical groups.
► Special procedures and operations.

Rather than simply telling you about icons, why don't I show you what I mean? Notice that the words "File Manager," the text description associated with the two-drawer file cabinet icon in Figure 3.3, are displayed in *inverse video*—that is, white letters on a black (or, possibly, blue) background. This identifies File Manager as the active icon. Let's change this.

 To Select a New Icon

1. Move your mouse until the mouse cursor points to the icon you want to select.

2. Click the left mouse button.   Windows highlights the selected icon to indicate it has been selected. □

Use this technique to select the Control Panel located just to the right of File Manager. Notice that this causes the words "Control Panel" to be displayed in inverse video, indicating that it is now the active icon. What exactly does this mean? This question is answered within our next topic of discussion: the Windows menus.

Using Menus

After an icon is active, you can use the different options accessed through the Windows pull-down menus to quickly perform a variety of operations on the file or group of files that icon represents. Let's look at what I mean by this.

 To Access a Menu

1. Move your mouse until the mouse cursor points to the item you want to select from a Windows menu bar.
2. Click the left mouse button.

Windows displays a pull-down menu associated with the option you chose. ☐

Use this technique to select the File option in the Program Manager menu bar. Your screen should now resemble Figure 3.4, which shows a pull-down menu containing those File options available in Program Manager.

Figure 3.4. The File menu lists file-related operations that you can perform on the active icon.

The availability of pull-down menus in Windows simplifies many PC operations by making them interactive. This means that Windows provides information about what you hope to accomplish and you, in turn, fill in the blanks to accomplish it.

Let's see what happens, for example, when you select the **C**opy option from the **File** menu.

✓ To Select the Copy Option

▶ Move your mouse until the mouse cursor points to the **C**opy option of the **Files** menu.

▶ Click the left mouse button.

This displays the dialog box shown in Figure 3.5.

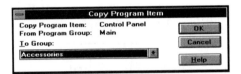

Figure 3.5. Windows automatically identifies the active icon as the item on which you want to perform the current Copy operation.

51

Notice that Control Panel has been entered into the field marked Copy Program Item. In other words, Windows assumes that, because Control Panel is the active icon, it is the program you want to copy. All you need to do to complete the **C**opy operation is specify where you want to copy Control Panel. You learn how to accomplish this in Chapter 5, "Managing a Windows Session." For now, let's return to the opening Windows screen so that we can continue our current discussion—the various procedures used to work effectively within the Windows GUI.

Canceling a Windows Operation

At this point, your display should still contain the Copy dialog box shown in Figure 3.5. Instead of completing this operation, however, let's assume you decided to leave the Control Panel right where it was, within the Main program group. Most Windows dialog boxes include a Cancel button you can use to cancel the current operation and return to where you were before the operation was initiated.

 To Cancel an Operation

1. Move your mouse until the mouse cursor points to the Cancel button.

2. Click the left mouse button.   The current operation is canceled—that is, not executed.   □

Cancel the **C**opy operation. This returns you to the opening Windows display shown in Figure 3.2—except that, as you might have noticed, Control Panel remains the active icon.

> **Note:** It's time to start cutting down on the complexity of the commands included in our exercises. By now you should have a good idea of the steps involved in selecting an icon, menu option, or as in the previous exercise, a Windows display button. For this reason, I'm going to start referring to this two-step procedure with a single word, *Choose*—the same terminology used in the Windows documentation. Now, therefore, whenever an exercise contains instructions to Choose an item, you should position the mouse cursor over that item and click the left mouse button. That's easy enough, isn't it?

Opening a Window

Icons also provide an easy way to open an *application window*—a window within Windows, containing a program or program group. To accomplish this, you use a special method called *double-clicking* an icon.

To Open a New Window

1. Move the mouse until the mouse cursor points to the icon representing the window you want to open.

2. Click the left mouse button twice in rapid succession.

The icon you selected is expanded to a full-sized window. □

For example, double-clicking the Accessories icon automatically expands that icon to a display window, as illustrated in Figure 3.6. Double-click this icon now. In this figure, a second window has been added to the opening Windows display. This second window contains the icons associated with the so-called Accessories Setup automatically installed in your Windows environment.

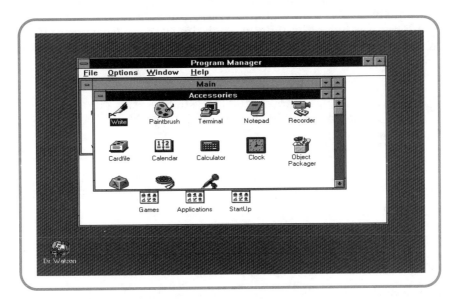

Figure 3.6. Double-clicking a Group icon automatically expands that icon to its own display window.

Now that we have two open windows, let's look at some additional features of the Windows GUI.

> **Note:** From now on, I'll describe this procedure using the same terminology you'll find in the Windows documentation—*double-clicking*. Whenever an exercise contains instructions to double-click an item, position your mouse cursor over that item and then quickly press and release the left mouse button twice.

Working with Multiple Windows

Notice that the title bar containing the name of the window, Accessories, you opened is now highlighted. This identifies Accessories as the active window. Conversely, the Main window, which was previously active, is now inactive, as indicated by the fact that its title bar is no longer highlighted. Each time you open a new window, Windows automatically places that window in the foreground of your display. Windows makes the new window active, too.

You can change the color scheme used to identify the various elements of your Windows display, such as the colors used to indicate active and inactive windows. We see how this is done in Chapter 4, "Customizing Windows."

How easily you manage, manipulate, and navigate even the most complex workspace is one of Windows' most impressive capabilities . Let's quickly look at a few examples of how this is accomplished.

Switching Active Windows

Suppose, for example, you need to access an icon located on the Main window. The quickest way to accomplish this is to make that window active again.

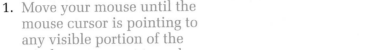

To Change Active Windows

1. Move your mouse until the mouse cursor is pointing to any visible portion of the window you want to make active.

2. Click the left mouse button.
   The selected window is made active and moved to the front of your display. □

Use this Quick Step to return the Main window to the foreground of your display and make it active. You could now select an item on this window by simply clicking on its icon.

Moving a Window

You also can change the location of a window on your display. This would be desirable, for example, if you wanted to be able to see more of an inactive window that is almost totally obscured in the default arrangement Windows uses when multiple windows have been opened.

Changing a Window's Position

1. Move your mouse until the mouse cursor is positioned on the title bar of the window you want to reposition.

2. Hold down the left mouse button.
   A broken-line border appears around the selected window.

3. Drag your mouse until this border is located at the desired window position.

4. Release the left mouse button.
   Windows moves the selected window to the specified location. □

Use this Quick Step to change the position of the Accessories window to the bottom-right corner of your workspace. (Remember to make it the active window, as outlined earlier, before doing this.)

> **Note:** Again, let's standardize our terminology. The Windows documentation refers to this procedure as *dragging* a display element. Sounds good to me. Whenever an exercise in this book contains instructions to drag an item, therefore, position your mouse cursor over that item, press and hold the left mouse button, move the mouse to a new location, and release the left mouse button.

When you've completed these steps, your screen should resemble Figure 3.7, in which the Accessories window has been moved to a new location on the Windows workspace. Admittedly, this new arrangement is less cluttered than before. Still, the actual Windows workspace seems crowded. It probably won't surprise you to find there is a way to enlarge the Windows workspace.

56

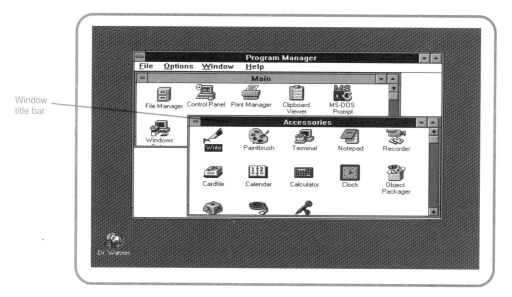

Figure 3.7. Move a window by dragging the mouse cursor on that window's title bar.

Window title bar

Resizing Elements of the Windows Display

It might help to think of your Windows display as resembling a typical desktop. As you've seen, it's easy to adjust individual windows within this display—in much the same way that, throughout the course of an average workday, you rearrange reports, folders, notepads, and so on, occupying your desk or workspace. If you're like me, however, there have probably been times when you wish your desk could be enlarged temporarily to make room for all the different projects you're working on at the time. Although it's impractical to think about doing this with a traditional work area, adjusting the size of the various elements comprising your Windows display is child's play. We'll begin by expanding the total Windows work area so that it occupies your entire display.

57

Maximizing the Windows Workspace

Notice the two boxes located to the far right of the Program Manager title bar. You can shrink and expand elements of your Windows display quickly by using these two boxes, called the Minimize box and Maximize box. (Refer to Figure 3.8, if necessary, to determine the location and appearance of the Minimize and Maximize boxes.)

 To Expand a Window to a Full-Screen Display

1. Position your mouse cursor over the Maximize box located in the title bar of the window you want to expand.
2. Click the left mouse button.

The selected window is expanded to fill your entire workspace. □

Use the previous Quick Step to expand the Program Manager. Your screen should resemble Figure 3.8 in which Windows has been enlarged to fill the entire display. This gives you much more room to work with when arranging the various elements of your Windows workspace. Now that we have all this additional space, let's take advantage of it.

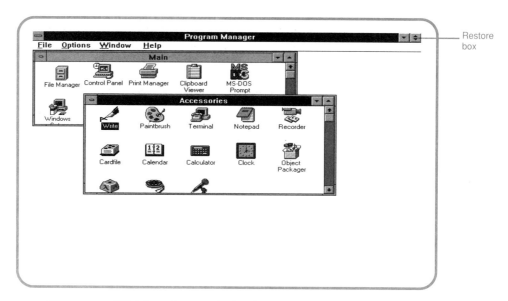

Restore box

Figure 3.8. Clicking the Maximize box expands your Windows display.

58

Expanding a Window Manually

Of course, there will be times when you'd like to enlarge a single window without having that window take over your entire display. This might be the case, for example, if you're working primarily in an application loaded into one window, but need to leave a small portion of a second window visible in order to reference specific material it contains.

In such a situation, it wouldn't make sense to use the Maximize box. Rather, you'd want to increase the size of your primary application window slightly. You can do this using Windows.

 Resizing a Window

1. Move your mouse until the mouse cursor is positioned on the appropriate border of the window you want to resize.

The mouse cursor changes to an arrow pointing vertically, horizontally, or diagonally, depending on how you are resizing the window.

2. Hold down the left mouse button.

A broken-line border appears around the selected window.

3. Drag your mouse in the appropriate direction to resize the window.

4. Release the left mouse button.

Windows redraws the selected window to the new dimensions. ☐

If you place the mouse cursor on the lower-right corner of the Accessories window, you can use this Quick Step to increase the size of the Accessories Window until the window resembles Figure 3.9. This figure shows the Accessories window slightly enlarged from its previous size. Depending on the border you drag, a window can be expanded horizontally, vertically, or as we did in the previous exercise, diagonally.

59

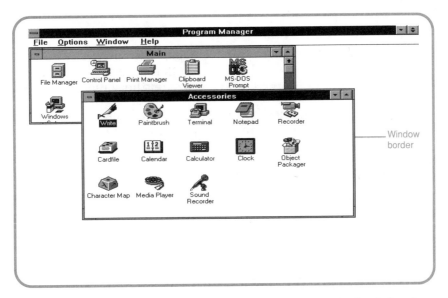

Window border

Figure 3.9. By dragging the mouse cursor on a window's border, you can alter dynamically the size of that window.

Tip: This same technique can be used to reduce a window's size. For example, positioning the mouse cursor on a window's right border and then dragging the mouse to your left would move the right border in, thus reducing the horizontal dimensions of that window.

Cascading Versus Tiled Windows

Until now, we've been working exclusively with Windows default layout, which sets up *cascading windows*—that is, a display arrangement where multiple windows are positioned to overlap one another, with each subsequent window you open automatically located slightly below and to the left of the previous one. Windows supports a second display option, called *tiling*.

 To Switch Your Windows Display to a Tiled Arrangement

1. Choose the Window option on the Program Manager menu bar. (Remember, this means to position your mouse cursor over the specified option and then click the left mouse button.)

   This displays the Window pull-down menu.

2. Choose Tile from Window options that appear in the subsequent pull-down menu.

   Open windows are arranged so that they are the same size on the screen. ☐

Windows automatically redraws your display to use tiled windows, as shown in Figure 3.10. With *tiled windows* in effect, multiple windows are positioned next to one another rather than in an overlapping configuration, as was the case with the default Cascade arrangement. Personally, I prefer the Cascade arrangement, so let's change back. In the process, we also can examine another Windows feature: keyboard shortcuts.

Using Keyboard Shortcuts

As I mentioned in Chapter 1, "Welcome to Windows," the availability of a mouse greatly simplifies most Windows operations. As is true of any general rule however, this one has some notable exceptions. In several cases, Windows provides alternate keyboard commands that you might find more convenient to use than the corresponding mouse sequences. When a keyboard shortcut is available, Windows lists it on its various option menus. Let's see how this works by taking another look at the **W**indow options menu used in the previous exercise. Choose the **W**indow option on the Program Manager menu bar.

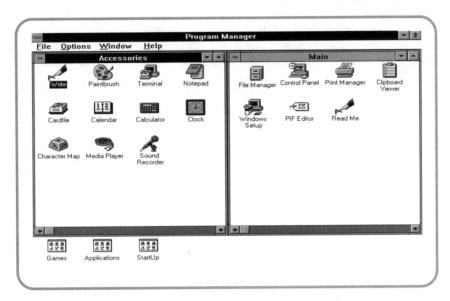

Figure 3.10. Tiled Windows.

Notice that the key sequence Shift+F5 appears next to the **C**ascade option. This is one example of a Windows keyboard shortcut.

> **Note:** Windows uses the plus sign (+) to indicate a multiple-key command sequence. In this case, for example, Shift+F5 indicates that you should hold down the Shift key while pressing F5. For the sake of consistency, I'll use this same notation to indicate multiple-key command sequences throughout this book.

✔ To Return Your Display to Cascading Windows

Press Shift+F5, or with the mouse, issue the **W**indows **C**ascade command.

61

This switches your display back to a cascading windows arrangement, as shown in Figure 3.11.

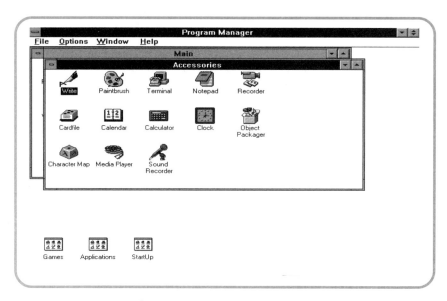

Figure 3.11. Keyboard shortcuts are available for many Windows operations.

In this chapter, we've looked at some of the basic procedures used to navigate and in some cases, modify the appearance of your Windows workspace. To be honest, we've only scratched the surface. You learn many more techniques associated with working in the Windows environment throughout the rest of this book as we examine additional components of the total Windows package. My main goal here was to introduce you to Windows and have you experiment just enough to feel comfortable with that program's GUI—to stick your head into Windows and then look around a bit. Now that I've gotten you into Windows, though, it's probably a good idea if I show you how to get out—that is, the steps required to end a Windows session.

Exiting Windows

Exiting Windows is a two-step process. First, any programs you have been running in the current Windows session should be closed. This guards against your losing the most recent work you've done. When these applications are closed, it's safe to exit the Windows GUI and return to DOS. Of course, we didn't open any applications in this, our first Windows session. Ending it, therefore, will be easy.

 To Exit Windows

1. Position your mouse cursor over the Control menu box located in the upper-left corner of the Program Manager title bar.

2. Click the left mouse button. This displays the pull-down Control menu.

3. Choose Close. Windows displays a prompt box, asking you to verify that you want to end the current session.

4. Choose OK. Windows returns you to the DOS system prompt. □

Step 2 displays the Control menu shown in Figure 3.12, which contains several options for managing either the current window or your total Windows environment. When available, selecting the Close option ends the current Windows session.

Each time you quit Windows, it displays a prompt box asking you to verify that you want to end the current session. This prompt box provides you with an opportunity to change your mind and return to the current session.

> **Note:** This prompt also provides a safeguard, so you can verify that you have closed any applications used during the current session.

63

You should now be back at the DOS prompt. Don't worry, we'll return to Windows in the next chapter.

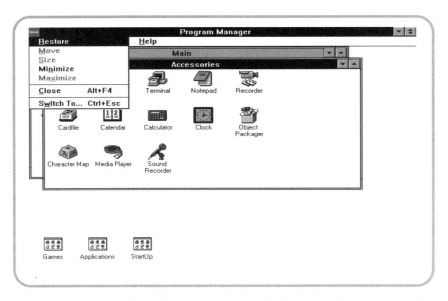

Figure 3.12. Select the Close option of the Control menu to end a Windows session.

What You Have Learned

▶ A typical Windows display contains a number of elements designed to simplify the process of working within a graphics-based environment. These include menu bars, pull-down option boxes, dialog boxes, scroll bars, and so on. Positioning the mouse cursor on these visual elements and performing the appropriate action makes working in the Windows environment an interactive process.

▶ Windows lets you modify the appearance and contents of the Windows GUI to complement your preferences and work habits.

Part Two

The Windows Environment

In the next two chapters, we look at the primary advantages associated with working within the Windows' GUI. Unlike standard DOS, which almost forces you to do things the way *it* thinks they should be done, Windows is extremely flexible. Windows enables you to set up a PC environment in which *you* feel comfortable working. A second major difference between DOS and Windows is the ease Windows brings to common PC operations such as copying files, creating directories, running application programs, and so on. Chapter 5, "Managing a Windows Session," describes how the improved Windows 3 File Manager simplifies such activities.

Customizing Windows

In This Chapter

▶ *The differences between Windows' two operating modes*

▶ *How to specify command parameters when starting Windows*

▶ *How to start applications from within Windows*

▶ *How to use Control Panel and Setup to modify your Windows environment*

I know you're probably eager to climb back into Windows. (Don't worry, we soon will.) Before we actually begin working in the various Windows applications, however, I want to make certain that Windows is set on your PC to run as efficiently as possible. This requires a short detour to examine the evolution of DOS-based personal computers—a topic that leads directly to a discussion of one of the most impressive features of Windows 3.1: its advanced memory management capabilities.

A Short History of PCs

I'm not going to get too technical here, I promise. My primary goal is to dwell on the subject only long enough to ensure that your Windows environment is configured to take full advantage of the memory installed on your PC. This said, let's forge ahead.

We begin by looking at the three general categories of personal computers on which Windows will run. Specifically, these include

▶ Systems built around the Intel 80286 microprocessor.
▶ Systems built around the Intel 80386 or i486 microprocessor.

It might look like we've swayed off-course here. Trust me, we haven't. As I'll explain shortly, the type of system you own directly influences the degree to which you can take advantage of Windows' advanced memory management features. Stay with me. Everything will be made clear as we move along.

Somewhere inside every PC sits a *microprocessor,* a special silicon chip designed to coordinate all other operations your PC performs. It is the heart and soul of that magical machine on which you rely so heavily. All microprocessors, however, are not created equal. As PC technology has evolved, so too have the microprocessors on which that technology depends. Each subsequent step up this ladder of electronic evolution has been accompanied by comparable improvements in the features and capabilities those microprocessors support. This is true especially in the area of memory management.

Early IBM and compatible personal computers—the so-called PC/XT models based on Intel's 8088 or 8086 microprocessor—were extremely limited in the amount of memory they were designed to support. Practically speaking, the largest amount of memory these first-generation PCs were capable of managing was 1 megabyte, or 1024 individual memory addresses.

If you'd like a useful analogy, picture a memory address as resembling a mail slot in an old-fashioned post office. Like the person distributing mail in our imaginary post office, your PC's microprocessor is responsible for constantly moving items in and out of these individual slots—making sure that the appropriate item (instruction or information) is placed in the correct slot and then knowing how to locate that item when it's needed. The original PC/XTs, therefore, could be compared to a post office with only enough space to accommodate 1024 slots. Admittedly, the manner in which your PC manages memory is more complex; for our purposes, however, this simple analogy suffices.

As if this 1-megabyte limit weren't restrictive enough, someone decided that over one-third of a PC's total memory, or 384K, should be reserved for controlling specific activities within that PC—coordinating its display, regulating the system clock, managing disk access, and so on. This left only 640K of *random access memory,* or RAM, available in which DOS could actually load and run any programs you planned to use, a figure condescendingly referred to as the *DOS 640K barrier.*

Life in PC land improved drastically with the introduction of a second generation of personal computers, dubbed AT systems, which were based on Intel's 80286 microprocessor. In essence, using an AT system resembles working in a post office with 16,384 mail slots, given that the 80286 chip is potentially capable of managing 16 megabytes (or 16 x 1024 bytes) of RAM. There was only one problem: DOS, by itself, still couldn't access these additional memory addresses—a dilemma not unlike building all those extra mail slots and then neglecting to have keys made to open them. Though potentially more powerful than the PC/XT models they improved on, at least in terms of the memory they could manage, 80286-based AT systems were still crippled by DOS. A frustrating situation for anyone who owned an AT? You bet. But the situation soon got better—or worse, depending on your perspective.

Unlike human evolution, which transpires over periods measured in millennia, improvements in computer technology come fast and furious. Even as it announced the 80286 chip, Intel was putting the finishing touches on its third-generation microprocessor, the 80386. Remember those 16,384 metaphorical mail slots incorporated into our previous postal annex? Well, how impressed would you be with a structure designed to hold *over 4 million* of them? Symbolically speaking, that's the 80386, which is theoretically capable of managing 4 gigabytes (4 x 1024 x 1024, or 4,194,304 bytes) of RAM! Now we're talking real PC power.

69

> **Note:** The recently released fourth-generation i486 chip is even more impressive. At some point, though, the numbers become so large their differences become inconsequential. Consequently, I'll limit our discussion to the three primary PC platforms, grouping the new i483 chip in with its immediate PC predecessor, the 80386.

Despite the availability of all this potential power, the advantages inherent in owning a PC more advanced than the original PC/XT remained largely unrealized. Anyone using standard DOS, even on a 386 system, was still destined to run smack up against the same impasse that existed before: that confounded 640K DOS barrier.

Did all this technological evolution merely represent an electronic exercise in futility? Hardly. Though fairly rigid, DOS's RAM restrictions are not impregnable. With the release of DOS 5.0 (and prior to that, by using memory management software), methods now exist so that you can climb over the 640K DOS barrier, even though you can't raze it completely. If that isn't the perfect cue to introduce the advanced memory management capabilities built into Windows 3.1, I don't know what is. See, I told you we'd get back to Windows, didn't I?

The Two Faces of Windows 3.1

As mentioned in Chapter 1, Windows 3.1 is designed to operate in two different modes:

Standard mode.
Enhanced 386 mode.

The existence of multiple alternatives in both PC platforms and Windows operating modes is no mere coincidence. The different configurations in which Windows can run is a direct result of the various types of DOS-compatible personal computers currently on the market. This isn't surprising, actually. You see, Microsoft planned it that way with the memory management techniques used by each of Windows operating modes designed to take full advantage of a specific generation of PC hardware.

Let's begin with a specific and rigid rule: you can't run Windows on a PC built around an 8086 or 8088 microprocessor, or so-called PC/XT systems. With earlier releases of Windows, doing so was impractical because of how slowly Windows ran on such systems. Starting with Windows 3.1, the impractical became impossible. You need at least an 80286-based AT system to run Windows 3.1.

Standard Mode

When operating in Standard mode, Windows 3.1 can access so-called high RAM memory located between 640K and the 1-megabyte memory address that DOS usually ignores. Standard mode also endows Windows with the capability of making *extended memory*—that is, RAM existing above the 1-megabyte memory address—available to those applications designed to take advantage of this feature. Consequently, programs that required the electronic equivalent of a crowbar to fit into previous releases of Windows, and then left precious little free memory for data storage when they were running, work fine under Windows 3.1.

The basic message lurking behind all this "technobabble" is a simple one: When operating in Standard mode, Windows no longer finds itself on a direct collision course with the dreaded 640K DOS barrier. If you have an AT system, therefore—or as I'll explain shortly, a 386 or 486 system with less than 2 megabytes of RAM—you'll probably want to force Windows 3.1 to run in Standard mode. I explain how to do this in a few paragraphs.

Enhanced 386 Mode

If your system is an 80386- or i486-based personal computer that includes 2-megabytes or more of RAM, you can run Windows 3.1 in its second and more advanced mode: Enhanced 386 mode. Enhanced 386 mode supports all the impressive features supported by Windows running in Standard mode, as well as providing a pair of additional capabilities only available in systems built around these two state-of-the-art microprocessors.

First, Enhanced mode enables a standard DOS application to run in its own window of a multiwindow display rather than automatically assigning such applications the entire screen, as happens when Windows is running in Standard mode. Second, and perhaps even more impressive, Enhanced mode enables Windows to convert available storage space on a hard-disk into *virtual memory*—a sort of artificial RAM created when disk space is temporarily used to store applications running in a Windows session—and then use this virtual memory to augment the actual RAM installed on your system. Consequently, the amount of memory available to Windows running in Enhanced 386 mode is ultimately determined by the amount of storage space available on your hard disk for Windows to use as a "swap file" to set up this virtual memory.

Using Command Switches

As I pointed out in Chapter 2, "Installing Windows," Windows tries to make a best guess as to how it should configure itself to run most efficiently on your PC. This includes selecting an initial operating mode, based on the hardware components Windows determines are installed on your system each time it is run. As a rule, there should be no reason to modify Windows's default configuration. If you ever do find it necessary to run Windows in a mode other than its default—as would be the case, for example, if Windows configures itself in Standard mode and you discover that some of your programs are designed to take advantage of the extended memory supported by Standard mode—there is an easy way to accomplish this.

When starting Windows, you can append one of two special switches to the WIN command, thus forcing Windows to run in a mode other than its default. These include

/S is used to force Windows to run in Standard mode.

/3 is used to force Windows to run in Enhanced 386 mode.

Typing the following command at the DOS system prompt, for example, would load Windows and instruct it to run in Standard mode:

```
WIN /S
```

As interesting as the technical aspects of personal computing might be, you are undoubtedly more interested in learning more about using Windows. Let's start another Windows session now from which we use the Control Panel and Setup accessories to complete customizing Windows to match your preferences. Restart Windows now by typing WIN and pressing Enter.

Tip: Entering the WIN command with the appropriate command switch forces Windows to run in a specified operating mode.

This reopens Windows and displays the screen shown in Figure 4.1. Notice that Windows displays the same workspace that was in effect when you ended the previous session. Each time you start a new Windows session, this feature, Windows' "memory" if you will, makes it easy to pick up where you left off. Now that Windows is running again, let's look at how you can use its Control Panel to further customize your Windows environment.

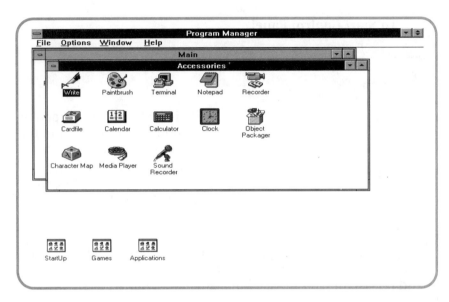

Figure 4.1. Each time you start Windows, it displays the workspace you had set up when you ended your previous session.

73

The Windows Control Panel

Control Panel provides a quick and easy way for you to modify several hardware and software settings associated with your system. The ability to access Control Panel from within a Windows session, combined with the fact that Windows immediately implements any modifications specified through its Control Panel, means that your Windows environment can be altered dynamically, as needed.

Starting Control Panel

You access Control Panel from within the Main program group.

 To Start Control Panel

1. Move the mouse cursor to any visible portion of the window containing the Main program group.

2. Click the left mouse button. This makes Main the active window and moves it to the front of your workspace.

3. Double-click the Control Panel icon. Windows displays a window containing the various Control Panel icons. ☐

74

> **Tip:** To open a Program group, remember to position your mouse cursor over the specified icon, then rapidly tap and release the left mouse button twice (double-click).

This opens a window from which you can access the various Control Panel options. Each option is represented by its own icon, as illustrated in Figure 4.2.

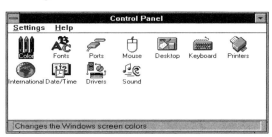

Figure 4.2. Use Control Panel to modify hardware and software settings associated with your Windows environment.

The Control Panel Options

Options available in the Control Panel window include

Color	Changes the colors used to display specific elements of the Windows GUI.
Fonts	Adds or removes fonts for your printer and display.
Ports	Specifies communication parameters for any serial ports installed on your system.
Mouse	Modifies mouse performance within the Windows environment.
Desktop	Modifies the appearance and other aspects of the Windows display.
Keyboard	Adjusts the keyboard repeat rate.
Printers	Installs and configures printers for your Windows environment.
International	Specifies international settings, such as the format used to display numbers and dates in your Windows environment.
Date/Time	Modifies the date and time recorded in your system clock.
Drivers	Installs, removes, and configures special files, called *drivers,* that control drivers such as special video and sound equipment connected to your PC.
Sound	Specifies whether Windows should generate a beep when it detects a potential error.

75

Two additional options might appear in the Control Panel window, depending on how Windows is configured to run on your system. These include

Network	Controls how Windows runs when installed on a network. (The Network option is only available if the system running Windows is installed on a network.)

386 Enhanced

Specifies how your system resources should be allocated among foreground and background applications when Windows is being used to run multiple programs in Enhanced 386 mode. (This icon only appears if Windows itself is operating in Enhanced 386 mode.)

To see how the Control Panel works, let's begin by installing a printer in your Windows environment.

Working with Printers

Windows' WYSIWYG (What-You-See-Is-What-You-Get) environment is ideal for creating printed documents. In truth, writing in Windows blurs the traditional lines that once existed between word processing and desktop publishing. As you'll see in Part Three of this book, even a simple letter created with the various Windows Accessories can be made extremely attractive, thus increasing its impact.

Of course, for that letter to impress someone, it first must be printed in hard copy. That's where your system printer comes in.

With standard DOS, each program you use must be set to recognize the specific type of printer you own. Beyond being inconvenient, the print drivers for all those different applications waste much disk space. Windows eliminates these hassles. When you install a single print driver in the Windows environment, that printer is available to every Windows application you run.

Accessing the Printers Dialog Box

You use the Printers dialog box to identify the types of printers you'll be using to print your Windows documents.

> **Tip:** If you selected the Custom Setup option, Windows
> might be set to recognize your printer. You should still
> read the following section, however, which outlines the steps
> you'll need to perform if you ever add a new printer to your
> system.

✓ To Access the Printers Dialog Box

Double-click the Control Panel Printers icon.

This displays the Printers dialog box shown in Figure 4.3. This dialog box provides an excellent example of how Windows simplifies many PC operations by converting them into interactive procedures.

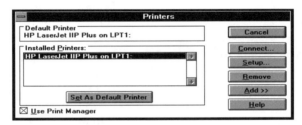

77

Figure 4.3. The Printers dialog box.

Installing a Printer

The first step in installing a printer into Windows is to identify what type of printer it is. Windows-supported printers are listed in a window in the lower-left corner of the Printers dialog box shown in Figure 4.3. After selecting a printer type, you can use the Install button to tell Windows to install that printer into your Windows environment.

Installing or Adding a Printer to your Windows Environment

1. Double-click the Printers icon in the Control Panel window.

Windows displays its Printers dialog box.

2. Click the Add button.

Windows displays a list of the different printers it supports.

3. Drag the button in the scroll bar to the right of the printer list until the type of printer you own is displayed in this window.

4. Click the name of your printer.

Windows highlights the name of the printer you selected.

5. Choose Install.

If necessary, Windows displays a prompt box requesting that you insert the distribution disk containing the print driver for the selected printer (see Figure 4.4).

78

6. Insert the specified disk and choose OK.

Windows copies the appropriate print driver from the distribution disk and adds the name of the printer you selected into the Installed Printers window in the Printers dialog box.

7. Choose Close.

Windows records any changes made in the Printers dialog box (see Figure 4.5) and returns you to the Control Panel. □

Tip: While installing a new printer, Windows might need to access a special file, called a *printer driver*. Printer drivers for a variety of printers are shipped on the Windows distribution disks. Make sure you have these disks handy before beginning the following exercise.

As mentioned in the previous tip, during printer installation Windows might use the dialog box shown in Figure 4.4 to request one of its distribution disks (see previous step 5). This dialog box identifies the distribution disk you need and indicates the drive where it should be inserted. As was true during installation, you can specify a different drive for this disk. To do so, simply replace the default drive letter A: with the appropriate drive for your distribution disks.

Figure 4.4. Windows identifies the disk on which the required print driver was shipped.

After step 5 in the Quick Step, you are returned to the Printers dialog box, and the printer you selected is added to your list of Installed Printers, as shown in Figure 4.5.

79

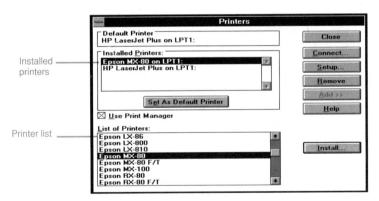

Figure 4.5. Windows adds the specified printer to its lists of Installed Printers.

Tip: Windows does a good job of letting you know when it needs a floppy disk to complete a given operation. Unfortunately, it rarely tells you when it's safe to remove that disk. Many's the time I've inadvertently left a disk in drive A of my PC, only to be greeted with a "Non-system disk" error message the next time I booted my system. Make sure you remove the distribution disk requested in the previous exercise and return it to your Windows box before continuing.

Using Multiple Printers

It's possible to have more than one printer installed on your PC. Many people, for example, use a dot-matrix printer for preparing preliminary drafts of their work and then rely on a laser printer for final copies. Windows simplifies this process by making it easy to install multiple printers and then switch between them for your various projects.

Let's apply the procedures outlined in the previous Quick Step to install a Panasonic dot-matrix printer in your Windows environment. If you have a different second printer, adjust your steps accordingly. If you don't have a second printer, don't worry. Go ahead and install this second printer as outlined below. You'll learn how to remove it in a few pages.

✓ To Install a Second Printer in your Windows Environment

▶ Scroll the printer list until the Panasonic KX-1180 option appears.

▶ Click Panasonic KX-1180.

▶ Choose the Install... button.

▶ If necessary, insert the requested distribution disk in the appropriate drive and click OK.

Again, after a few seconds, you are returned to the Printers dialog box. Notice that your new printer has been added to the Installed Printers list. Notice also that the previously installed printer remains the Default Printer. You can easily change this if you want.

Selecting a Different Default Printer

One printer in your Windows environment is always defined as the default printer. As a rule, this should be the printer you plan to use for the majority of your print operations. Changing the default printer is a simple, two-step operation.

 Changing the Default Printer

1. Double-click the Printers icon in the Windows Control panel.	Windows displays the Printer dialog box.

2. Click the printer you want
   to use as your default printer
   in the Installed Printers list.

   The printer you selected
   is highlighted.

3. Choose Set As Default Printer.

   The name of the selected
   printer is placed in the
   Default Printer box.   □

Modifying a Printer's Settings

Each print driver shipped with Windows uses certain default settings for printing. Whenever you install a new printer, therefore, it's
always a good idea to check its default settings to make sure they
reflect your personal preferences.

 To View a Printers Default Settings

1. Double-click the Printers
   icon in the Windows Control
   Panel.

   Windows displays its
   Printers dialog box.

2. In the Installed Printers list,
   click the printer for which
   you want to view the default
   settings.

   Windows highlights the
   printer you selected.

3. Choose Setup.

   Windows displays the
   settings for the selected
   printer.   □

81

   Choosing Setup displays a dialog box containing the default
settings for the selected printer. For example, Figure 4.6 shows the
default settings for an HP LaserJet IIP, one of the printers installed
in my Windows environment.

   As this sample screen shows, print options I can modify for my
LaserJet IIP include

▶ Resolution—how many dots-per-inch the HP LaserJet uses to
   print characters and graphic images.

▶ Paper Size—the type of paper on which I print.

▶ Memory—how much memory is installed in the HP LaserJet.

▶ Orientation—whether the LaserJet uses a vertical or horizontal orientation when printing a page.

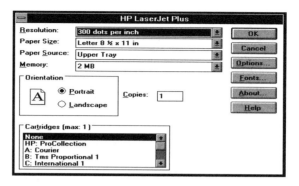

Figure 4.6. You can modify the default settings Windows uses for its installed printers.

The specific settings available differ from printer to printer. For example, the HP LaserJet supports print resolutions of 75, 150, and 300 dots-per-inch. Other printers might use different resolutions. (In case you're interested, a higher dpi setting increases the clarity and, therefore, the quality of your final printouts. Unfortunately, increasing the resolution also increases the amount of time it takes to print a document.)

As is true so often when working in Windows, the interactive nature of this dialog box makes it easy to modify the default settings for your printers. For example, I would use the following steps to increase the Memory setting for my HP LaserJet, which has 1.5 megabytes of installed memory.

1. Click the option arrow for **M**emory.
2. Click 2MB in the resulting pull-down option list.
3. Choose OK.

That's all there is to it. This increased memory amount would now become the default setting for my HP LaserJet and Windows would return me to the Printers dialog box shown in Figure 4.5.

Using the Windows Print Manager

Notice that you can choose between using the Windows Print Manager and printing your documents directly through DOS by setting one of the options in the Printers dialog box. Advantages associated with using the Windows Print Manager include

▶ Documents can be printed in the background, as you continue working in your Windows environment. When printing in Standard DOS—that is, outside Windows—you cannot use your system for anything else until printing is completed.

▶ Using Print Manager, you can send more than one document to your printer at a time, even if the various documents were created using different applications. When printing through DOS, you must wait until one document has finished printing before you can send a second document to the printer.

Background printing and multidocument handling greatly reduce traditional bottlenecks in PC productivity. As a rule, therefore, you'll want to leave this option set to its default setting, so you can take advantage of the Windows' Print Manager.

Removing a Printer

83

Nothing lasts forever, including PC hardware. Old hardware wears out or more likely, is replaced by newer, more powerful equipment. The **R**emove button in the Printers dialog box makes it easy to remove unused printers from your Windows environment.

 To Remove an Installed Printer

1. Double-click the Printers icon in the Windows Control Panel.

   Windows displays its Printers dialog box.

2. In the Installed Printers list, click the printer you want to remove from your Windows environment.

   Windows highlights the printer you want to remove.

3. Choose **R**emove.

   Windows displays a prompt box, which verifies that you want to remove the selected printer.

4. Click Yes in the subsequent prompt box.

   Windows removes the selected printer and returns you to the Printers dialog box.

Use the previous Quick Step to remove the Panasonic printer installed earlier. Windows is an extremely conscientious environment. For example, it does everything possible to guarantee that you have not accidentally selected the **R**emove option. Before actually deleting a printer from the Installed Printers list, Windows displays the prompt box shown in Figure 4.7. Choosing No cancels the **R**emove command and returns you to the Printers dialog box.

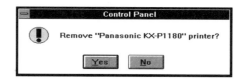

Figure 4.7. Windows guards against your accidentally removing a printer.

Saving Your Printer Settings

When your print environment is configured properly, have Windows save it for future use. To save the current printer settings

Choose Close in the Printers dialog box.

Windows records the new settings, closes the Printers dialog box, and returns you to the Control Panel.

A Metaphorical Desktop

In Windows parlance, your display is considered a "desktop." The choice of this word is not arbitrary. Comparing your Windows environment to a traditional desktop can help you understand what Windows does, how Windows works, and how it can help you get work done.

Think about it. Over the course of a typical day, as you shift from project to project, you're constantly rearranging objects on your desktop. You might pull a file from the bottom of a stack of papers and shift it to the top to make it more convenient to get to. You might take a notepad and move it over to the side of your desk, placing it temporarily out of the way. This kind of shuffling probably occurs frequently each day.

With Windows you can perform the same types of activities on your PC. Opening a new application program, for example, corresponds to removing a file from a file cabinet and placing it on your desk. Bringing an open window to the front of your display is not that different from shifting a file to the top of a stack of papers. Furthermore, rearranging individual display windows is not that different from moving physical items around on a desk.

Accessing the Desktop Dialog Box

You use the Control Panel's Desktop dialog box to define the basic "ground rules" for the organization of this metaphorical Windows desktop. Items specified with the Desktop dialog box include

85

▶ A pattern or image to serve as the background for your Windows' desktop.

▶ The arrangement of icons and their descriptions on your Windows display.

▶ Whether this desktop should include a "magnetic" grid that makes it easier to align the various elements in your Windows display.

▶ Whether your desktop includes a "screen saver," which can prevent possible damage to your monitor's screen.

▶ Additional features of your desktop's appearance, including the width of window borders and the rate at which the cursor blinks on your display.

 To Access the Desktop Dialog Box

1. Open the Control Panel window.

2. Double-click the Control Panel Desktop icon.

Windows displays the Desktop dialog box.   □

Double-clicking the Desktop icon displays the dialog box shown in Figure 4.8. Notice that this dialog box contains options corresponding to the various items described previously.

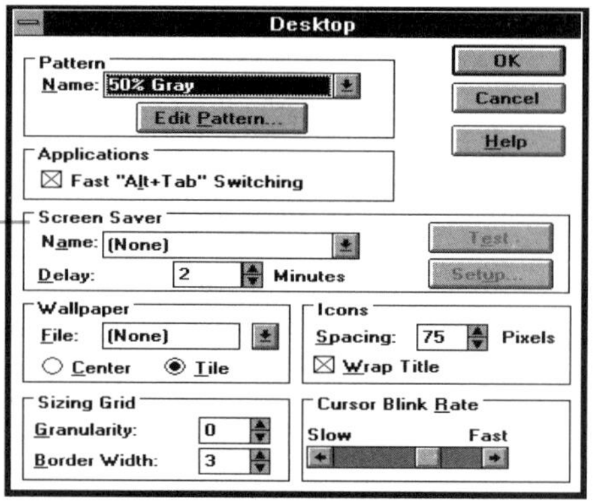

Figure 4.8. The Desktop dialog box.

Selecting a Screen Saver

86

Most of the options in the Desktop dialog box relate to personal preferences—that is, the unique "look and feel" you wish to establish for your metaphorical desktop. One item, the Screen Saver option, should interest everyone.

The graphic nature of the Windows environment might look attractive, but it also represents a potential danger to your monitor. Over time, sustained graphics can "burn into" a monitor's screen and appear as a ghost image, even when your system is turned off. The danger of this happening is highest when you're not actively working in Windows and the same display remains on the screen for a long time.

One way to avoid this problem is to have Windows temporarily blank out its display during extended periods of inactivity. Desktop's Screen Saver option is used to select a moving pattern to replace the Windows display, thus preventing screen burn-in. Using a second option, Delay, you can specify the period of time after which you want the Screen Saver activated.

Q **To Select a Screen Saver Pattern ▸**

1. Double-click on the Desktop icon in the Control Panel.

   The Desktop dialog box appears.

2. Click the down-arrow button located to the right of the Name field in the Screen Saver portion of the Desktop dialog box.

Windows displays a list of patterns available to Screen Saver.

3. Select the pattern you want to use.

This displays the Setup dialog box for the Screen Saver you chose.

4. Select the various options you want to use with this Screen Saver.

5. Click OK.

Setup box closes.

7. Click OK.

The Desktop dialog box closes, and your screen saver is activated. □

Step 2 displays a pull-down window containing a selection of Screen Saver patterns shipped with Windows. Any of these patterns can prevent burn-in. To easily personalize your desktop environment, use the Marquee option.

Use the Quick Step to select the Marquee screen saver. Selecting the Screen Saver Setup button displays the Marquee Setup dialog box shown in Figure 4.9. You use the Text section of this dialog box to enter the text you want to appear on your display during periods of inactivity.

87

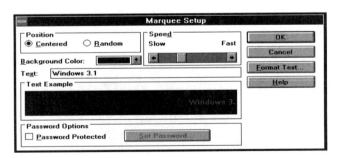

Figure 4.9. Marquee Setup lets you personalize your Windows Screen Saver.

Let's create a personalized Marquee for your Windows display:

1. Position the mouse cursor in the Text box.

2. Click the left mouse button.

3. Use the Del and Backspace keys to remove the default text that is in this box.

4. Type **This Windows desktop has been designed by** followed by your name.

5. Choose OK.

Windows records your personalized message and returns you to the Desktop dialog box shown in Figure 4.8. To see the results of your work, let's test the screen saver.

 To Test Screen Saver

1. Click the Test button in the Screen Saver portion of the Desktop dialog box.	The monitor goes blank, and your screen saver is activated.
2. Press any key or click the left mouse button.	You are returned to the Desktop dialog box. ☐

88

 Tip: If desired, use the Screen Saver Delay option to specify a period of inactivity other than the default 2-minute setting.

 To Exit the Screen Saver Dialog box

Click OK.

Assigning a Password to Your Windows Desktop

Password protection prevents unauthorized individuals from accessing the Windows desktop when the Screen Saver is activated. This feature is helpful especially if you regularly work on sensitive material in your Windows applications. After selecting a Screen Saver, you use the Password Options in the Setup dialog box to specify a password for your Windows environment.

Password Protecting Your Windows Environment

1. Double-click the Desktop icon in the Control Panel window.

   Windows displays its Desktop dialog box.

2. Select a Screen Saver.

3. Choose the Setup option in the Screen Saver portion of the Desktop dialog box.

   Windows displays a Setup dialog box containing the Password Options for the specified Screen Saver (see Figure 4.9).

4. Click **P**assword Protected.

5. Choose **S**et Password.

   Windows displays the Change Password prompt box (see Figure 4.10)

6. Enter the password you want to use in the **N**ew Password field and press Tab.

   Asterisks are displayed as you enter your password.

7. Re-enter your selected password in the **R**etype New Password field.

   Windows verifies that you entered the exact same password in the previous fields.

8. Choose OK.

   Windows stores your password and returns to the Desktop dialog box.

9. Choose OK.

   Windows records any changes made with Desktop, including your new password, and returns you to the Control Panel. □

89

Step 3 returns you to the Setup dialog box, shown in Figure 4.9. You use the Password Options portion of this dialog box to activate password protection and select the password used to redisplay your desktop after Screen Saver has been activated.

Selecting **S**et Password in step 5 displays the dialog box shown in Figure 4.10. You use this dialog box to enter a password that is required to deactivate the Screen Saver and return to your Windows desktop.

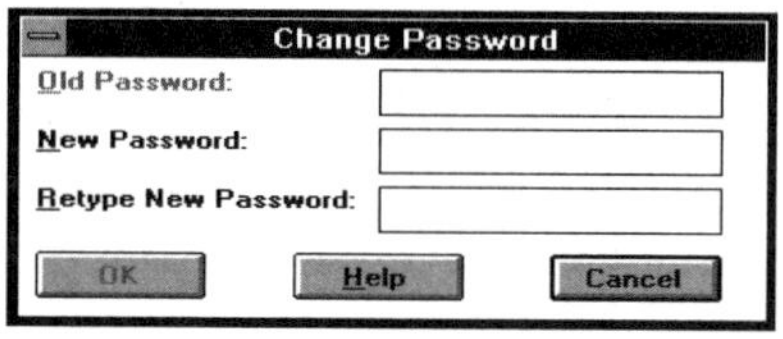

Figure 4.10. You can assign password protection to your Windows environment.

Note: Windows forces you to verify your selection, each time you create or change a password. This prevents a mistyped password from locking you out of your Windows desktop.

Windows records your new password and returns you to the Setup dialog box. To see what you've accomplished, use the following Quick Step:

90

To Test a New Password

1. Double-click the Desktop icon in the Windows Control Panel.

   Windows displays its Desktop dialog box.

2. Choose the Test option in the Desktop dialog box.

   Windows blanks the screen and displays your screen saver.

3. After the Screen Saver is activated, press any key or click your mouse button.

   Windows displays the Password dialog box.

4. Type the password you selected in the previous exercise and press Enter.

   The Windows display is restored.

Before Windows deactivates the Screen Saver, Windows displays the dialog box shown in Figure 4.11, informing you that your desktop is protected and requesting that you enter the appropriate password. Anyone who does not know the correct password can't access your Windows environment.

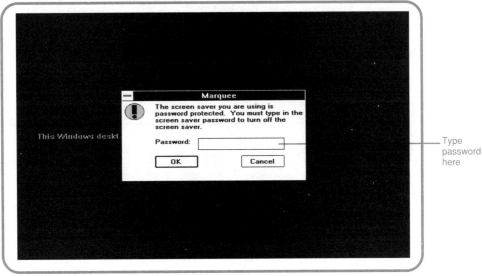

Type
password
here

Figure 4.11. You must enter a password to turn off the screen saver.

This turns off the screen saver and returns you to the Desktop dialog box, which is where you were prior to testing your password protection.

> **Tip:** As is true of any security device, a Windows password is only as effective as you make it; a dead bolt protects your home more efficiently than a simple turn lock. You should keep this same principle in mind when selecting a password for your Windows environment. For example, don't use an obvious password like your last name or the first name of your spouse. Any knowledgeable individual truly interested in accessing your Windows applications certainly will try entering such an obvious selection at the password prompt. Instead, you should specify a password that even people who know you will have difficulty figuring out. It also is a good idea to change your password from time to time as an additional security precaution.

As the previous two examples illustrate, you can fine-tune your Windows environment using the various Desktop options. Of course, when the Desktop settings reflect your personal preferences, you'll want Windows to save them for future use.

Follow the previous Quick Step if you wish to password-protect Windows.

✓ To Exit the Desktop Dialog Box and Return to the Windows Control Panel

Click OK.

Working with Fonts

One major appeal of Windows is its reliance on a WYSIWYG design, the so-called What-You-See-Is-What-You-Get nature of the Windows interface. Despite this sobriquet, however, early versions of Windows only approximated on the screen the final appearance of printed documents. In other words, what you saw on the Windows display was almost what you got in your printouts. (Should we more correctly call this a WYSIAWYG approach?) That's because of the font technology, or character styles, used by Windows 3 and earlier releases.

Beginning with Windows 3.1, Microsoft added support for a new feature called True Type to the Windows package. True Type overcomes the previous weakness in Windows WYSIWYG design by making it possible to install fully scalable fonts in the Windows environment.

What Are Scalable Fonts?

Professional typesetters spend years learning the "ins and outs" of font technology. Unfortunately, we only have space for a brief overview.

Stated simply, a specific typeface is defined by a combination of two attributes:

▶ The way in which the letters it contains are designed, called the *font*.

▶ The size of those letters, commonly referred to as *point size*.

With standard fonts, different files, consisting of different sets of letters in various sizes, must be available to create multiple typefaces. One file, for example, would contain letters in Helvetica font of 24-point size—in other words, a 24-point Helvetica type-face—a second file would be required to generate a 16-point Helvetica typeface, and so on, for all the available Helvetica typefaces. With a scalable font, on the other hand, a single font file can be used to create typefaces of virtually any point size. Thus, a single scalable font file containing Helvetica-style letters can generate a 24-point Helvetica typeface, a 16-point Helvetica typeface, and almost any other Helvetica typeface you want to use.

Certain types of printers have supported scalable fonts for years. Until version 3.1, however, the Windows display was limited to using only predefined font sizes. Microsoft's new True Type technology guarantees that what you see on your Windows display is really what you get when you print. (WYIRWYGWYP? See how easy it is to create impressive looking computer acronyms?)

93

With scalable fonts, one file is used for both the printer and the display, which is why you get WYSIWYG. Scalable fonts (called True Type fonts by Windows) get their name from the fact that only one file is used for the various point sizes; it is "scaled" up or down as necessary. The result of using True Type fonts is that you get better quality output, while reducing the amount of font files on your hard drive.

The Fonts Dialog Box

Several fonts, of both the True Type and traditional variety, are included with Windows. In most situations, these built-in fonts suffice. For certain applications—desktop publishing comes imme-diately to mind—you might wish to expand your Windows font library beyond its original size. Additional Windows-compatible fonts are available from a number of software companies. You use the Control Panel's **F**onts option to add a new font set to your Windows environment.

 To Access the Fonts Dialog Box

Double-click the Fonts icon in the Control Panel.

Windows displays its Fonts dialog box.   □

Selecting Fonts displays the Fonts dialog box, shown in Figure 4.12. This dialog box can be used to add and remove fonts and to specify how you want the new True Type technology applied to your Windows environment.

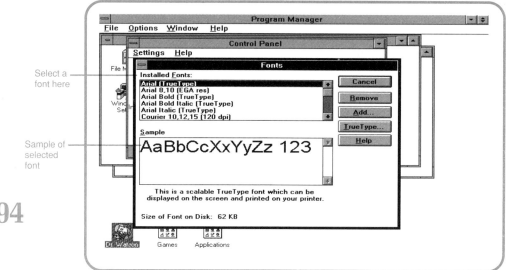

Select a font here

Sample of selected font

Figure 4.12. Windows 3.1 added some impressive font capabilities to the Windows environment.

Each time you send a document to the printer, Windows checks the current printer driver to see whether it supports all the fonts that document contains. If the driver supports all the fonts, the final printout will look exactly as it did in your Windows' display. If a specific font is not supported by your printer, Windows attempts to substitute a screen font from the Windows font files available on your system. These fonts are listed in the Installed Fonts window of the Fonts dialog box.

The Sample Font window shows a sample of the currently active (highlighted) font in all available sizes. If only a single font size is shown, as is the case with the Arial font shown in Figure 4.12, you are viewing a scalable font. (Notice that the Arial font is identified as a scalable font within the Installed Fonts listing.)

As you might suspect, the Add and Remove buttons are used to add to and remove fonts from the Installed Fonts list, respectively. Choosing the Add button takes you to a second dialog box, which you use to tell Windows where to find the files containing any new fonts you might purchase independently or receive with a specific application.

> **Caution:** Never attempt to remove the MS Sans Serif fonts installed by Windows. These fonts are used in most Windows dialog boxes. Removing them from your Windows environment makes for some interesting and frustrating experiences.

Two other items worth noting are the pair of options available by clicking the True Type button in the Fonts dialog box.

▶ The Enable True Type Fonts option tells Windows whether to make the True Type technology available to your Windows environment. If you do not anticipate using True Type fonts in your documents, turn off this option to free system memory for other uses.

▶ The Show Only True Type Fonts in the Application option is used to tell Windows you are working exclusively with True Type fonts. Turning this option on is another way to free memory for other uses, but doing so restricts you to using only True Type fonts in your documents.

95

> **Note:** Changes made to the **True** Type settings with these last two buttons modify the WIN.INI file (a special file in which Windows stores your default configuration) and therefore, do not take effect until you exit Windows and restart Windows again.

√ **To Exit the Fonts Dialog Box and Return to the Windows Control Panel**

Choose Cancel.

As you can see, the Control Panel provides several methods for customizing the Windows environment to meet your specific needs. Using additional Control Panel options, you can change the colors used in your Windows display (Color), configure your serial ports (Ports), modify how dates, times, and numbers are represented in your Windows applications (International), reset your system clock (Date/Time), adjust the sensitivity of your mouse (Mouse) and keyboard (Keyboard), and turn on or off the Windows warning beep (Sound). Selecting any of these options displays a dialog box that you use to perform the desired operation.

Control Panel is useful for changing attributes of Windows itself. Next, let's look at how Windows' Setup program can be used to modify elements of your system configuration without forcing you to completely reinstall Windows, as was required in earlier versions.

✓ To Exit the Windows Control Panel

Double-click the Control Panel Control button.

Using Setup to Modify Your System Configuration

Early Windows releases forced you to run Setup from the DOS prompt. Consequently, if you upgraded your display, for example, you had to reinstall Windows completely before it would recognize this new purchase—a major inconvenience, as almost any Windows veteran will attest. Beginning with Windows 3, Microsoft made it possible to access the Windows-based portion of Setup from within a Windows session. System components you can upgrade with Setup include

▶ Display
▶ Keyboard
▶ Mouse
▶ Network

Starting Setup

You start Setup just as you would any other Windows applications.

To Start Setup

1. Open Main window
2. Double-click the Windows   Windows displays its
   Setup option in the Main   Setup option box.
   window.   □

This displays the Windows **S**etup option box shown in Figure 4.13. You use this option box to identify the element(s) of your Windows environment that need to be modified.

Figure 4.13. You can modify system components of your Windows environment by using the Windows Setup program.

97

Setup is slightly different from other Windows applications in that you must use its pull-down **O**ptions menus to select the item you want to modify. To see how this works, let's assume you've added a network to the system on which Windows is installed. In this situation, you would use the following steps to configure Windows to be compatible with that network.

> **Caution:** Unless you really do need to configure Windows for a network, make sure you follow the steps in the following Quick Step exactly. It is being presented here only as an example of the procedures used to modify a **S**etup option. Do not perform this Quick Step now. Make sure you close all applications and save files before configuring your system for a network. At the end of this procedure, you will be forced to exit Windows and reboot your system.

 To Configure Windows for Network Compatibility

1. Choose **O**ptions from the   Windows displays its pull-
   Windows Setup menu bar.   down Setup Options menu.

2. Choose Change System Settings from the resulting pull-down menu.	Windows displays its Change System Settings dialog box.
3. To see the Networks Windows supports, choose the down arrow to the right of the Network option.	Windows displays a list of networks it supports.
4. Select your Network from the list.	The network you select is highlighted.
5. Click OK.	Setup prompts you to insert a disk with the network driver file.
6. Insert the disk with the network driver file.	Setup copies the necessary files.
7. Select whether to Restart Windows now or Return to MS-DOS.	You must reboot your system before using Windows. □

Step 2 calls the dialog box shown in Figure 4.14. Notice the down arrow to the right of each option displayed in this box. Clicking one of these arrows displays a listing of available settings for the corresponding item that are compatible with Windows 3.1.

Figure 4.14. The Change System Settings dialog box displays those items you can reconfigure using the Windows Setup utility.

Note: Compatibility is critical when modifying Setup options because Windows must have access to a device driver capable of supporting the specified item. In those cases, where Windows itself does not support a specific device, check to see whether the manufacturer provides its own device driver so that its product runs with Windows.

To identify the network installed on your system, choose that network from the resulting list of Windows-compatible network drivers, shown in Figure 4.15.

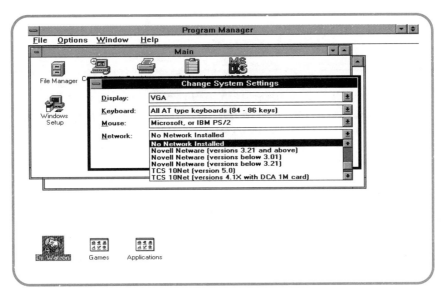

Figure 4.15. Windows displays lists of hardware with which it is compatible in each Setup category.

Now that you've seen how Setup works, let's back out of the current exercise without actually installing a network driver.

Q To Exit Setup Without Modifying Your System Configuration

1. Choose the Control menu box of the Change System Settings window.

2. Choose Close.

   This returns you to the Windows Setup option box.

3. Choose the Control menu box of the Windows Setup window.

   Windows displays a pull-down menu listing the Setup Control options.

4. Choose Close.

   Windows closes the Setup utility and returns you to Program Manager.   □

This closes the Setup window and returns you to the Program Manager with the Main group still the active window.

What You Have Learned

▶ Windows 3.1 can run in two different operating modes—Standard and Enhanced 386—each of which is designed to provide maximum support for different types of personal computers. Which mode you should run Windows in depends on the specific hardware comprising your PC system.

▶ It's possible to override Windows' default operating mode by including the appropriate command switch with the WIN command used to start a Windows session.

▶ Using the Control Panel and Setup utilities, you can modify your Windows environment. As a general rule, use Control Panel to change settings internal to Windows itself—display colors, fonts, your desktop layout, icon placement, and so on. Setup, on the other hand, provides a way to tell Windows when new or different hardware has been added to your system configuration. You access Control Panel and Setup just as you would any other Windows application.

Managing a Windows Session

In This Chapter

▶ *How the Windows Program Manager Works*
▶ *How to Use the Windows File Manager*
▶ *How to Create and Maintain Program Groups*

Until now, we've discussed the more general aspects of the Windows GUI. For example, you now know how to install, customize, and interact with Windows (on a cursory level). From here on out, the discussion gets a little more specific—to open Windows a little wider and look around—such as, the procedures you use regularly when running actual applications within the Windows environment. You begin by looking at Program Manager and File Manager, two features of Windows 3.1 that you use to organize and manage the programs and data files comprising your total PC environment.

The Windows Program Manager

Microsoft designed its Windows Program Manager to accomplish something that simply can't be done with standard DOS. Specifically,

Program Manager lets you organize your disk files logically—that is, based on how those files will be used—rather than strictly reflecting their physical location on your hard disk. That's not self-explanatory, is it? Maybe I'd better use an example.

The DOS Directory Structure

Using the standard DOS directory structure is similar to organizing paper documents with a traditional filing cabinet. On a given hard disk, for example, you might choose to store files associated with your word-processing program in one directory, analogous to a single manila folder in a file cabinet. Then create a second directory to hold the documents your word processor generates. You also could make a third directory for your spreadsheet program, a fourth directory to store your spreadsheet files, and so on, creating one directory for each of your application programs and a second dedicated to its corresponding data files.

102

Although better than no organization at all, DOS's strict reliance on how files are physically stored on a disk leaves much to be desired, especially when you consider how most people work. When was the last time you put together a project that relied on a single application program? Perhaps a better question would be, have you ever worked on a project that could be completed using a single program? Odds are the answer is no. More likely, the work emanating from your PC contained elements from several sources.

An annual report, for example, might include text files created with a word processor, some tables generated with a spreadsheet program, a graphics file or two designed visually to emphasize a point, and so on. The problem is, DOS's reliance on directories and subdirectories provides little help in organizing such tasks—forcing you, as it does, to scramble hither and yon through the physical layout of your hard disk when the time comes to gather all the various elements of a given project. The Windows Program Manager provides a more logical approach.

A More Logical Approach

Unlike DOS, which organizes your files based strictly on their physical location, you can use the Windows Program Manager to gather multiple files into a single program group, regardless of those files' storage location within a disk's directory structure. Sticking with our previous example for a moment, you can use the Windows Program Manager to create a program group called Annual Report. This group, in turn, would contain an icon representing your word processor, a second for a spreadsheet program, a third for a graphics program, as well as individual icons associated with each of the data files created by these various applications, files that ultimately will be combined to produce your final report. Whenever it is time to work on this project, all you have to do is open this program group, and you have immediate access to all the application and data files you need.

Program Manager provides additional convenience so that you can include the same application or data file in more than one program group. The same word-processing program file assigned to the Annual Report group, for example, could be included in a program group you've created to manage and organize your personal correspondence. This, again, differs from the standard DOS disk structure, where the only way to have a file exist in more than one directory is to create multiple copies of that file, a waste of valuable storage space.

103

Beyond providing a logical alternative for organizing program and data files, Program Manager includes several additional features designed to simplify managing your PC activities. Rather than merely describing the various capabilities built into the Windows Program Manager, however, why don't you return to your previous Windows session and see just what you can accomplish with this impressive new organizational tool?

Using the Program Manager

You might not realize it, but you already are familiar with the Windows Program Manager. The Program Manager starts automatically when you begin a Windows session. Consequently, you've been working in the Program Manager almost exclusively throughout the previous two chapters. Furthermore, at least three program groups—possibly more, depending on what types of programs Setup discovered when you installed Windows on your hard disk—exist in your Windows environment. Instead of letting Setup have all the fun, however, let's create our own program group, one designed to hold the programs and data files you work with in Part III, "The Windows Accessories."

Creating a Program Group

You create a program group using the New command, one of the
options listed in the Program Manager File menu.

 To Create a Program Group

1. From the Program Manager menu, choose File.

   Windows displays its pull-down menu.

2. Choose New.

   Windows displays its New Program Object dialog box.

3. Choose Program Group.

4. Choose OK.

   Windows displays its Program Group Properties dialog box.

5. Type the name of the new group in the Description box.

6. Press Enter to specify OK.

   Windows creates a New Program Group window. □

Use the previous Quick Step to create the new Program Group,
Book Exercises. When you create a new Program Group, Windows
displays the New Program Object dialog box shown in Figure 5.1.
Like most Windows operations, creating a new program group is an
interactive procedure: Windows requests the details it needs, and
you provide the proper information.

*Figure 5.1. Use the New Program Object dialog box to supply
initial information about your new group.*

First, Windows needs to know whether you want to create an
entirely new program group or add a new program to an existing
group.

The Program Group Properties dialog box, shown in Figure 5.2,
is what you use to assign a group name to your new program group.
The name you enter in the Description field appears in the title bar

whenever this group is active. At other times, a group's name is displayed beneath its icon.

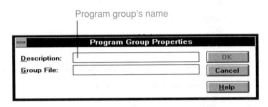

Figure 5.2. Windows uses information entered in the Description field as the new program group's name.

Tip: Group names are not limited by the eight-character DOS file-naming conventions. Consequently, it's possible to specify a group name that adequately describes a group's function. Keeping group names short prevents them from overlapping one another and conserves space on your Windows display.

105

Each time you create a new program group, Program Manager creates a group file, which Windows subsequently uses to keep track of any program and data files assigned to that group. Group files are named by combining a derivative of the specified group name with the file extension .GRP. Unless you want a specific name assigned to a group file, therefore, you should leave the Group File field in the Program Group Properties dialog box blank.

After setting up the required files, Program Manager automatically displays a blank window for the new group, as shown in Figure 5.3. At this point, you can begin assigning items—program and data file icons—to your newly created Book Exercises group.

There are three ways you can add items to a group.

1. By using the mouse to move or copy icons from one program group to another.
2. By manually identifying the program item you want added to a group.
3. By using the Windows File Manager to create new program item icons for a program group.

In the following sections, we look at the first method, which was outlined previously. The other two techniques are covered later in this chapter when we examine the Windows File Manager.

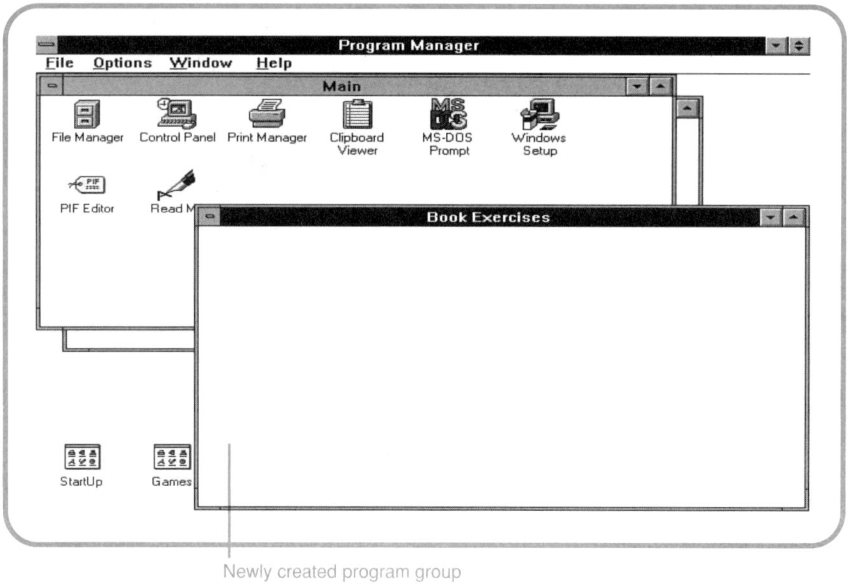

Newly created program group

Figure 5.3. Program Manager automatically displays the new program group as the active window.

Moving Icons Between Program Groups

The easiest way to add a new item to a program group is to move or copy that item from an existing group. This method is especially convenient when you need to include an application program in multiple groups. You will probably want to assign your word-processing program, for example, to every group that uses document files. That's exactly what you're going to do with the Windows Write program.

To Copy Programs Between Groups

1. Position the mouse cursor over the icon associated with the program you want to copy to a program group.

2. Press and hold down the Ctrl key.

3. Press and hold down the left mouse button.

This selects the icon.

4. Drag the mouse until the icon is located within the program group you're copying it to.

A duplicate image of the icon moves across the screen as you move your mouse.

5. Release Ctrl and the left mouse button.

Windows creates a copy of the original icon in the target program group.   ☐

We use the previous Quick Step to add some programs to our new Book Exercises group. First, choose **W**indow from the Program Manager menu bar. Choose **A**ccessories.

This makes the **A**ccessories group the active window and brings it to the foreground of your Windows display, as shown in Figure 5.4.

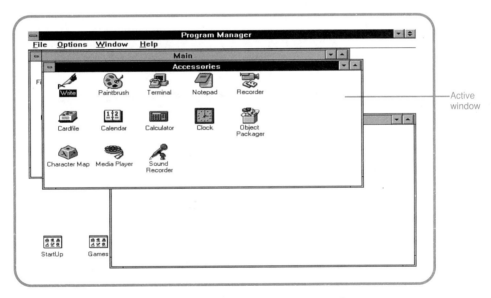

Figure 5.4. The first step in transferring an icon between program groups is to make the group containing that icon the active window.

Tip: You could have displayed the Accessories group by clicking any visible portion of its window. Given that most of the Accessories window was obscured, however, I opted to use the menu bar Window command.

At this point, you have two options for transferring an icon from the Accessories group to your new Book Exercises group.

1. Dragging an icon exclusively with the mouse moves it from Accessories into the new group. That is, the program associated with that icon no longer exists in the Accessories group when the move operation is completed.
2. Depressing the Ctrl key as you drag an icon replicates that icon in the new group. That is, the program associated with that icon is assigned to both groups when moved in this manner.

We are employing the second method so that you can access the Windows Write program from both the Book Exercises and Accessories groups. Follow the steps included in the previous Quick Step to add Write to the Book Accessories group.

Your display now resembles Figure 5.5, which shows a copy of the Write icon located in the Book Exercises window. You can now access Write directly by double-clicking either of the two Write icons that now exist in your Windows environment.

108

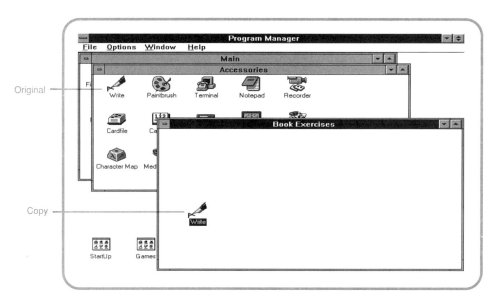

Figure 5.5. Dragging the Write icon with the Ctrl key pressed places a copy of that icon in the Book Exercises window.

Keep in mind, however, that a single copy of Windows Write still is on your hard disk. This is one of the major advantages associated with using the Windows Program Manager to complement standard DOS, which would require that you actually copy a program file in a different directory if you wanted that program directly associated with other files in a program group—a misnomer in itself, because DOS doesn't support the creation of program groups.

Before moving on, let's copy a few other Windows accessories into the Book Exercises program group, so they are available for use in Part III, "The Windows Accessories." Using the same procedures outlined in the previous exercise, replicate the Paintbrush and Cardfile icons in the Book Exercises program group. When you're finished, your screen should resemble Figure 5.6.

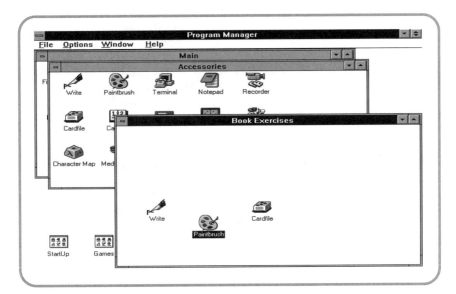

Figure 5.6. We use the Windows accessories now assigned to the Book Exercises group in Part III.

Note: Your display might differ slightly from Figure 5.6, depending on where you positioned the Paint and Cardfile icons while copying them from the Accessories window. What's important here is to make certain that you transfer all three of the specified icons into the Book Exercises program group. As I mentioned earlier, we use them in Part III, "The Windows Accessories."

Now that the necessary icons exist in your Book Exercises program group, let's arrange them more conveniently for subsequent use.

 To Rearrange Icons in a Newly Created Group

1. If necessary, click the mouse cursor on any visible portion of the program group in which you want to rearrange icons.

   This makes the selected window the active program group.

2. Choose the Window option of the Program Manager menu bar.

   This displays the pull-down menu.

3. Choose Arrange Icons.

   Windows organizes the icons in the active window. □

Use the previous Quick Step to rearrange the icons in the Book Exercise group. The previous exercise redraws your Windows display, automatically rearranging the icons in the Book Exercises program group to resemble Figure 5.7.

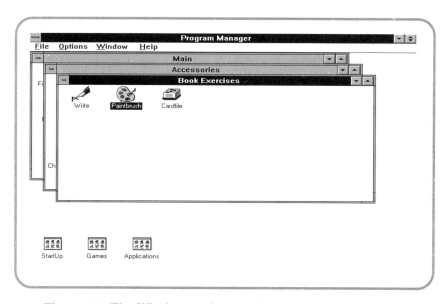

Figure 5.7. The Window options make it easy to organize your desktop.

Now that we have the beginnings of a program group dedicated to future exercises, let's move over to the Windows File Manager to complete this work.

Using the Windows File Manager

File Manager resembles the Windows Program Manager in that it simplifies working with various elements of your PC environment. Although you use Program Manager to manage programs and groups of programs, File Manager, as its name implies, is designed to help you organize your files and disk directories. File Manager works much like other traditional DOS shells, such as XTree or Norton Commander. One major benefit File Manager has over its standard DOS counterparts is that, being a Windows application, File Manager takes full advantage of the Windows GUI.

111

> **Note:** Microsoft first introduced File Manager in Windows 3. That initial version of File Manager, although useful, was extremely primitive, to say the least. Beginning with Windows 3.1, this Windows-aware DOS shell truly came into its own. The examples and exercises in the remainder of this chapter are based on the File Manager introduced in Windows 3.1. Anyone with an earlier version of Windows can't use these examples and exercises as presented. When you folks with a pre-3.1 Windows release see what you're missing, however, it's a pretty sure bet that you'll want to upgrade to a newer version of Windows. When you do, what follows will be familiar territory, indeed.

Starting File Manager

During installation, **S**etup automatically included File Manager in your Main program group. Before actually starting File Manager, therefore, if you've been working in another window, you need to make the Main program group your active window.

To switch to the Main Window and start File Manager

1. Position your mouse cursor on the title bar of the Main window.
2. Click the left mouse button.
3. When the Main window appears, double-click the File Manager icon.

After a few seconds, during which Windows analyzes your system components and the contents of the currently active disk drive, you see a window resembling Figure 5.8.

Note: The specific items listed in your File Manager window will differ from those shown here, which reflect the disk drives and directories on my system.

112

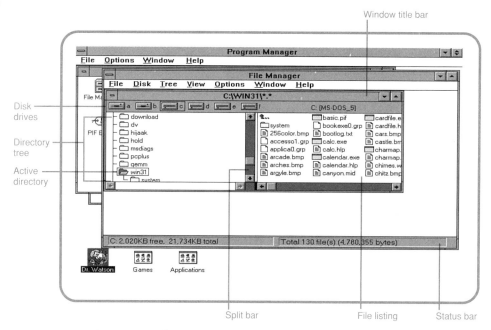

Figure 5.8. The File Manager window.

File Manager Basics

As mentioned earlier, File Manager resembles a traditional DOS shell. As such, you can manage the disks, directories, and files comprising your PC environment without forcing yourself to memorize the often complicated and potentially confusing command syntax employed by standard DOS—that is, when you're beginning PC operations directly from the DOS system prompt.

Remember the example I presented in Chapter 1, where a simple Windows procedure replaced the following two standard DOS commands:

```
COPY C:\DOS\ANSI.SYS D:\WINDOWS
DEL C:\DOS\ANSI.SYS
```

And, as I pointed out in that earlier example, this is a simple activity. The more complex your day-to-day PC activities, the greater the advantages you realize from relying on Windows' File Manager instead of working in what I call "naked DOS."

113

Common DOS operations that can be performed from within the Windows File Manager can be broken down into three major categories including

- ▶ Disk-related operations—changing the active disk drive, formatting, copying, and labeling disks.
- ▶ Directory-related operations—changing the active directory and creating and removing directories.
- ▶ File-related operations—copying, moving, renaming, and deleting files, searching your disks and directories for specific files, changing the appearance and contents of file listings, and printing the contents of a file to your system printer.

In addition to these standard DOS operations, File Manager can be used to perform the following operations relating more directly to the Windows environment:

Windows-related operations—running an application within the Windows environment, creating associations between data files and the applications that created them, adding an application program and its associated data files to a Windows program group, and specifying which DOS operations require confirmation before being initiated from within Windows.

Best of all, with File Manager, you can initiate each of these operations using the familiar point-and-click techniques previously introduced in this book. Later portions of this chapter contain exercises that demonstrate the specific steps used to perform these activities. Before pointing and clicking our way down into the depths of File Manager, however, let's analyze the various components of its display, as illustrated by Figure 5.8.

The File Manager Display

Notice first, the similarities that exist between the File Manager screen and displays we've seen in previous exercises. We can start with the familiar title bar, which identifies this as a File Manager window. There's also a menu bar, listing the various options available when you're working within File Manager. Finally, the File Manager window contains **C**ontrol, Ma**x**imize, Mi**n**imize, and **Re**store boxes, which can be used to change the size and location of this window quickly.

In addition to these standard items found in every Windows window, the File Manager window in Figure 5.8 includes the following display elements:

▶ Disk drive icons—identify all storage devices installed on your system with different icons used to represent floppy disks, hard disks, network drives, RAM disks, and CD-ROM devices. Figure 5.8, for example, lists three drives, A-C, of which A and B are floppy disks. (No network drives, RAM disks, or CD-ROM devices are represented in this figure.)

▶ Active drive—surrounds the icon on the line directly below the menu bar. Figure 5.8 indicates that drive C is currently active.

▶ Workspace—consists of two distinct, vertically arranged elements: a visual representation, called a directory tree, of those directories that exist on the current drive and a file listing for the currently active directory. These are located in the left and right portions of Figure 5.8, respectively.

▶ Title bar—indicates the currently active disk drive, directory, and files that are included in the file listing portion of the File Manager display, c:\win31*.* in Figure 5.8.

▶ Active directory—win31 in Figure 5.8.

► Scroll bars—automatically included when more files exist in the current directory than can fit across the bottom of the directory listing portions of the display window, as shown in Figure 5.8. (Scroll bars also appear below the directory tree if more directories exist on the active drive than will fit in the File Manager display.)

► Types of files—associated with a variety of icons resembling file folders, pieces of paper, display windows, and so on. (Don't worry, I'll explain what each of these icons represents as we move along.)

► Status line—runs across the bottom of the file manager and reveals storage-related information about the currently active disk and directory. The section of this status line directly below the directory tree lists the total size and amount of storage space still available on the active drive (Figure 5.8, for example, indicates that my hard disk, drive C, is 41,374KB, or approximately 41-megabytes, in size and still contains 24,550KB, or slightly more than 24-megabytes, of available storage space).

► Similar status line (below the file listing)—indicates the number and total storage requirements of files in the currently active directory. (The section of this status line below the file listing indicates that my win31 directory contains 92 files that occupy 3,654,722, or just over 3.5-megabytes, of disk space.)

Now that I've outlined the various elements contained in the File Manager display, let's see how they are used to organize and manage your disk, directory, and file related operations.

Working with Disks

Without disks, your PC would be useless. Almost everything stored in a computer's memory is lost when you turn your computer off. If there were not some way to preserve the work being done when you shut down your system, therefore, you would have to begin all over—start from scratch—each time you booted your PC. That's where disks come in. Even after your PC is turned off, your efforts are preserved.

To understand what I mean, imagine your personal computer as resembling a typical office. Within this imaginary office, the system unit itself, with its various memory chips and microprocessors, corresponds to a desktop. (In fact, as I explained in the previous chapter, Windows exploits this desktop metaphor to provide a comfortable and familiar work area.)

Chances are one of the first things you do when you arrive at your office each morning is assemble, on your desktop, all the items and information you think you'll need to complete whatever project you plan to work on that day. This would be analogous to loading program and data files into your PC's memory. Where do those different items and all that information come from? Your desk probably has drawers. Your office also might contain a file cabinet or two. These locations, the various places where you store the tools of your trade, serve the same function as disks do within your PC system.

If you've followed along in previous chapters, you will not have any trouble initiating the File Manager disk-related operations. The basic procedures for using File Manager are virtually identical to those you've been using throughout this book. Before looking at specific disk-related activities, however, let's expand the workspace in our current File Manager display.

✓ To Expand the File Manager Workspace

Click the Maximize box (the up arrow) located to the extreme right of the File Manager window.

This changes your Windows display to resemble Figure 5.9. Notice how the file listing was adjusted automatically to take advantage of the larger display area.

With this larger work area available, we can begin examining the disk-related operations you can perform from within the Windows File Manager. But before we do, let's learn some basics about disk types.

There are two different sizes of disks, 3 1/2" and 5 1/4". The 3 1\2" size disks are covered in a hard plastic which protects them from most damage. Both sizes of disks come in two types: high density and double density.

The density of a disk determines the amount of data that it can hold. A high density disk can hold twice as much data as a double density disk of the same size.

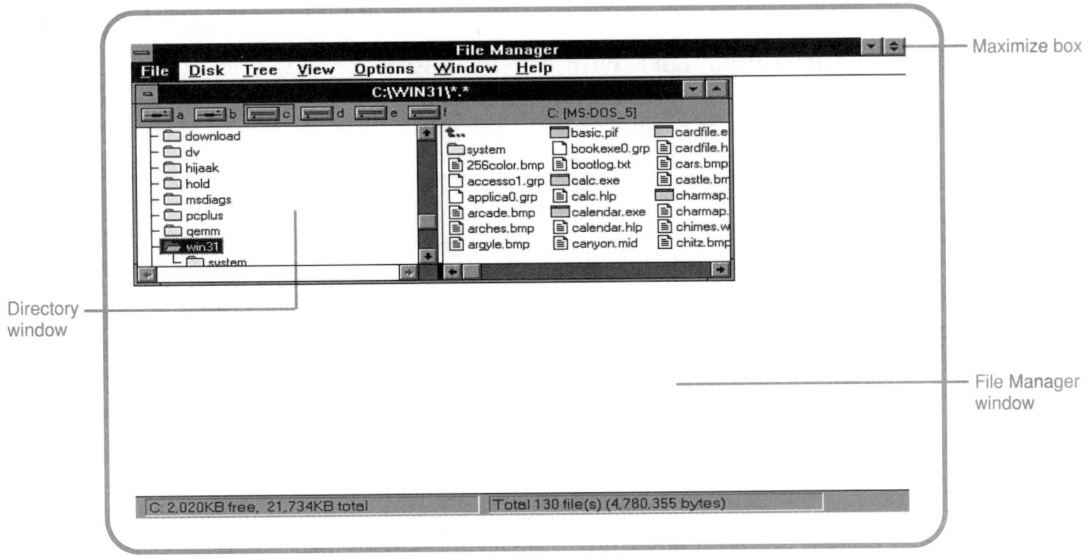

Figure 5.9. Clicking the Maximize box expands the File Manager window to full-screen size.

Caution: It is important to use the right type of disk for the drive that your PC has. To determine the type of drive that your PC has, check your operating manuals.

Formatting Disks

We begin by looking at how you use File Manager to format a disk, a critical step that must be performed on any disk before it can be used by your PC. All disks start as a tabula rasa—a blank slate on which virtually any information can be recorded. Before formatting, the same disk could be used in any number of PCs, running under a variety of operating systems. Formatting a disk with File Manager takes a disk, this blank slate, and overlays it with the specific information subsequently used by DOS (the operating system under which Windows runs) to find any files it contains.

Caution: Formatting a disk effectively eliminates all files it currently contains. For this reason, you should make certain that the disk you use in the following exercise contains no important programs or data files.

Formatting a Disk with File Manager

1. Choose **D**isk from the File Manager menu bar.

   The pull-down Disk option menu appears.

2. Choose **F**ormat Disk.

   The Format Disk dialog box appears. You use this box to identify the drive containing the disk to be formatted and select the storage capacity to which you want it formatted. Formatting options include assigning this disk a volume label, specifying whether it should be formatted as a system disk and if you use MS-DOS 5 or higher, whether this should be a Quick Format.

3. After marking all the desired options in the Format Disk dialog box, choose OK.

   A confirmation box is displayed.

4. At the Confirm Format prompt, choose Yes.

   Windows displays a message box reporting on the percentage of the format operation that has been completed, followed by a prompt box asking whether you want to format another disk.

5. Choose No to end the format operation and return to File Manager.

   Windows returns you to the File Manager display. ☐

118

Follow the previous Quick Step to format a disk. Step 2 displays the pull-down **D**isk menu, shown in Figure 5.10. You use the various options on this menu to begin disk-related operations from within File Manager.

Step 3 displays the **F**ormat Disk dialog box shown in Figure 5.11. You use this dialog box to tell Windows how the current format operation should be performed.

Figure 5.10. The File Manager Disk options.

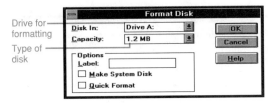

Figure 5.11. The Format Disk dialog box.

119

Note: The actual information shown in your Format Disk dialog box might differ from the contents of Figure 5.11. During installation, Windows analyzed your PC and recorded information about its various system components, which it uses to set default values for subsequent operations. Drive A on my PC is a 5 1/4-inch, high-density disk drive, which supports disks with a maximum storage capacity of 1.2-megabytes. Your Format Disk dialog box reflects the default values Windows determined should be used to format disks in drive A of your system.

You use the Format Disk dialog box to specify information about the current format operation, including

▶ The drive containing the disk you want to format.

▶ The storage capacity to which you want this disk formatted.

▶ An optional label (name) to be assigned to this disk.

▶ Whether the disk should be bootable—that is, whether you want the disk to contain the DOS system files.

▶ Whether DOS should perform a quick format by only erasing its directory and file allocation table. (This option is only available if your PC is using MS-DOS 5 or higher.)

For this exercise, format a disk using the default values for each of these fields.

At Step 4, Windows displays the **C**onfirm Format Disk message box shown in Figure 5.12. This message gives you an opportunity to change your mind and cancel the current format operation before Windows actually erases any data it contains.

Figure 5.12. Windows verifies that you want to format this disk.

While formatting your disk, Windows displays a message box reporting on the percentage of the format operation that has been completed. This message is updated continually as the format proceeds until the disk is 100 percent formatted, and then Windows displays the prompt box shown in Figure 5.13. In addition to showing the storage capacity of the newly formatted disk, this prompt box offers you the option of formatting another disk, using the same format parameters. Choosing Yes would initiate the second format operation. For now, choose No.

Figure 5.13. You can format more than one disk in a single Format Disk operation.

> **Note:** On your display, the actual values in Figure 5.13 might differ from those shown here, depending on what type of disk was formatted in drive A.

Now that we have a formatted disk in drive A, let's use the disk to examine additional features of the File Manager.

Changing the Active Disk Drive

Reiterating an earlier metaphor, disk drives and the disks they contain are similar to the filing cabinets found in traditional offices. As you often need information stored in several filing cabinets, you find yourself using program and data files stored on different disk drives while working with your PC. Using File Manager, changing the active disk drive is a simple matter of clicking that drive's icon.

 To Change the Active Disk Drive

Click the drive icon of the drive you want to make active. (Drive icons are located below the menu bar of your File Manager window.)

The file listing display changes to list files for the selected drive.

☐

You should now be looking at a boring display. Specifically, it has no directory tree and the only item its file listing contains is a message stating No Files Found. As you might have surmised, this happens because the disk in drive A is completely blank. Let's change back to drive C again and in the process, see another neat trick you can perform from within File Manager. Return drive C to active status by double-clicking the drive C icon.

Again, you see a window containing the directory tree and file listing for drive C. This time, however, you notice a small portion of what might be a second window behind it. To get a better idea of what this window contains

1. Position the mouse cursor on the title bar of the drive C window.
2. Hold down the left mouse button.
3. Drag your mouse down and to the right until the resulting outline for the drive C window does not completely obscure this second window.
4. Release the left mouse button.

Your screen now resembles Figure 5.14. As this figure illustrates, double-clicking the drive C icon actually placed the information for drive C in a second window. The File Manager window for drive A still is open.

121

File listing for drive A

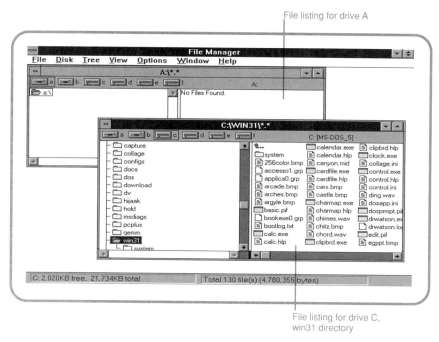

File listing for drive C,
win31 directory

Figure 5.14. Using File Manager, you can open multiple drive windows concurrently.

Later in this chapter, you see that accessing multiple drive windows simplifies certain File Manager operations. For now, however, let's return drive A to active status so that we can examine more disk-related operations.

Return drive A to active status by clicking any visible portion of the drive A window.

Labeling Disks

Identifying your disks with a volume label is convenient. Suppose, for example, that you're working on a multiyear budget plan. This project might involve several disks, each containing files relating to a specific year. How do you tell one disk from the other? Certainly, you can stick an identifying paper label to each disk, and most people do. What if that paper label comes off, as paper labels sometimes do? Then, you're the one who's stuck. Assigning volume labels to a disk eliminates this problem, because it actually encodes on the disk an identification of its purpose.

As you saw earlier, you can instruct Windows to label a disk during formatting. This is a convenient feature, if you happen to know what type of data will be stored on a disk when it's formatted. This isn't always the case, however. For example, what if you're formatting a whole pack of new disks and have no idea what type of files they ultimately will hold? In this situation, you could use File Manager's Label Disk command to assign a volume label to a disk after you know how it will be used.

 To Label a Disk

1. Choose Disk from the File Manager menu bar.

   This displays the pull-down Disk menu.

2. Choose the Label Disk option from the pull-down Disk menu.

   This displays the Label Disk dialog box shown in Figure 5.15. You use this dialog box to enter the volume label you want assigned to the currently active disk.

3. Assign a volume label to the disk by typing its name.

4. Choose OK.

   The newly assigned name appears in the File Manager window. □

123

Figure 5.15. You can use the Label Disk option to assign a volume label to formatted disks.

Assign a volume label to the disk by following the Quick Step. Use the name SYSTEM_DISK. When the File Manager display returns, the selected volume label, SYSTEM_DISK, appears in the drive A File Manager window to the right of the drive icons. This disk, however, wasn't formatted as a system disk, that is, a disk containing the MS-DOS system files. That's easily taken care of, using another File Manager option.

Transferring the DOS System Files to a Disk

As my short dissertation on disk labels implied, it would be nice if we always knew exactly what we wanted to accomplish each time we started something. Unfortunately, life doesn't always work like this. Going back to our example of formatting an entire pack of new disks, what if you discovered later that you wanted some of these to be system disks—that is, disks from which you could boot a PC? Would you have to reformat them? Luckily, no you wouldn't. File Manager provides a quick and easy way to transform a nonsystem disk into a system disk.

 To Format a Disk as a System Disk

1. Choose Disk from the File Manager menu bar.	This displays the pull-down Disk menu.
2. Choose Make System Disk from the pull-down Disk menu.	The Make System Disk dialog box is displayed.
3. Specify the floppy drive you want to use.	
4. Choose OK.	Windows displays a dialog box asking you to verify that you want to transfer the DOS system files to the disk in the active drive.
5. Choose Yes.	File Manager displays a Make System Disk prompt box, asking you to identify the drive containing the disk you want to make a system disk. □

Before File Manager actually transfers the DOS system files to the specified disk, it asks you to verify that this is indeed what you want to do, as illustrated in Figure 5.16. Again, Windows is watching out for your best interests, by making sure you don't perform a potentially destructive operation accidentally.

Use the previous Quick Step to transfer the DOS system files to the disk in drive A

When the File Manager display returns, a new file, COMMAND.COM, is in the file list for drive A, indicating that the transfer of system files was successful. This disk can now be used to start an IBM-compatible personal computer running under the same version of DOS as your system.

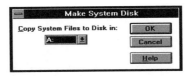

Figure 5.16. Windows verifies that you want to create a system disk.

Now that we have a work disk in drive A formatted, labeled, and set as a system disk, let's use this disk to examine some directory-related options available in File Manager.

Working with Directories

125

Returning to our office metaphor for a moment, where we drew the analogy between PC disks and file cabinets, directories and subdirectories comprise the drawers that cabinets usually contain. As such, directories provide a method for organizing the voluminous information a disk potentially can contain.

One way to understand exactly how directory structures work is to visualize a disk's different directories and subdirectories as resembling the various headings in a traditional outline. Each subsequent heading (subdirectory) branches from the heading (directory) that immediately precedes it. The following diagram reflects a directory structure created by Setup when it installed Windows on your hard disk:

```
C:\                          (the root directory)
    \WIN31
    \WIN31\SYSTEM
```

Setup could have stored all the Windows files in the root directory of my hard disk, as there's no law to stop you from throwing all your important paper files into one, large cardboard box. Doing so, however, opens the door to chaos and confusion whenever you need to find a specific file. By organizing the Windows files into subdirectories, Setup avoided this potential problem. Using a few simple File Manager procedures, you can build onto the directory structure considerate installation programs like the one Windows' Setup created on your disks.

Creating Directories

Let's start our examination of File Manager's directory related operations by creating a new directory on the disk in drive A.

 To Create a New Directory on the Active Drive

1. Choose File from the File Manager menu bar.

   Windows displays its pull-down File menu.

2. Choose Create Directory.

   Windows displays the Create Directory dialog box.

3. Enter the name you want assigned to your new directory.

4. Choose OK.

   The new directory is added to the File Manager display.   □

> **Note:** Before beginning the following series of exercises, make drive A the active drive, if necessary, using the procedures outlined in the previous section.

Follow the Quick Step to create a directory on drive A called NEWDIR. Step 1 displays the pull-down File menu shown in Figure 5.17. You use the various options listed in this menu to begin many directory- and file-related operations from the Windows File Manager.

```
File
  Open                Enter
  Move...             F7
  Copy...             F8
  Delete...           Del
  Rename...
  Properties...       Alt+Enter

  Run...
  Print...
  Associate...

  Create Directory...
  Search...
  Select Files...

  Exit
```

Figure 5.17. The File menu.

Selecting **C**reate Directory in step 2 causes File Manager to display the dialog box shown in Figure 5.18. You use this dialog box to enter the name of your new directory.

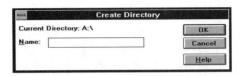

Figure 5.18. The Create Directory dialog box.

When the File Manager display returns, you can see this new directory in two places: within the directory tree and as a new entry in the file list, preceding COMMAND.COM, as shown in Figure 5.19.

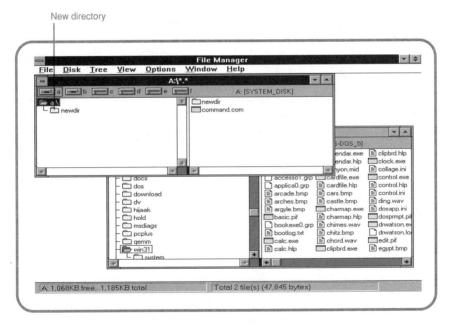

Figure 5.19. File Manager creates the new directory and includes it in the drive A display window.

Notice that, within the directory tree, the name of the new directory is slightly indented just below a:\. This identifies this directory as a subdirectory running off the root directory of drive A. Remember that outline analogy I used earlier? Well, File Manager emulates this familiar format when it displays its directory trees.

127

We'll come back to this in a moment. First, let's add still another directory to the disk in drive A, running off the one we just created.

Changing the Active Directory

By default, Windows adds new directories as subdirectories running off the currently active directory. Before expanding our directory structure further, therefore, let's make NEWDIR the active directory.

 To Make a Directory the Active Directory

1. In the directory tree listing, position the mouse cursor over the directory you want to make active.

2. Click the left mouse button.

File Manager makes the selected directory the active directory and displays the files in that directory. □

Follow the previous Quick Step to make the new directory, NEWDIR, the active directory. Notice that the highlight bar, previously located over the root directory of drive A, moves down to the NEWDIR directory. We can create a new subdirectory off the new active directory.

 To Add a New Directory Under an Existing Directory

1. Select the directory under which you want the new directory to appear.

2. Choose **File** from the menu bar.

Windows displays the pull-down menu.

3. Choose Create Directory.

This displays the Create Directory dialog box.

4. When the Create Directory dialog box appears, enter the name of the new directory you want to create.

5. Choose OK.

File Manager adds the new directory to the active disk. □

Use this Quick Step to make a new directory called NEWDIR2 under the NEWDIR directory created earlier. Now there are two new directories on your floppy disk: NEWDIR and NEWDIR2. In computer parlance, you have begun to create a *hierarchical directory tree*, where certain directories exist as children, branching from their parent directories.

Managing Directory Trees

Right now, the directory on drive A is straightforward. As the directory structure of a disk grows more complex, however, it would be convenient if there were some way to expand and condense the visual tree these branches create. When you're working in File Manager, there is a way to resize this tree. Before moving on, though, let's display the pull-down Tree menu and examine the terminology File Manager uses to describe its directory trees.

 To Display the Pull-Down Tree Menu

Choose the Tree option on   File Manager displays its
the File Manager menu bar.   pull-down Tree directory. ☐

Because the NEWDIR directory is itself both a child and parent directory; that is, it is a subdirectory of the A:\ root directory and has the NEWDIR2 directory running off it. This exercise displays a pull-down menu containing all the File Manager Tree options, as shown in Figure 5.20.

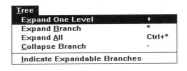

Figure 5.20. The Tree menu.

Let's look at what these individual options describe.

Expand One Level   In File Manager parlance,
                          level is a single layer of
                          subdirectories, directly
                          underneath the currently
                          active directory.

Expand Branch	A branch is the current directory plus all directories and subdirectories underneath it.
Expand All	Selecting this option causes all directories and subdirectories on the current drive, at all levels, to be included in the File Manager display.
Collapse Branch	As you've probably guessed, this option removes from the File Manager display all directories and subdirectories running off the active directory.

130

The characters after each option indicate keyboard shortcuts you can use to expand and collapse the directories included in File Manager's directory tree. There is, however, an even easier way. To see how this works, let's let File Manager provide visual clues about the complexity of your directory structure.

 To Have File Manager Provide Visual Clues to Your Directory Structure

1. Select the Tree option of the File Manager menu bar.	The pull-down **Tree** menu is displayed.
2. Choose Indicate Expandable Branches.	A plus sign will appear on any icon whose directory is not yet expanded, and a minus sign will appear on any icon whose directory is expanded. □

Notice that minus signs (–) have been added to the stylized file folders to the left of both the root directory and its NEWDIR directory listing in the directory tree. This symbol indicates that each of these two directories can be collapsed within the directory tree. (Do you remember that the minus key was the keyboard shortcut for the Collapse Branch option?)

To Collapse a Directory Branch

Double-click the file folder to the left of the directory (marked with a minus sign) you want to collapse.

File Manager removes from your display any subdirectories running off the selected directory.

Collapse the Root Directory using the previous Quick Step. This removes all the subdirectories running from the root directory of the directory tree. Notice also, the minus sign previously located within the root directory file folder has been replaced with a plus sign (+). This indicates that the root directory has at least one directory running from it, which can be displayed by expanding the root directory branch.

 To Expand a Directory Branch

Double-click the file folder (marked with a plus sign) of any directory branch you wish to expand.

File Manager displays any subdirectories running off the selected directory.

131

Expand the Root Directory using the previous Quick Step. Voilà! NEWDIR reappears. Not only that, but the NEWDIR file folder now contains a plus sign, indicating the presence of still more directories under it. Clearly, navigating a complex directory structure is easier using the Windows File Manager than it ever was with standard DOS commands.

We're not finished with File Manager yet, not by a long shot. Using File Manager, you easily can move around your disks and directories, as well as manage the files those disks and directories contain, as we see in the next section.

Working with Files

Welcome to the trenches. Why the trenches? Because down here, at the file level, is where the true PC productivity takes place. Most of the files you use on your PC fall into two main categories:

▶ Program Files
▶ Data files

Stated simply, virtually everything that happens in your PC is from running a program file and using it to work with data. For example, I'm writing this book using a word-processing program, so I can enter and revise the text (data) the file contains. Each time I finish a chapter, I save the text it contains to an appropriately named data file. What actually happens inside my computer is more complicated and technical than this, but the basic concept applies.

File Manager visually identifies program and data files by representing them with different icons. To see what I mean, let's look at the file listing for your \WIN31 directory.

To view the contents of the \WIN31 directory

1. Click any visible portion of the drive C window.
2. If necessary, click WIN31 to make this the active directory.

Your display now resembles Figure 5.21. Notice there are three different types of icons associated with the various file names on this screen.

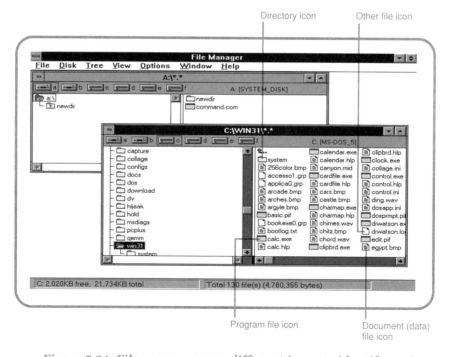

Figure 5.21. File manager uses different icons to identify various file types.

We've encountered the stylized file folder next to the listing for the \WIN31\SYSTEM subdirectory which **S**etup created running off \WIN31. This represents a directory.

Now, look down the column below the \WIN31\SYSTEM directory until you find a file called CALC.EXE. Notice that the icon to its left looks like a stylized display window. File Manager uses this icon to indicate executable files—that is, program files ending with .EXE, .COM, or .BAT that when selected, execute any commands they contain.

Directly below CALC.EXE should be a file called CALC.HLP, to the left of which is an icon resembling a piece of paper with a corner folded over. This is the icon File Manager uses to identify data files— or to be more precise, any file that does not end with .EXE, .COM, or .BAT.

File Manager does more than make your files look good. It also provides several ways to manage and organize those files as you go about your day-to-day duties.

Personal computer operations usually are dynamic. One of the greatest strengths of the personal computer is its flexibility, its penchant for adapting to diverse and ever-changing situations. As circumstances change, so too can the way you organize your personal computer resources. File Manager is designed to simplify this process as much as possible.

133

Note: Many file-related activities can be started from File Manager's pull-down **F**ile menu. For example, one way to move files that I alluded to earlier in this book is by selecting the **M**ove option on that menu. As easy as using File Manager's interactive menus and dialog boxes might be, however, nothing is more convenient than the point and click procedures that lie at the heart of a GUI like Windows. For this reason, these procedures are my focus in the following exercises.

Copying Files

Imagine having to enter a command similar to the following each time you wanted to copy a file from one disk or directory to another.

```
COPY C:\WIN31\ARCADE.BMP A:\NEWDIR
```

That's exactly the kind of complicated command syntax required to copy files from the DOS system prompt. File Manager changes all this. How dramatically? To find out, try the following Quick Step, and copy the ARCADE.BMP file from your WIN31 directory to the NEWDIR directory on drive A.

 Copying Files from One Directory to Another

1. Position the mouse cursor over the name of the file you want to copy.

2. Hold down the Ctrl key.

3. Hold down the left mouse button.

This selects the file you're pointing to.

4. Drag your mouse until the resulting mouse cursor (a data file icon) is located over the directory where you want to copy the selected file.

A file-folder icon follows your mouse movements.

5. Release the Ctrl key and your left mouse button.

Windows displays a Copy Confirmation dialog box.

6. Choose Yes.

The selected file is copied to the specified directory. □

In Step 5, File Manager responds with the dialog box shown in Figure 5.22, asking you to verify that you want to perform the requested file copy.

Figure 5.22. Copying a file with File Manager is a simple matter of dragging it to a new location.

File Manager displays a message box, letting you know that the requested copy operation is being performed. To verify that the new file exists

1. Click your mouse cursor on any visible portion of the drive A window.

2. If necessary, click NEWDIR to make this the active directory.

You should see a copy of ARCADE.BMP in the NEWDIR file listing for drive A.

> **Tip:** Strictly speaking, it's not necessary to hold down the Ctrl key when copying files between different disks. Simply dragging the icon to its destination on the new disk is enough. Using the Ctrl key to copy files works in all situations, however, so it's a good habit to develop.

Moving Files

Notice that the original ARCADE.BMP file still exists in your WIN31 directory. Copying a file creates an exact duplicate of that file in a new location. This is useful if you want to keep an archival copy of a file to protect against losing crucial data—a process similar to making photocopies of important papers.

135

More common, though, is the process of reorganizing your disks by removing files from one directory and relocating them in a new directory. This corresponds to removing file folders from one cabinet and transferring them to a second location, something people who rely on a paper-based filing system do every day.

Move the ARCADE.BMP file from the NEWDIR directory to the NEWDIR2 subdirectory using this Quick Step:

Q Move a File from One Directory to Another

1. Position the mouse cursor over the name of the file you want to move.

2. Hold down the Alt key.

3. Hold down the left mouse button.

   This selects the file you're pointing to.

4. Drag your mouse until the mouse cursor is located over the directory where you want this file moved.

   A file icon follows your mouse movements.

5. Release the Alt key and your left mouse button.

Windows displays the Confirm Mouse Operations dialog box.

6. Choose Yes.

The selected file is moved to the new directory. □

In Step 5, File Manager displays the dialog box shown in Figure 5.23, asking you to verify that you want to perform the requested file move.

Figure 5.23. Moving files with File Manager is equally easy.

File Manager displays a message box, letting you know that the requested move operation is being performed. When this message disappears, so has the ARCADE.BMP file.

To verify that the ARCADE.BMP file was moved to the specified location: double-click the NEWDIR2 file folder in the drive A display windows.

> **Tip:** As was true when using Ctrl key for Copy operations, it's not necessary to hold down the Alt key when moving files between directories on the same disk. Simply dragging the icon to its new destination is enough. Using the Alt key to move files, however, works in all situations and is therefore a good habit to develop.

Renaming Files

In some cases, reorganizing your files is a simple matter of renaming them. You might, for example, choose to identify older files that you no longer use regularly, but don't want eliminated completely with an .HLD file extension—a form of DOS shorthand commonly used to identify a hold file. Use the following Quick Step to rename ARCADE.BMP to ARCADE.HLD.

To Rename a File

1. Click the file you want to rename.	This makes the selected file the active file.
2. Choose **File** from the File Manager menu bar.	File Manager displays its File menu.
3. Choose Re**n**ame from the pull-down **File** menu.	This displays the Rename dialog box.
4. Type the name you want assigned to the file.	
5. Choose OK.	File Manager renames the selected file. □

In Step 3, File Manager displays the dialog box shown in Figure 5.24, asking you to enter a new name for the selected file.

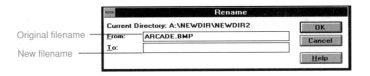

Figure 5.24. The Rename dialog box.

Deleting Files

Of course, the usefulness of a file, like all good things, ultimately must end. When this happens, the best you can do is free the disk space it occupies for more productive purposes. ARCADE.HLD has served us well, but now is as good a time as any to get rid of it. Use the following Quick Step to delete ARCADE.HLD.

 To Delete a File

1. Click the name of the file you want to delete.	This selects the file.
2. Choose **File** from the File Manager menu bar.	File Manager displays its File menu.
3. Choose **D**elete from the pull-down **File** menu.	This displays the Delete dialog box (see figure 5.25).

4. Choose OK.   A confirmation box is displayed.

5. Choose Yes.   The file is deleted.   □

In Step 3, the File Manager displays a dialog box containing the name of the file you have selected to delete.

As it has done so many times before, Windows attempts to stop you from accidentally performing a potentially destructive task by displaying the confirmation prompt box shown in Figure 5.25. Choosing the OK button would complete the delete operation. For now, however, choose Cancel.

Selecting No cancels the `Delete` command and returns you to the File Manager display with the ARCADE.HLD file still intact. Don't worry. We will get rid of it. Before we do, however, I want to demonstrate how Windows lets you control the degree to which it holds your hand, so to speak, as you manage your PC files.

Figure 5.25. The Delete Confirmation prompt.

Confirming Operations

When you're first learning your way around File Manager, Windows' penchant for protectiveness can be a real lifesaver. As you grow more familiar with the Windows environment, however, the need to constantly respond to confirmation prompts becomes not only frustrating, but counterproductive. At some point, therefore, you might feel comfortable enough to deactivate some of Windows' safeguards.

 To Modify File Manager's Default Confirmation Settings

1. Choose Options from the File Manager menu bar.   File Manager displays its pull-down Options menu.

2. Choose Confirmation.   This displays the Confirmation options box shown in Figure 5.26. An X indicates a Confirmation

option is currently active—
that is, performing that
procedure requires your
confirmation.

If you're feeling confident, let's deactivate a Confirmation
option:

√ To Deactivate File Delete Confirmation

▶ Click **F**ile Delete.

▶ Click OK.

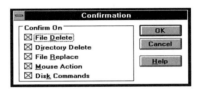

Figure 5.26. The Confirmation options box.

139

Now, let's have another go at deleting our ARCADE.HLD file.

√ To Delete ARCADE.HLD

1. If it is not the active file, click the ARCADE.BMP file in the
    drive A file listing.
2. Choose **F**ile from the File Manager menu bar.
3. Choose **D**elete from the pull-down **F**ile menu.
4. Choose OK.

As before, File Manager displays the name of the file you have
selected to delete. Even with **C**onfirmation deactivated, a list appears, so you can verify that the selected files are indeed the ones you
meant to specify.

This time, however, when you click OK, Windows completes
the **D**elete operation without prompting for confirmation.

> **Caution:** Until you feel comfortable working in File
> Manager, it might be a good idea to leave all **C**onfirma-
> tion settings turned on. Every PC user, from old pro to relative
> neophyte, knows at least one horror story about work he or she
> has lost to an incorrectly entered DOS command or as is more
> likely in Windows, a hastily executed point and click proce-
> dure or a delete key.

Organizing File Listings

By default, File Manager organizes its file listings in alphabetical order, based on file name. There are times, however, when you might find it advantageous to alter this order. This might be the case if you quickly wanted to review all the files of a particular kind—for example, Windows' bit-mapped files—on your hard disk. You can review a particular kind of file by having File Manager arrange its file listings based on type.

> **Note:** Options selected from the **V**iew menu effect only the currently active window. Consequently, file listings in multiple windows can be organized in different ways.

 To Arrange File Listings to Your Preference

1. Click any visible portion of the window in which you want to change the sort order.

   This makes the selected window active.

2. Choose **V**iew from the File Manager menu bar.

   File Manager displays its pull-down View menu.

3. Choose the sort order you want.

   Files on the active drive are sorted in the specified order. □

When you chose **V**iew, Windows displayed the pull-down menu shown in Figure 5.27. This menu lists the various options available for organizing the File Manager file listings.

Use the previous Quick Step to arrange your files in the WIN31 directory of drive C by **T**ype. Files having the same extension, such as .BMP, are now grouped together near the beginning of the WIN31 file listing.

As the options in the **V**iew menu demonstrate, Windows affords you great latitude in the manner in which you can structure and arrange your File Manager display. In addition to rearranging the order of your file listings, you also can change the actual information displayed for each file. You can, for example, expand the file listing to include the size of each file, its attributes, and the date on which it was last modified.

View
√ Tree and Directory
Tree Only
Directory Only
Split
√ Name
All File Details
Partial Details...
√ Sort by Name
Sort by Type
Sort by Size
Sort by Date
By File Type...

Figure 5.27. File Manager's View Options.

✓ To Include Additional Information in a File Listing

▶ Choose **View**.

▶ Choose **P**artial Details.

▶ Click **S**ize.

▶ Click **L**ast Modification Disk.

▶ Click **F**ile Attributes.

▶ Choose OK.

141

Your display now resembles Figure 5.28, which shows a file listing that includes the additional information. Well, not all of the information. The file listing window is too small to hold everything we requested. Specifically, the file attributes have been pushed off to the right side of the drive C window. Through File Manager, you can adjust the relative size of the directory tree and file listing to avoid this problem.

Q To Adjust the Size of the File Listing

1. Choose View.	File Manager displays its pull-down **View** menu.
2. Choose Split.	A vertical bar appears, which you can use to adjust the relative size of the directory and file listings.
3. Use the mouse or the arrow keys to adjust the position of the split bar.	
4. Press Enter or click the left mouse button.	The size of the file listing is adjusted. □

Date of last
modification

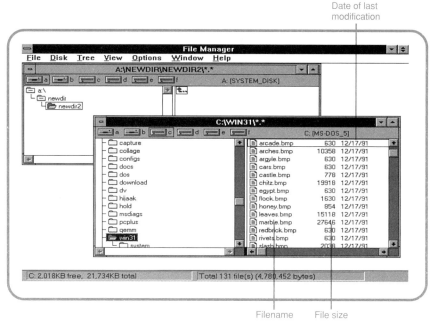

Filename   File size

Figure 5.28. You can specify what types of information you want included in your file listings.

This causes a vertical bar to appear in the current display window for drive C. You use this bar to adjust the border separating the directory tree and file listing portions of this window.

✓ To Increase the Space Allocated to Your Current Listing

▶ Move your mouse until the vertical bar is located just below the drive C icon.

▶ Click the left mouse button.

As Figure 5.29 illustrates, this increases the size of the file listing, making it wide enough to include the file attributes requested in the previous exercise.

As these few examples demonstrate, the View menu makes it possible for you to format your file listings in a variety of ways. As you perform the following exercise, take a moment to analyze how each step modifies the appearance and contents of the drive C window.

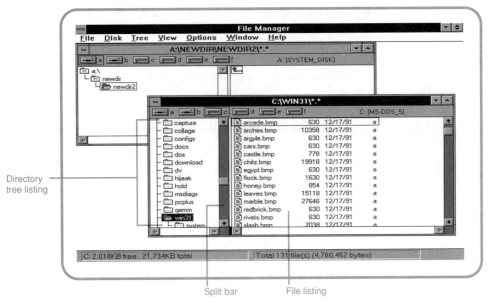

Directory tree listing

Split bar   File listing

Figure 5.29. You can adjust the relative size of the directory tree and file listing with the Split option.

143

✓ To Review the View Options, Use the View Menu to

▶ Choose **Tr**ee and Directory displays both the directory tree and file listing in side-by-side windows.

▶ Choose **Tr**ee Only displays only the directory tree.

▶ Choose Directory **O**nly displays only the file listing.

▶ Choose Sp**l**it adjusts the vertical bar that splits the display window.

▶ Choose **N**ame displays only the filenames.

▶ Choose **A**ll File Details displays filename, size, date, and time of last modification.

▶ Choose **P**artial Details displays only the details you select.

▶ Choose **S**ort By Name sorts filenames alphabetically.

▶ Choose Sort **B**y Type sorts filenames by the filename extension.

▶ Choose Sort By Si**z**e sorts filenames by size.

▶ Choose Sort By **D**ate sorts filenames by date of last modification.

▶ Choose By File **T**ype displays only the file types you select.

When you're finished cycling through these variations, your drive C window will look exactly as it did at the beginning of this section. Selecting the individual **V**iew options, however, provided several dramatic examples of the flexibility File Manager offers, when examining and managing the contents of your disks. We're not done yet. Until now, we've used File Manager to work with a single file. Specifically, we copied, moved, removed, and deleted the ARCADE.BMP file. You also can manage multiple files concurrently with File Manager.

Working with Multiple Files

You can select multiple files in two different ways when working in a single File Manager window.

▶ Use the Shift key in conjunction with your mouse to select *contiguous* file names.

▶ Use the Ctrl key in conjunction with your mouse to select *noncontiguous* file names.

Contiguous filenames are filenames that appear immediately before or after one another in your file listing. On the file listing for the WIN31 directory shown in Figure 5.30, for example, BOOTLOG.TXT, CALC.EXE, and CALC.HLP would be considered contiguous filenames. ACCESSOR.GRP, BOOTLOG.TXT, and CALENDAR.EXE, on the other hand, are an example of three noncontiguous filenames.

Let's look at the different procedures used to select multiple files.

✓ To Select Contiguous Filenames

▶ Click BOOTLOG.TXT in the WIN31 file listing.

▶ Position the mouse cursor over CALC.HLP.

▶ Hold down the Shift key.

▶ Click the left mouse button.

▶ Release the Shift key.

Your screen should now resemble Figure 5.31, which shows that you have selected the following three files:

BOOTLOG.TXT

CALC.EXE

CALC.HLP

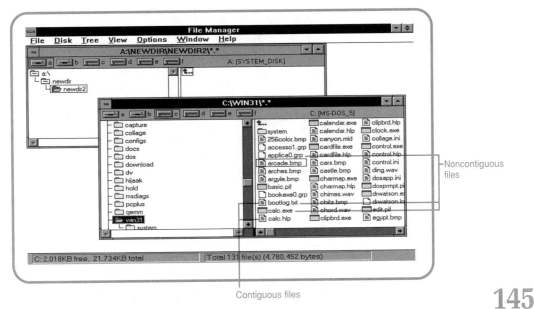

Figure 5.30. *Whether files are contiguous or noncontiguous depends on where they appear in a file listing.*

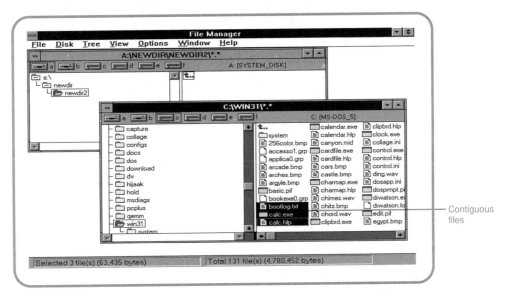

Figure 5.31. *You use the Shift key to select contiguous files.*

✓ To Select Noncontiguous Filenames

▶ Click ACCESSOR.GRP.

▶ Hold down the Ctrl key.

▶ Click BOOTLOG.TXT.

▶ Click on CALENDAR.EXE.

▶ Release the Ctrl key.

Your screen should now resemble Figure 5.32, which shows that you have selected the following three noncontiguous files:

ACCESSOR.GRP

BOOTLOG.TXT

CALENDAR.EXE

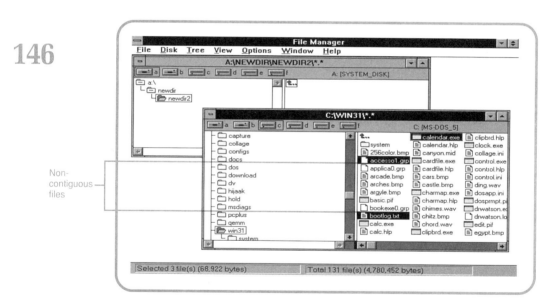

Figure 5.32. You use the Ctrl key to select noncontiguous file names.

What can you do with multiple files after they're selected? The quick answer to this question is, virtually anything you can do with a single file. To see what I mean, try the following exercise:

1. With the mouse cursor positioned over CALENDAR.EXE, hold down the Ctrl key.

2. Hold down the left mouse button.

3. Drag your mouse until the mouse cursor is positioned over the NEWDIR directory in the drive A display windows.

4. Release the Ctrl key and the mouse button.

   This displays our old friend the Confirm Mouse Operation dialog box. (See Figure 5.22.) To complete the copy operation

5. Choose Yes.

Now go ahead and click the \NEWDIR directory icon in the drive A display window. As the file listing shows, ACCESSOR.GRP, BOOTLOG.TXT, and CALENDAR.EXE were copied to drive A with this single procedure, as shown in Figure 5.33.

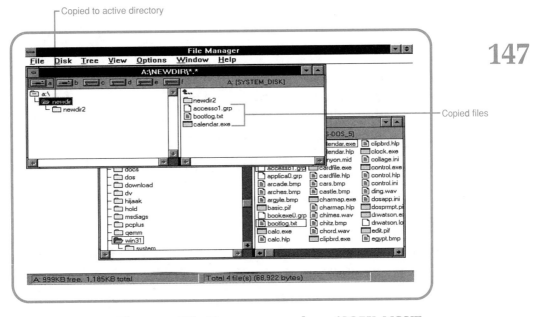

Figure 5.33. The same File Manager procedures (COPY, MOVE, and so on) can be applied to both multiple files and single files.

> **Caution:** Be sure to deselect your files after completing any procedure you want to perform on the current group of files. Otherwise, any files you previously selected remain active as you add new ones to the list.

Selecting Multiple Files

1. Click the first file you want to select.	File Manager highlights the selected file name.
2. Point to the last file in a contiguous list of file names you want to select.	
3. Hold down the Shift key and click the left mouse button.	File Manager highlights a contiguous list of files, including the last file you clicked.
4. Point to another file you want to select.	
5. Hold down the Ctrl key and click the left mouse button.	File Manager adds this new file as a noncontiguous file to your selected list. □

148

It's possible to select multiple files in a directory based on elements of their names, using the Set Selection option on the File Manager **File** menu. One convenient use for this feature is to quickly select all the files in a directory.

To Access the Set Selection Option for a Directory

1. Click the directory you wish to set selection options for.	This makes the directory for which you want to change selection options the active directory.
2. Choose **File** from the File Manager menu bar.	File Manager displays its pull-down File menu.
3. Choose **S**elect Files.	This displays the Select Files option box. □

This displays the Select Files dialog box, shown in Figure 5.34. Using standard DOS wildcards, you use this dialog box to identify a group of files you want to mark for additional processing. In this figure, for example, the * . * selection criteria identifies all files.

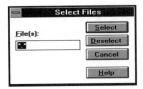

Figure 5.34. The Select Files dialog box lets you quickly mark groups of files.

✓ To Select All Files in a Directory and Return to File Manager

▶ Click the **S**elect button.
▶ Click the **C**lose button.

With everything selected, let's empty the NEWDIR directory.

✓ To Remove All the Contents of Your NEWDIR Directory

▶ Choose **F**ile from the File Manager menu bar.
▶ Choose **D**elete.
▶ At the **D**elete prompt, choose OK.
▶ Choose Yes.

149

File Manager begins to delete automatically all items in the NEWDIR directory, with one important exception. When File Manager encounters the NEWDIR2 subdirectory, called a subtree in the Windows vernacular, it displays the confirmation prompt shown in Figure 5.35. By differentiating between regular files and directories, it gives you an opportunity to preserve NEWDIR2, if you choose. Let's not.

Figure 5.35. File Manager protects you against accidentally deleting subdirectories.

That floppy disk in drive A has certainly come in handy. At this point, however, it's served its purpose. Let's close the File Manager display window.

To Close a File Manager Window

Double-click the control box   This closes the window.
in the upper left corner of
the window you want to
close.

Use this Quick Step to close drive A. Drive C now should be the only window remaining in your File Manager display.

Program Manager and File Manager, a Dynamite Pair

150

Okay, pay attention now. Instructions are going to get a little tricky as we use both Program Manager and File Manager to prepare our total Windows workspace for the Book Exercises that follow in Part III, Chapters 6-12, of this book. Along the way, we also examine some File Manager features that go beyond DOS operations and relate directly to the Windows environment.

✓ To Modify the Size of Your File Manager Window

1. Click the maximize button in the upper-right corner of your drive C display window to expand it to full-screen size.
2. Click the split button in the upper-right corner of the File Manager window.
3. Position the mouse cursor on the left border of the File Manager window. (The mouse cursor changes to a horizontal double-arrow.)
4. Press and hold the left mouse button.
5. Drag your mouse to the right until the resulting outline is located in the middle of your display.
6. Release the left mouse button.

When you've finished these steps, your screen should resemble Figure 5.36, which shows the File Manager window occupying approximately half of the Windows display.

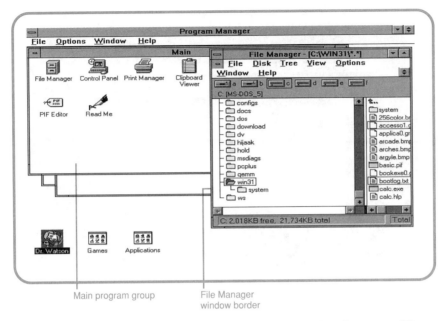

Main program group   File Manager
                            window border

151

Figure 5.36. Drag your mouse on a window's border to modify the size of that window.

Next, let's do the same to the Program Manager window, but position it on the opposite side of your display.

✓ To Modify the Size of Your Program Manager Window

1. Position the mouse cursor on any visible portion of the Program Manager window.
2. Press your left mouse button to make this the active window.
3. Choose **W**indow from the Program Manager menu bar.
4. Choose Book Exercises to make this the active window.
5. Position the mouse cursor over the Maximize box in the upper-right corner of the Program Manager screen, which now shows two small arrows pointing up and down.
6. Click the left mouse button.

Your screen now resembles Figure 5.37, which shows a resized Program Manager workspace in which Book Exercises is the active window.

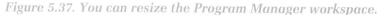

Figure 5.37. You can resize the Program Manager workspace.

Next, I'm going to let you work with the Program Manager on
your own. Using the techniques you've learned, modify your display
until it resembles Figure 5.38, which shows the Program Manager
and File Manager running side by side in the File Manager workspace.

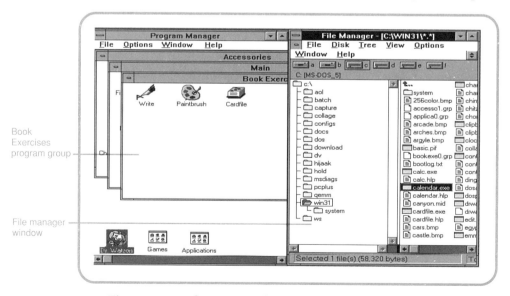

*Figure 5.38. When you've finished, Program Manager and File
Manager should be sharing your Windows display.*

> **Tip:** Remember that dragging the mouse on a window's title bar changes the positioning of that window within your total workspace. Altering a window's size, on the other hand, is accomplished by dragging the mouse cursor on the border corresponding to the direction in which you want its size increased or decreased. Dragging the mouse at the corner of a window expands that window horizontally and vertically.

When you've established the appropriate positioning for Program Manager and File Manager, clicking the Maximize box for the C:\WIN31 directory listing expands the directory to occupy the full size of the File Manager window. Get all this right—a process that really is easier than it sounds—and you see a display resembling Figure 5.38 on your PC monitor.

Now that we've set the appropriate Windows workspace—but keep in mind, one that still only hints at the true flexibility of the Windows GUI—let's use the tools you've established to finish creating the Book Exercises program group that we work in throughout the rest of this book.

Creating a Directory

First, make a special directory to hold the various data files you create in Part III of this book. Doing so makes it easier to organize these files later.

✔ To Create a WINBOOK Directory

▶ Position the mouse cursor on any visible portion of the File Manager window.

▶ Click the left mouse button to make this the active window.

▶ Click \WIN31 in the directory tree to make this the active directory.

▶ Choose **F**ile from the File Manager menu bar.

▶ Choose **C**reate Directory.

▶ Type **WINBOOK** and press Enter.

File Manager creates the new directory and adds its name to the directory window for \WIN31, placing it in alphabetical order immediately after the \WIN31\SYSTEM directory.

153

Using File Manager to Add an Item to the Program Manager

Next, let's add a program listed in the File Manager file listing to a program group. Specifically, we include the Windows Calculator in our Book Exercises group.

Note: This differs from earlier exercises, where we copied items from the Accessories group to Book Exercises, in that it provides an easy way to incorporate files into one program group that are not associated with another group. (Yes, I realize Calculator is also in the Accessories group; I needed something to demonstrate this technique.) You could, for example, use the following method to include your word processor in a program group set to organize your personal correspondence.

✓ To Add Calculator to the Book Exercises Group

▶ Position the mouse cursor on filename CALC.EXE in the File Manager file listing.

▶ Press and hold down the left mouse button.

▶ Drag your mouse to the left until the resulting icon shadow is located within the Book Exercises window.

▶ Release the left mouse button.

When you've finished these steps, your screen resembles Figure 5.39, which shows a Calculator icon added to the Book Exercises program group.

Automatically Loading a Data File with an Icon

The last step we perform in this chapter is to create a special icon, in the Book Exercises program group, that not only loads the Windows Write program, but also automatically opens a special document file each time that icon is selected. You accomplish this using the **New** option, which is located in the Program Manager File menu.

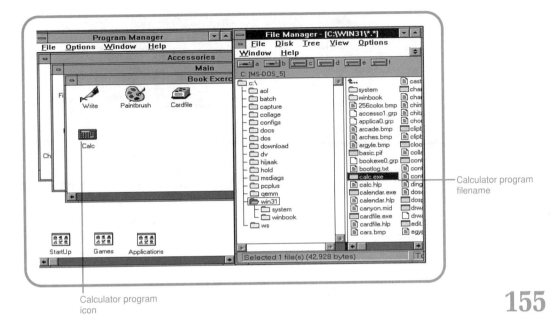

Calculator program
filename

Calculator program
icon

Figure 5.39. It's easy to add items to a program group from a File Manager directory window.

 To Add a Program Item to a Program Group

1. From the Program Manager menu, choose File.

   This displays the File menu.

2. Choose New.

   This displays the New Program Object dialog box.

3. Click Program Item.

4. Choose OK.

   This displays the Program Item Properties dialog box shown in Figure 5.40. You use this dialog box to describe the new item and tell Windows what should happen when this item is selected.

5. Type a description and a command line for the new program item.

6. Click OK or press Enter.

   The new program icon is added.

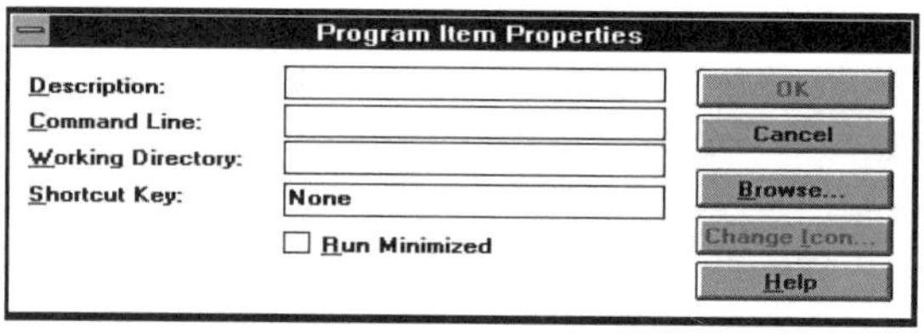

Program Item Properties		
Description:		OK
Command Line:		Cancel
Working Directory:		
Shortcut Key:	None	Browse...
	☐ **Run Minimized**	Change Icon...
		Help

Figure 5.40. Selecting New from the File menu displays the Program Item Properties dialog box.

For this exercise, we add a file called SAMPLE.DOC to our Run Exercises group.

√ To Add SAMPLE.DOC to the Book Exercises Group

▶ Type **Sample Document** in the Description box

▶ Press Tab to advance the cursor to the Command Line box

▶ Type **WRITE C:\WIN31\WINBOOK\SAMPLE.DOC**

▶ Press Enter or click the OK button

When you've completed the previous steps, your screen resembles Figure 5.41, which shows that the new item has been added to the Book Exercises program group. Notice that Windows automatically assigned a stylized pen icon to this new item, identifying it as a Windows Write application.

 Note: You might need to maximize your Book Exercises window to see this new icon.

We've examined several Windows procedures in this chapter. Specifically, we used the Windows Program Manager and File Manager to create and refine a program group designed to help you organize the various exercises contained in Part III of this book, "The Windows Accessories," which begins in the next chapter.

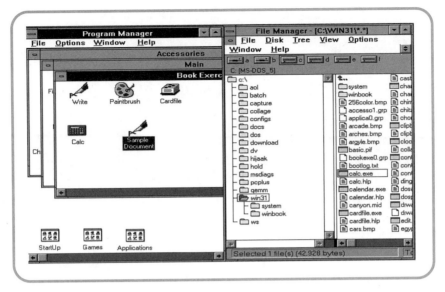

Figure 5.41. Program Manager adds the new item to the current program group.

What You Have Learned

▶ You use the Windows Program Manager to organize your files into program groups. Instead of relying strictly on the DOS directory structure, you can manage your PC activities more logically with the Program Manager, because it organizes files according to how they are used, instead of by their physical location on a disk. You can assign the same file to multiple groups using Program Manager, thus making more efficient use of your valuable storage space.

▶ By performing interactively from a Windows-like graphical interface, File Manager simplifies file-related operations. For example, you create a directory in File Manager by selecting the **C**reate Directory menu option, and then entering a name for your new directory in the subsequent dialog box.

▶ Working together, Program Manager and File Manager help you create a personalized Windows workspace, custom designed to help you optimize your PC productivity.

Part Three

The Windows Accessories

Now that you've installed and, to some degree, customized Windows for your PC, it's time to look at the individual accessories Microsoft includes in the Windows package. Basically, these accessories include a number of miniprograms designed so that you can begin using the Windows GUI quickly and productively. The seven chapters comprising Part Three contain a series of exercises that illustrate how the Windows accessories work and the types of work each enables you to accomplish. Chapter 12, "Putting It All Together," the final chapter in Part Three, demonstrates how the Windows Clipboard can be used to combine data elements from multiple accessories into a single file.

Windows Write

In This Chapter

▶ *How to use the Windows Write accessory*
▶ *How to access the editing features of Write*
▶ *How to format a document with Write*

How Write Lets You Process Words

If statistics can be believed, people love to process words with their personal computers. One recent study, for example, revealed that 78 percent of those surveyed identified word processing as the primary task for which they use their personal computers. Perhaps more than any other activity, word processing has assured the success of the personal computer. And why not? Processing words on a personal computer turns an otherwise tedious chore, writing, into the creative activity it should be.

You're probably more interested, however, in the professional advantages inherent in a word processor's workings. To be more precise, you're probably interested in how Write, the word processor included in the basic Windows package, can place the power of word processing at your fingertips.

What Is Write?

Put simply, Write is one of the accessories included with every copy of Windows. At its most basic level, Write converts your personal computer into an electronic typewriter. Words you enter at the keyboard when working with Write appear on your display monitor as they would on paper if you were using a manual typewriter. You can do more than send words to the screen by composing text with an electronic word processor like Write.

Used properly, Write can simplify the writing process by putting several advanced editing and formatting capabilities at your fingertips.

▶ Margins of a Write document can be justified or not justified, depending on whether you want that document to look factual (both margins justified—that is, vertically lined up with each other), formal (all margins centered), friendly (ragged right margin), or fanciful (try justifying only the right margin to accomplish this).

▶ Assigning different margin settings for different portions of a Write document is a simple point-and-click mouse operation.

▶ Words, phrases, even entire paragraphs can be emphasized using the underline, boldface, and italics features supported by Write.

▶ Should you need to make a point more strongly, Write can even print portions of a document using different type sizes and styles—from that tiny-print footnote that readers love to hate to large, dramatic headline-style type fonts. (Try doing this with a traditional typewriter.)

▶ Write lets you automatically generate headers and footers, information printed at the top and bottom, respectively, on every page of your finished document.

▶ You can copy, move, and delete entire passages within your document, using Write's variety of electronic editing tools, with only a few, simple menu-driven commands.

▶ Write also supports advanced find-and-replace operations. Suppose, for example, that you write a long article about Ms. Brown and, just before that article is completed, Ms. Brown marries Mr. Smith. If you're using Write, updating your document to reflect this new marital status is a simple matter of finding all occurrences of the words Ms. Brown and replacing them with the words Mrs. Smith. Now we're talking simple revisions!

► You can even incorporate graphic images created with other Windows applications (such as Windows own Paintbrush accessory, which we discuss in Chapter 9, "Paintbrush") into your Write documents.

Perhaps most important, Write's reliance on the Windows GUI makes learning to perform these various operations as simple as learning to press a mouse button. As you can see, Write does more than emulate a traditional typewriter. Write also transforms your personal computer into a personal typesetting system and does so without forcing you to become a computer scientist in the process.

There I go again, extolling the virtues of a Windows product when I should be showing you how to use it. Let's get "Write" down to it and begin writing.

163

Starting Write

Before we actually start Write, let's modify our Windows workspace to one more conducive to working in a single application. Begin by closing File Manager, which was left running at the end of Chapter 5, " Managing a Windows Session."

✓ To Close the File Manager Window

► Choose **F**ile from the File Manager menu bar.
► Choose E**x**it.

> **Note:** Like Program Manager, File Manager includes a **S**ave Settings feature. When the **S**ave Settings feature is activated, any settings specified with the **V**iew or **O**ptions menus remain in effect the next time you open File Manager.

Next, let's return to our Program Manager window, that currently occupies only the left half of your screen, to a full-screen display and organize our book exercise icons.

✓ **To Expand the Program Manager to a Full-Screen Display**

▶ Choose the Maximize box.

▶ Choose **W**indow from the Program Manager menu bar.

▶ Choose **A**rrange Icons.

 Note: Arranging icons is an easy way of adjusting icon placement to reflect any changes you've made in a window's size, contents, and so on.

We're ready to use Write to compose a sample document. The document you create here is used in future chapters, as we examine how the various Windows accessories work together to enhance all your PC operations.

Q **To Start Write**

Double-click the Write icon.   The Write opening menu
                                is displayed.   □

This loads the Windows Write accessory and displays its initial editing screen, shown in Figure 6.1. Notice that this screen is almost empty, resembling a blank piece of paper. That analogy, as you will soon see, is certainly apropos.

The Write Menus

As is true of all Windows accessories, Write's command menus are neatly tucked away, where they won't interfere with your primary work area. Specifically, Write commands are accessed from the Write window's menu bar, which, logically enough, runs across the top of the Write window. As was true in previous chapters, use your mouse to display Write's pull-down command menus. Let's see how this works.

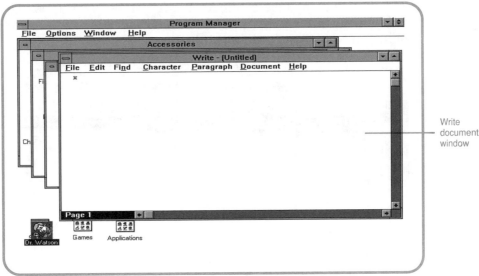

Write
document
window

Figure 6.1. Write initially displays a blank editing screen.

165

 To Access the Write File Menu

Choose File from the Write menu bar.

This displays a pull-down menu listing the various Write File operations (see Figure 6.2). □

Some of these include starting a new document (**N**ew), loading an existing Write file (**O**pen), saving your current document to a disk file (**S**ave or Save **A**s), and printing a Write document (**P**rint). Because we're in the Write menu bar, let's look at some other Write command menus. Press the right arrow to display the **E**dit menu.

The arrow keys provide a quick method for moving between Windows menus, one that might be more convenient than using the mouse if you're working at the keyboard. Each time you press the right arrow key, Write displays a different pull-down menu. As you've seen previously, each menu lists multiple options.

You might notice, as you move through the various Write menus, that only certain options are *active*—that is, displayed in clear, legible type—at any given time. For example, because no text currently exists in this Write file, several of the options on the **E**dit menu would accomplish nothing. These options are therefore *disabled*—listed in light colored, or alternately fuzzy type. The remaining Write menus contain additional disabled options, depending on what you are doing at the time.

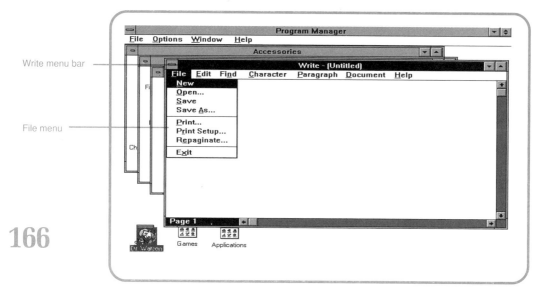

Figure 6.2. *Like all Windows accessories, Write uses pull-down command menus.*

Go ahead and use the arrow keys to familiarize yourself with the various Write menus. After you're finished, press Esc to return to the opening screen.

> **Tip:** This consistency between different programs is one of the biggest advantages of working in the Windows environment. After you're familiar with how one program works, learning the other Windows accessories is simplified.

Navigating a Write File

I've spent a lot of time extolling the virtues of using a mouse whenever possible when you're working within the Windows environment. Usually, this reliance on the mouse is useful. However, Write is a little different. It's only natural that, as you create your Write documents, you spend a lot of time entering text at the personal computer keyboard. For this reason, Windows provides several keyboard-based shortcuts for quickly moving from one location to another within a Write file, shortcuts that might actually be more convenient to use than their mouse-driven counterparts.

Keyboard shortcuts available in Write are included in Table 6.1.

Table 6.1. The Write keyboard shortcuts.

Key(s)	Function
left arrow	Moves the cursor one character to the left
right arrow	Moves the cursor one character to the right
up arrow	Moves the cursor one line up
down arrow	Moves the cursor one line down
Home	Moves the cursor to the beginning of the current line
End	Moves the cursor to the end of the current line
PgUp	Moves you one window up in your document
PgDn	Moves you one window down in your document
Ctrl+right arrow	Moves the cursor to the next word in the document
Ctrl+left arrow	Moves the cursor to the previous word in the document
Ctrl+Home	Moves the cursor to the beginning of the document
Ctrl+End	Moves the cursor to the end of the document

167

 Tip: You can quickly navigate even the longest Write documents by familiarizing yourself with these shortcuts.

Okay, it's time to begin working on our sample Write document. Before we begin, however, let's expand our Write window to maximum size.

✓ **To Maximize the Write Window**

Click the Maximize button in the upper-right corner of the Write window.

Defining Page Layout

The whole purpose of using Write is to write. That sounds logical, doesn't it? We'll start writing shortly. Before we do, however, let's define the most elementary aspect of a document's page layout and margin settings.

 To Define Margin Settings for a Document

1. Choose Document.   Write displays its pull-down document menu.

2. Choose Page Layout.   Write displays the Page Layout dialog box (see Figure 6.3).

3. Press Tab.   The cursor moves between fields.

4. Type the appropriate values into any Page Layout fields you want to modify.

5. Press Enter to accept the new values.   Write adjusts the page layout of the current document to reflect your modification. □

Use the previous Quick Step to change the left and right margins to 1.5. In Step 2, choosing the **P**age Layout option displays the dialog box shown in Figure 6.3. Use the **P**age Layout dialog box to specify margin settings for the current document.

Change the left and right margin setting to 1.5 inches each, acceptable margins for a business letter like the one we are writing for our sample document.

Before composing our sample letter, let's make one more modification to the default Write settings. Specifically, we're going to tell Write to display its on-screen ruler to simplify document formatting.

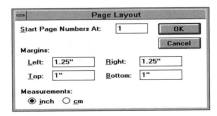

Figure 6.3. Use the Page Layout dialog box to specify margin settings for your Write documents.

 To Display Write's On-Screen Ruler

1. Choose **Document**.

   Write displays its pull-down Document menu.

2. Choose **Ruler On**.

   This adds an on-screen ruler to the Write display (see Figure 6.4). □ **169**

   As you see a little later in this chapter, using your mouse with the ruler icons can simplify the process of formatting individual paragraphs and blocks of text within your document.

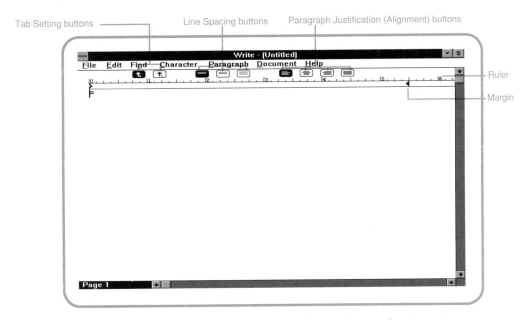

Figure 6.4. Mouse owners can use the various ruler icons to simplify document formatting.

> **Note:** Notice that the ruler displays a small marker be-
> tween 5 and 6. This identifies the actual width of the text
> comprising your document as 5-1/2 inches wide, a figure
> arrived at by subtracting the two 1.5-inch margins you set
> earlier (or 3 inches) from the width of a standard 8 1/2-inch wide
> piece of typing paper. How Write uses this right margin setting
> becomes clear in the next section.

With our initial page layout defined and the on-screen ruler easily accessible, we're ready to write with Write, if you'll forgive my redundancy.

Entering Text in a Write Document

Let's begin with the basics by adding a few blank lines to the beginning of our new document and then typing a simple salutation.

1. Press Enter twice.
2. Type **Dear valued customer,** and press Enter twice.

As this simple beginning demonstrates, composing a document with Write is much like using a traditional typewriter. What you enter at the computer keyboard appears within the Write window. It's all straightforward and not radically different from the way you've written in the past—at least, at this stage of the game.

At this point, let's add some more text to our document.

1. Type the following passage:

   We recently reaped the harvest of a substantial drop in the purchase price of materials used to manufacture our best-selling Wonderful Widgets. Consequently, we're able to pass these savings on to you, our customers, through a special price reduction on new orders.

2. Press Enter.

> **Tip:** As you type in the first sentence of this passage, notice that Write moves to a new line each time you reach the right margin. This feature, called *word wrap*, is one of the big advantages a word processor has over a traditional typewriter, where you have to anticipate where each line should end and manually press the Return key before you reach the right margin setting. When working in a word processor, the only time you need to press Enter to move to a new line is between paragraphs.

When you have completed these steps, your display resembles Figure 6.5, which shows the document elements entered to this point. We'll add more to our sample document in a moment. First, let's take a short detour to perform an important operation.

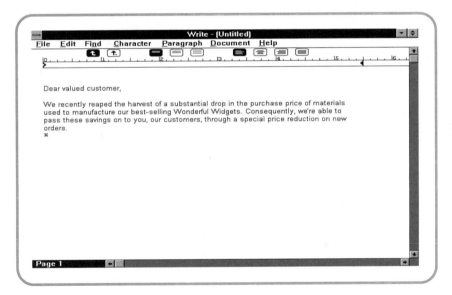

Figure 6.5. This screen shows how the sample Write letter should appear on your display.

Saving a File

Although your personal computer is dependable, it is not infallible. All kinds of things can cause either immediate or potential problems, some over which you have no control. Suppose, for example, that the power goes out while you're composing and editing a letter in Write. Bye, bye, PC—at least temporarily. Also, bye, bye Write file—if you haven't saved it to disk. You should cultivate the habit of regularly saving your work-in-progress to a disk file. While working in Write, you accomplish this with the **S**ave command, located on the **File** menu.

 To Save a Write File

1. Choose File to access the File menu.

   Write displays its pull-down File menu.

2. Choose Save.

   The File Save dialog box is displayed.

3. Type the name of the file.

4. Double-click the directory you wish to save the file in.

   The directory name changes.

5. Click OK or press Enter.

   Write saves your work using the filename you typed.   ☐

Use the procedures outlined in this Quick Step to save your current work to a file called SAVELET. Choose **S**ave. Because this is the first time you have saved the sample file, Windows displays a File Save **A**s dialog box, as shown in Figure 6.6. You can specify several items about the new file using the File Save As dialog box, including

▶ A name for this file.

▶ The directory in which to store the file.

▶ Whether Write should maintain a backup copy as future modifications are made to this file.

▶ The file format in which the current file should be stored.

✓ To Assign a Name and Location to the File

▶ Type **SAVELET**.

▶ Double-click the WINBOOK directory listing.

▶ Click Backup.

▶ Press Enter or choose OK.

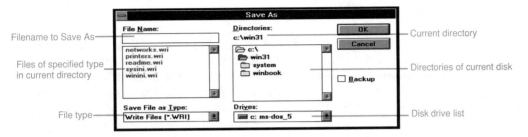

Figure 6.6. *Saving your files regularly guards against lost data.*

Note: You need to specify this last item only if you want your document stored in a format other than the default Write format, a procedure generally used to share Write files with other applications. Specifically, if desired, you can save your document as an ASCII file (Text Only) or in a file format compatible with Microsoft's popular word processing program, Word (Microsoft Word Format).

173

The top line of the Write screen used to indicate that the current file was Untitled, it now lists the name assigned to the current file. Notice also that Write added extension .WRI to the file name you specified. Windows uses the .WRI file extension to identify files created with Write. Because this file has been named, whenever you select the **S**ave option from this point on, Windows does not take time to display the File Save **A**s dialog box. Rather, it saves your updated work to the file called SAVELET.WRI.

Tip: It's always a good idea to name files in a way so that you can identify their contents or purpose later. In this instance, for example, we named the letter announcing our impending price reduction SAVELET. Although it isn't the King's English, this representative name should remind us of what our sample letter is about.

Now that we've protected the initial draft of our letter against accidental loss, let's go back to Write and begin adding some polish to its admittedly mundane appearance.

Adding Formatting Elements to a Write Document

One big advantage to working in the Windows GUI, even when composing and editing a text document, is that its graphics-based display more precisely reflects the final appearance of your document. In computer parlance, this is referred to as the What-You-See-Is-What-You-Get (or WYSIWYG, pronounced *wis-e-wig*) paradigm. How does working in a WYSIWYG environment differ from using more traditional DOS programs? I'm glad you asked.

Formatting Characters

174

Suppose, for example, that you wanted the product name, Wonderful Widgets, to appear in boldface in our sample letter. If you were using a traditional text-based word processor rather than Write, you'd need to insert special codes in your file to indicate where you wanted certain formatting elements—boldface, italics, underlining, and so on—applied. Furthermore, you wouldn't see these enhancements until the document was actually printed. How would you accomplish this same thing using Write? Quite easily.

 To Boldface a Word or Phrase

1. Position the mouse cursor (now a vertical line) in front of the word or phrase you want to boldface.

2. Press and hold down the left mouse button.

3. Drag the mouse to your right until all text you want to boldface is highlighted—that is, displayed in reverse video.

   This marks your text.

4. Release the left mouse button.

   This selects the specified text.

5. Choose Character from the Write window menu bar.

   Write displays its pull-down Character menu.

6. Choose Bold.   Write boldfaces the selected
                                             text and returns you to your
                                             document.   □

Use this Quick Step to bold the words Wonderful Widgets. This
formats the selected text, Wonderful Widgets, to boldface, as shown
in Figure 6.7.

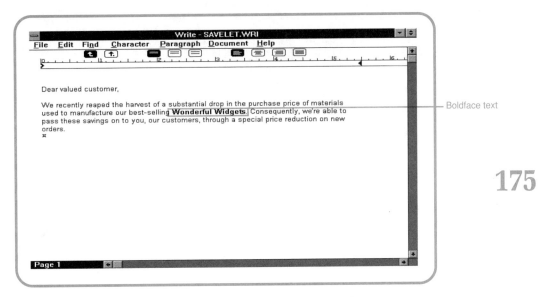

Figure 6.7. *To modify the appearance of a Write document,
use Window's WYSIWYG interface.*

Formatting Paragraphs

In the previous example, you altered the font for a selected passage.
With Write, you can modify entire paragraphs using the formatting
icons located above the on-screen ruler. To see how this feature
works, reformat the opening paragraph so both its left and right
margins are fully justified.

 To Specify Full Justification

1. Make sure the mouse cursor
   is located somewhere within
   the body text of the paragraph you want to justify.

175

2. Click one of the Justify icons.   Write justifies the selected paragraph in the manner indicated.   □

Write reformats the selected paragraph to full justification, as illustrated in Figure 6.8.

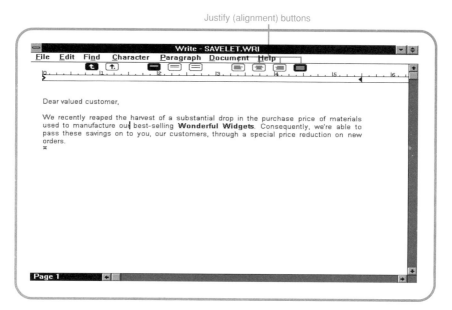

Justify (alignment) buttons

Figure 6.8. Use the ruler icons to reformat quickly entire paragraphs in your Write document.

> **Tip:** Each of the ruler icons represents a command available in the pull-down Paragraph menu. There might be times when selecting a menu option is more convenient than clicking the corresponding ruler icon.

Creating Headers and Footers

With Write, you can create *headers and footers*—text that appears on the top and bottom of each printed page, respectively—for your documents. Optionally, you can tell Write to number the pages of your printout in either of these two areas. Let's use this last feature to see how you specify headers and footers when working in Write.

Use the following Quick Step to create a Footer with centered page numbering.

 To Include Page Numbers Within a Footer

1. Choose **Document** from the Write window menu bar.	Write displays its Document menu.
2. Choose **Footer**.	Write displays a blank window and the Page Footer dialog box (see Figure 6.9).
3. Click the **Center** icon (the third icon from the right).	This centers your footer text.
4. Choose **Print** on First Page.	This causes your footer to be included on every page of your document.
5. Choose **Insert** Page #.	The word (page) will appear in the Footer window. This causes page numbering to occur automatically in your footer.
6. Choose **Return** to Document.	Write creates the specified footer and returns you to your document. □

177

Choosing the **Footer** option (Step 2) displays a blank window and the Page Footer dialog box, as illustrated in Figure 6.9. It helps to think of headers and footers as being subdocuments to your main document. Use the blank portion of the Footer screen, for example, to enter any text that should appear in your footer. Furthermore, various menu options are available to format this text. Additional options located in the Page Footer dialog box include indicating placement of your footer text, as well as specifying whether the footer should include page numbering. We'll use the Footer screen to specify page numbering, centered on the document margins.

Replacing Text

One of the most convenient features associated with using a word processor like Write is that you can quickly find selected words and phrases, regardless of where they are located in your document. You can even tell Write to replace these passages with something else. Let's see how this works by changing the phrase price reduction in our sample letter to another word discount.

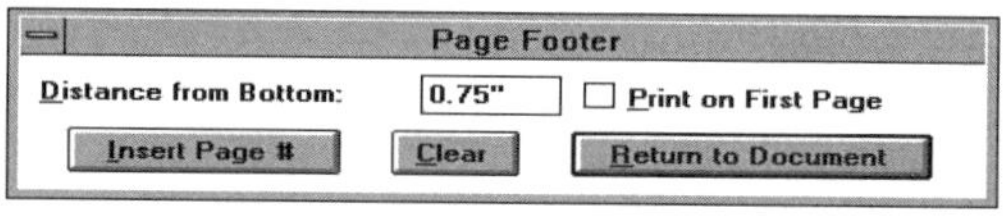

Page Footer		
Distance from Bottom:	0.75"	☐ Print on First Page
Insert Page #	Clear	Return to Document

Figure 6.9. You can have Write automatically include headers and footers in your documents.

Ｑ Global Find and Replace

1. Choose Find from the Write menu bar.

   Write displays its pull-down Find menu.

2. Choose Replace.

   The Replace dialog box appears (see Figure 6.10).

3. Enter the word or phrase you want to change in the Find What input box.

4. Press Tab.

   The cursor advances to the Replace With input box.

5. Enter the new text you want substituted for the word or phrase entered in the Replace With input box.

6. Choose Replace All.

   Write scans the entire file, making the requested changes.

7. Press Esc.

   Write returns you to your document.   ☐

Use this Quick Step to change price reduction to discount. Choosing the Change option displays the dialog box shown in Figure 6.10. Use this dialog box to enter information about the current find-and-replace operation.

Replace	
Find What: price reduction	Find Next
Replace With: discount	Replace
	Replace All
☐ Match Whole Word Only	Close
☐ Match Case	

Figure 6.10. Find-and-replace is one of the most convenient features associated with word processing.

Selecting the Replace **All** option causes Write to perform the Replace operation across the entire file, finding all occurrences of the specified **Find** What text and replacing it with whatever you entered into the Replace With field. When this process is completed, Write leaves the Replace dialog box displayed for future use. Because we have no additional changes, pressing Esc returns us to our sample letter.

 Tip: Although find-and-replace might not seem like an extremely useful feature when used to revise a single-page letter like the one we've been working with, it can be a godsend when you need to convert text across a long document. (Remember that Ms. Brown to Mrs. Smith file conversion I mentioned earlier?) Believe me, if you do much writing, you soon learn to love Write's find-and-replace feature.

179

We're about finished with our initial examination of the Windows Write accessory. (We come back to this sample letter several times in the next few chapters.) Before we move on, however, I'd like to demonstrate one more powerful feature of Write, its Undo option.

Using the Undo Feature

Write keeps a record of the latest edit you have performed so that you can use a special **Undo** option to reverse the results of the previous edit operation quickly. When selected, **Undo** restores your document to however it was before the most recent edit command was executed. Right now, for example, **Undo** would reverse the find-and-replace procedure from the previous exercise.

To Reverse a Previous Edit Operation

1. Choose **Edit** from the Write window menu bar.	Write displays its Edit menu.
2. Choose **Undo**.	Write reverses your last edit and returns you to the document. ☐

Notice that selecting Undo changed discount back to price reduction. Stated simply, Undo reversed the previous find-and-replace operation and then marked any blocks of text affected by this procedure for additional processing, as illustrated in Figure 6.11.

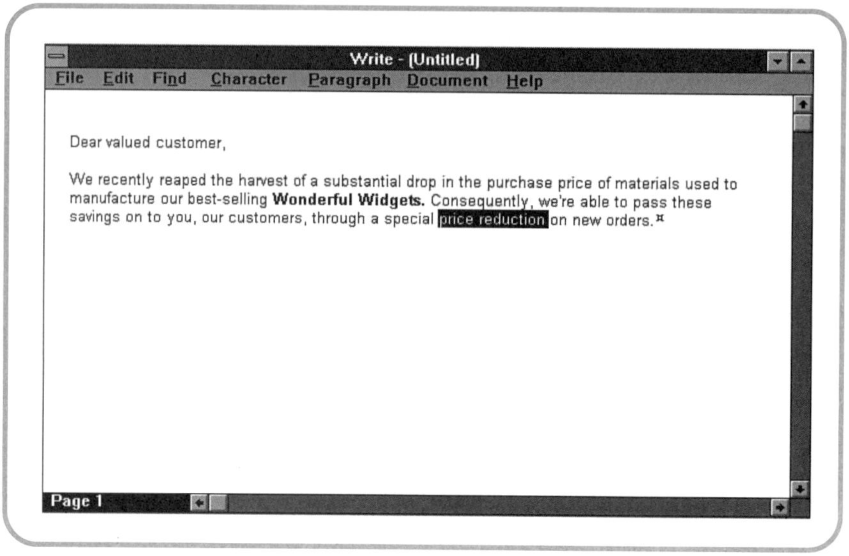

Figure 6.11. Write's Undo feature can be used to quickly reverse previous changes to a document.

180

Exiting Write

Although the letter is not finished, let's take a short break and end this introductory Write session. Use the **Exit** option in the Write **File** menu to return to the Windows Program Manager.

✓ To End a Write Session

▶ Choose **File** from the Write window menu bar.

▶ Choose **Exit**.

▶ Press Enter or choose the Yes button.

Whenever you exit a Windows accessory, that program checks to see whether you've made any modification to the current file since the most recent **S**ave operation. If changes have been made, Windows displays a prompt box similar to the one shown in Figure 6.12, asking whether the revised version of the file should be saved to disk. This safeguards against your inadvertently losing work by prematurely closing a Windows accessory.

Figure 6.12. Write checks to see whether you have saved the most recent revisions to your files before returning to the Program Manager.

After storing the latest version of SAVELET.WRI on disk, Windows returns you to its Program Manager screen. As I mentioned earlier, we return to our sample letter in future chapters, when we look at how Windows combines elements created with several programs into a single file.

181

What You Have Learned

▶ Write is the Windows word processor. You use Write to create, revise, and print documents.

▶ Working with a word processor like Write is much easier than using a traditional typewriter. For example, by using Write, you can easily revise and even reformat a document without having to retype that document's contents completely.

▶ Write can run in so-called WYSIWYG mode using the Windows GUI, where changes you make to your document on-screen are reflected in that document's final printed appearance.

▶ Write includes an advanced search-and-replace feature that can be used to make global changes in the contents of your text documents.

Chapter 7

Cardfile

In This Chapter

► *A definition of database management*
► *How to manage records in a Cardfile database*
► *How to design and create a Cardfile database*

What Is Database Management?

Database management typifies everything a personal computer does well. Managing the kinds of information a PC database generally contains is repetitive and tedious work. What's involved in managing data in a PC database? How does database management work? What things can you accomplish with a database manager such as Cardfile? And how do you use a database manager such as Cardfile? We have many questions to answer. Never fear—the answers provide the foundation for this chapter's discussion of Cardfile, the database manager included as part of the basic Windows package.

Database Fundamentals

A *database* is a file that contains some kind of information, just like any other PC file. The information contained in a database file, however, is organized in a precise manner, using specific data elements. A database contains *records*, each consisting of one or more fields. Each *field* represents a particular piece of information. In a database designed to keep track of names and addresses, for example, all the information about a given individual is a record. Within that record are several fields—first name, last name, address, telephone number, and so on.

Another term you encounter regularly in any discussion about database management is form. Basically, a *database form* is the screen you use to enter information into a database file. As such, a database form resembles the more traditional paper forms we've grown familiar with in this age of burgeoning bureaucracy, where virtually every move we make must be meticulously recorded. As its name implies, Cardfile uses a form resembling a typical 5-by-7-inch index card to record information stored in your database files.

PCs, the Perfect Information Managers

As implied earlier, the personal computer is the ideal tool for keeping track of the types of information each of us must manage regularly. Consider for a moment the steps involved in extracting a particular piece of information from a manila folder stored in a traditional filing cabinet, an organizational technique with which most of us are familiar.

Even easy procedures become tedious and bothersome when done repeatedly. First, you must get up from your desk (or wherever you're working at the time) and walk to the filing cabinet. Next, you must identify the drawer in which the folder you are seeking resides. After opening the correct drawer, there's still the little matter of tracking down the actual file folder containing the specific information you need. Transport this folder back to your desk and you're (finally!) ready to review the information you need.

Wouldn't a more ideal situation be to have all the information you need readily available and easily found, quite literally at your fingertips, whenever you need the information? When you use a PC database like Cardfile, the information is available.

PC databases not only are convenient, but they also are flexible. Referring to the previous example, consider for a moment some different methods of organizing those manila folders stored within that imaginary filing cabinet, the one designed to keep track of names and addresses. Do you arrange your folders alphabetically? This would work, providing you always look up information based on some alphanumeric value—for example, a person's last name. Suppose instead, you need to track down information about someone living at a specific address. In this case, having your file folders organized alphabetically by last name provides no help at all. What if you need to find the names and addresses of everyone living within a particular state? If you still depend on an old-fashioned record keeping method like a filing cabinet stuffed full of manila folders, you're really facing an organizational nightmare.

The Advantage of Using Cardfile

185

Using an electronic database like Cardfile eliminates all these hassles. To begin with, you can enter information (individual records) into a Cardfile database in totally random order. Cardfile couldn't care less. In fact, Cardfile doesn't even worry about organizing the individual records its databases contain unless you tell it to. Only when you specify does Cardfile concentrate on arranging the records a database contains into some structured order. Cardfile, furthermore, arranges these records in the precise order you specify. The next time you look up information, if you request a completely different organizational structure, that's okay. Cardfile won't complain. It simply goes about its assigned task, fulfilling your latest request quietly and, as I implied earlier, more efficiently than you ever could.

Ask Cardfile to print an alphabetical listing of names and addresses contained in a customer database, arranged by company name, and it does. If you ask Cardfile to generate the same list five minutes later, but this time you want your customers grouped together by their respective zip codes, it complies quickly with your new request. If your only alternative was pulling a pile of paper folders out of a traditional filing cabinet and manually rearranging them, Cardfile complies quicker than you ever could.

Now let's look at how to do some of Cardfile's various database management functions that were previously outlined. We'll begin by using Cardfile to design and create a sample database.

Using Cardfile

Cardfile is Windows' generic database manager. Using Cardfile, you can store and manage information on a wide range of topics. Some specific applications for which you might use Cardfile include

▶ Maintaining sales and inventory records—an invaluable tool for anyone who runs a small business.

▶ Organizing your collection of record albums or compact discs—who recorded them, what style of music they are, when they were recorded, which songs they contain, where they are located, and so on.

▶ Keeping track of your critical tax records (Who, facing this nightmare, hasn't wished he or she could sleep through midnight, April 15th?).

▶ Keeping a recipe file.

186

Because you design each Cardfile database to contain only the information you want, this list could be several pages long. In fact, the number and types of items you can organize using Cardfile are limited only by your personal data management needs and imagination. Perhaps more than any other potential use of a personal computer, database management is the most personal. Given this fact, my goal in this chapter is to discuss the basic steps involved in creating and using a Cardfile database. How will you ultimately apply this elementary information to your personal database management activities? In this respect, the sky's the limit.

Starting Cardfile

By now, you should be familiar with this particular step of working within the Windows environment.

 To Start the Cardfile Accessory

Double-click the Cardfile icon.

Windows opens a Cardfile window. □

After a few seconds you see the Cardfile display, shown in Figure 7.1. Admittedly, this display does not look overly impressive. In this case, however, looks definitely are deceiving.

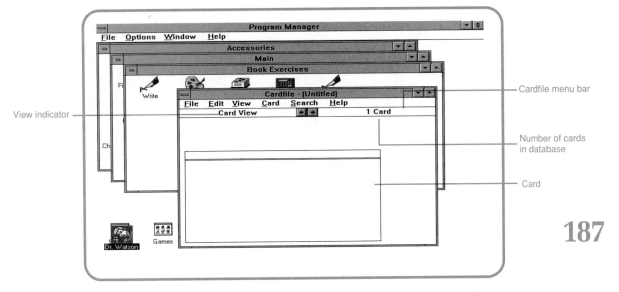

Figure 7.1. Cardfile's display is deceptively unsophisticated.

187

Notice that, as was true with Write, Cardfile creates an untitled file the first time you start it. We'll name our new database in a few minutes. Before we do, though, let's provide some information for this database to manage.

Adding Records to a Cardfile Database

As I mentioned earlier, the Cardfile screen is designed to emulate a traditional 5-by-7-inch index card. To create individual records in a Cardfile database, enter information into these cards by selecting the **A**dd option from Cardfile's **C**ard menu.

> **Caution:** When you add a record, you will be asked to choose an index for the card. This index is used to identify that card within the database, and the index cannot be changed.

To Add a Record to a Cardfile Database

1. Choose Card from the Cardfile menu bar.
   Cardfile displays its pull-down Card menu.

2. Choose Add.
   Cardfile displays the Add dialog box (see Figure 7.2).

3. Type the index value and press OK.
   Cardfile displays the index value in the upper-left corner of a new card. □

This displays the Add dialog box, shown in Figure 7.2. Use this dialog box to enter information that will appear on the first line of a Cardfile card—information that in turn serves as the primary index for that card within its database file.

Figure 7.2. Use the Add dialog box to enter the first line of a Cardfile record.

Tip: Like Write, Cardfile is another keyboard-intensive application. Consequently, it is often more convenient to use the F7 function key—the keyboard **A**dd command—rather than its mouse alternative, to initiate an **A**dd operation.

Selecting an Effective Index

Expanding on an earlier analogy, Cardfile uses its *index field* (the first line of each record) the same way you would depend on folder tabs within a traditional filing cabinet. This field provides Cardfile with a method for quickly scanning a database to locate a specific record, a procedure similar to your scanning the tabs on folders in a file drawer to find the one you want. Consequently, you should design a Cardfile database so that, whenever possible, the value you use most often to access records within that database is stored in its index field.

Suppose, for example, you own a manufacturing company and want to set up a Cardfile database to record information about the customers to whom you regularly sell the bread and butter of your product line, the Wonderful Widget. In such a case, a logical choice for the index field would be the individual company names of these customers. In fact, this is exactly the type of information that is recorded in the sample Cardfile database you're going to create in the following exercises.

Entering the Index Line

The first step in adding a record to a Cardfile database is to enter that record's index value in the Add dialog box.

Type **MiniCorp, Inc.** and press Enter.

Cardfile adds a new card to the current file and automatically displays this new card within the Cardfile window for additional data entry, as illustrated in Figure 7.3.

189

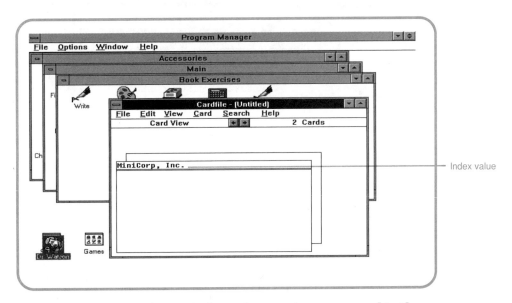

Figure 7.3. Entering an index value creates a new card in the current Cardfile window.

Completing a New Card

After you specify the Add field, complete the record as if you were typing information on a typical 5-by-7-inch index card. To complete the first record,

1. Type **1234 First Avenue** and press Enter.
2. Type **New York, NY 10012** and press Enter.
3. Type **1-212-555-1234** and press Enter.
4. Type **Contact: James Doe** and press Enter.

When you're finished, your screen resembles Figure 7.4, which shows the information you entered. All that remains now is to save this information as a record in the Cardfile file.

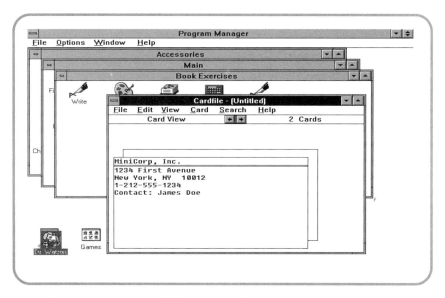

Figure 7.4. Use Cardfile to record important information about your business contacts.

Let's go ahead and add a few more entries now, so that we'll have some sample records to work with later.

✓ To Add Additional Records to the Cardfile File

▶ Press F7 to access the **A**dd dialog box.

▶ Type **Conglomerate, Inc.** and press Enter.

▶ Type **456 Second Street** and press Enter.

▶ Type **Anywhere, USA** and press Enter.

▶ Type **555-3456** and press Enter.

▶ Type **Contact: Betty Brown** and press Enter.

▶ Press F7 to access the Add dialog box.

▶ Type **The Buyer's Club** and press Enter.

▶ Type **3333 Third Street** and press Enter.

▶ Type **Cincinnati, Ohio 45255** and press Enter.

▶ Type **1-513-555-4567** and press Enter.

▶ Type **Contact: Bill Brown** and press Enter.

Your display now resembles Figure 7.5, which shows the three cards you just created within the Cardfile window. These three records will suffice for our purposes here.

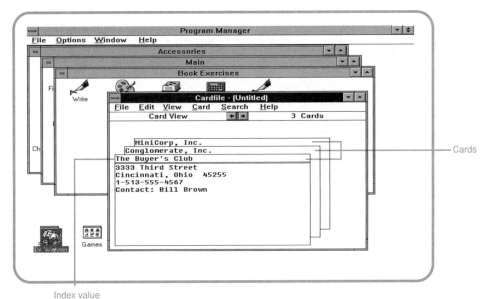

Figure 7.5. Cards are added to the Cardfile display each time you record a new entry.

Viewing Cardfile Records in List Mode

Information in your Cardfile databases can be viewed in one of two ways. Until now, we've been working exclusively in Card mode, where records are displayed using the simulated index cards alluded to earlier. You also can examine a database's contents with Cardfile in **L**ist mode. Let's switch to this second mode and see what information is available there.

 To Switch to List Mode

1. Choose **V**iew from the Cardfile menu bar.

   Cardfile displays its pull-down **V**iew menu.

2. Choose **L**ist.

   Cardfile changes from Card to List View.   ☐

192

Your screen now resembles Figure 7.6, which shows the Cardfile List display. When running in List mode, Cardfile displays the first line of any records stored in the current file, its index line.

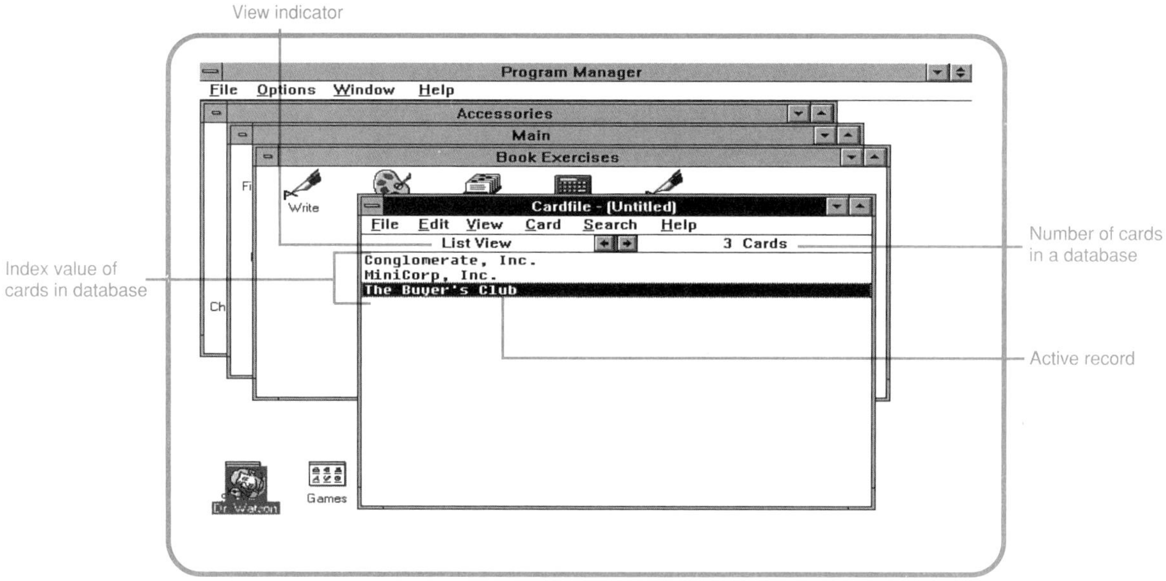

View indicator

Index value of cards in database

Number of cards in a database

Active record

Figure 7.6. List mode displays the first line of records in the current Cardfile database.

If you look carefully at Figure 7.6, you notice several items that provide information about how Cardfile works.

▶ Records in a Cardfile file automatically are organized in alphabetical order, based on the initial character in the first line of each record (notice, for example, that even though you entered information for MiniCorp, Inc. first, it is the second line displayed in Figure 7.6.).

▶ The *status line* indicates the number of records stored in the current database (Figure 7.6, for instance, shows that you have added three records to this file).

▶ When you work in Cardfile, the record on which the previous operation was performed remains the *active record* (for example, the line containing The Buyer's Club should be highlighted on your display, because that was the last record added to the current file).

> **Tip:** Clicking the right and left arrows displayed in the status line of the Cardfile window enables you to move forward and backward one record at a time within the current database. These scroll arrows provide a convenient method for quickly scanning individual cards within a Cardfile database.

Saving a Cardfile Database

As was true in Write, unless told otherwise, Cardfile begins each new session working in an untitled database. Because this is the first time you've used Cardfile, none of the records entered before now has been identified with a named file. The file you're working is currently identified as Untitled on its title bar. Let's assign your new database a file name.

Again, a convenient feature of working in Windows is that similar tasks are performed using similar procedures. Consider, for example, how much the following exercise resembles the steps you used to save your Write document in the previous chapter.

▶ Choose file from the Cardfile menu bar.

▶ Choose Save **As**.

Cardfile displays a dialog box, asking you to enter a filename under which the records comprising this database should be saved.

✓ **To Save Cardfile Records**

▶ Type **Practice**.

▶ Double-click the WINBOOK file folder.

▶ Choose OK.

Notice that the specified filename, PRACTICE.CRD, now appears in the title bar of the Cardfile window.

Note: Should you enter any new records and then attempt to exit Cardfile without first saving those records to a file, you will be asked whether you wish to save before returning to the Windows Program Manager.

Before looking at some specific activities you can perform with Cardfile, let's examine the various keyboard commands that Cardfile uses to simplify its use.

Cardfile Key Commands

As mentioned earlier, when you're working in Cardfile you rely heavily on keyboard input. For this reason, Cardfile provides a number of keyboard commands to simplify entering and finding records in the current file without forcing you to switch to the mouse for menu selection. These commands are included in Table 7.1.

Table 7.1. Cardfile keyboard shortcuts.

Key	Function
Ctrl+Home	Brings the first entry in the current database to the front of the Cardfile window

Key	Function
Ctrl+End	Brings the last entry in the current database to the front of the Cardfile window
PgDn	In **C**ard mode, scrolls forward one card in the current file; in **L**ist mode, moves forward one page (window) group of records
PgUp	In **C**ard mode, scrolls backward one card in the current file; in **L**ist mode, moves backward one page (window) group of records
Down arrow	Scrolls forward one card in **L**ist mode
Up arrow	Scrolls backward one card in **L**ist mode
F4	Initiates a **S**earch from the keyboard

Scanning a Cardfile File

Scanning the records in a Cardfile file is analogous to thumbing through our imaginary file drawer when it's filled with index cards. Pressing Ctrl+End in Card mode, for example, is comparable to flipping back to the last index card in that drawer. Conversely, pressing Ctrl+Home is like pulling and looking at the first card the drawer contains. The other Cardfile keyboard file scanning commands work in similar ways. Let's use our three sample records to demonstrate what I mean. First, switch back to the Card view.

1. Choose **V**iew from the Cardfile menu bar.
2. Choose **C**ard.

Your Cardfile window shows the record for The Buyer's Club, the last record we entered into this database. Go ahead and press Ctrl+Home. This brings the first card (record) in our PRACTICE.CRD file, the record for Conglomerate, Inc., to the front of the display window. Now, let's quickly move to the end of the file.

 To Display the Last Record in the Current File

Press Ctrl+End.

Cardfile displays the last record in the current file. □

The record for The Buyer's Club reappears (and, yes, pressing Ctrl+Home right now would just as quickly redisplay the record for Conglomerate, Inc.). Admittedly, this isn't an impressive feat with only three records in a file, but you can use the Cardfile command keys to navigate as quickly through a file that contains hundreds of names, addresses, phone numbers, and other information. And best of all, Cardfile doesn't limit you to linear scans. As is true of any PC application program, the ease with which you can find a specific piece of information located in one of Cardfile's records is the real strength of this accessory.

Searching a Cardfile's Index

You can use Cardfile's **S**earch command to quickly find specific records in a file. We're going to see how this works, but first let's make the first record in our PRACTICE file the active record.

 To Display the First Record in the Current File

Press Ctrl+Home.	Cardfile displays the first record in the current file. □

Suppose you had a large Cardfile database and needed to look up the name of your contact at MiniCorp, Inc. Scanning this Cardfile file alphabetically, therefore, would be impractical. So, what could you do? We'll attempt to use the Cardfile **S**earch command to see whether we can find the record containing the name of our sales representative contact at MiniCorp, Inc.

 To Find a Record Quickly

1. Choose **S**earch from the Cardfile menu.

   Cardfile displays its pull-down Search option menu.

2. Choose **G**o To.

   Cardfile displays the Go To dialog box (see Figure 7.7).

3. Enter the index value of the record you want to find in the Go To dialog box.

4. Choose OK.

   Cardfile scans the current file's index field and displays the first record that matches the specified search criteria. □

Have Cardfile display the MiniCorp record by using the previous Quick Step. At Step 2, Cardfile displays the Go To dialog box, shown in Figure 7.7. Use this dialog box to enter the index value you want Cardfile to find in the current file.

Figure 7.7. Use the Go To command to find a specific record in a Cardfile file.

Cardfile initiates a file search based on the criteria you specified—that is, with instructions to stop searching when it finds a record containing the text string "MiniCorp" in the index field. In our sample file, therefore, this search brings the card containing information for MiniCorp, Inc., to the front of your Cardfile window.

197

Searching for Nonindexed Text

Regardless of where a specified string exists, the Find command locates the specified text string within a database file. This feature is useful if you need to perform a random search on your database for information you know is not contained in an Index field.

Suppose, for example, you were planning a trip to Cincinnati and wanted to know what customers in our PRACTICE database were located in that city. Obviously, an index Search would be useless in this situation. Instead, you would want to use the Find command.

 To Have Cardfile Find Specific Nonindexed Information Within a Record

1. Choose Search from the Cardfile menu bar.	Cardfile displays its pull-down Search menu.
2. Choose Find.	Cardfile displays the Find dialog box.
3. Type the information you want to find. You can also choose to match case and change the direction of the search (up or down). Press Enter.	Cardfile scans the current file for the first incidence of the specified search criteria.

4. Press Alt+F4 to close the Find Dialog Box.

Cardfile highlights the requested information within the record. □

Use this Quick Step to search for the word Cincinnati. In Step 2, Cardfile displays a Find dialog box similar to the Go To dialog box shown in Figure 7.7. Use this dialog box to enter the text string you want Cardfile to locate within records in the current file. In this case, we want to find all customers located in Cincinnati.

Cardfile initiates a file search based on the Find criteria you specified—that is, with instructions to stop searching when it finds the text string Cincinnati anywhere in a Cardfile record. Using our sample records, therefore, this search ends when Cardfile reaches the card containing information for The Buyer's Club and moves the card to the front of your Cardfile window, as illustrated in Figure 7.8. Notice that Cardfile automatically highlights the specified text string within the display window.

198

> **Tip:** The Find Next button in the Find dialog box lets you scan multiple records containing the requested information.

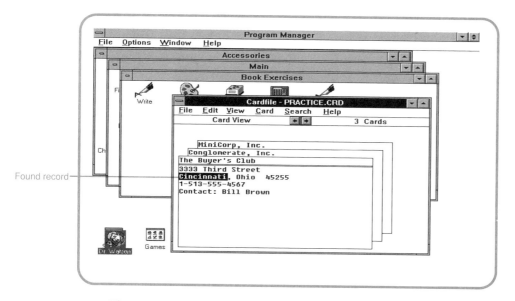

Figure 7.8. To search a database for a text string located any-where in a Cardfile record, use the Find command.

The Cardfile Autodial Feature

If you own a Hayes or Hayes-compatible modem, you can have Cardfile automatically dial phone numbers contained in a Cardfile database. Before testing the Cardfile autodial feature, however, perform the following steps:

1. Press F7 to add a new Cardfile entry to the PRACTICE database.
2. Type the name of someone you know and press Enter.
3. Type that person's phone number and press Enter.

Are you ready? Okay, here we go. Complete the following Quick Step to see how the autodialer works.

> **Tip:** You might want to call manually first and let your friend know that he or she is about to become part of a small experiment in automation.

199

Q Using the Cardfile Autodial Feature

1. Use the Cardfile Search options to display the record containing the phone number you want to dial.
2. Choose Card from the Cardfile menu bar.

   Cardfile displays its pull-down Card options menu.
3. Choose Autodial.

   Cardfile displays a prompt box containing the phone number recorded on the current record and options for using dialing prefixes for this call (see Figure 7.9).
4. Specify a prefix and select Use Prefix if this call requires one.
5. Choose OK.

   Cardfile uses your modem to dial automatically the selected phone number. ☐

In Step 2, Cardfile displays the dialog box screen shown in Figure 7.9, which contains the phone number associated with the current record. If you configured Windows to recognize your modem during installation, choosing OK causes Cardfile to dial this number.

Figure 7.9. Cardfile displays the number that is about to be dialed.

 Note: Of course, the actual telephone number shown in your Cardfile display differs from the one shown here.

After you choose OK, you hear a series of beeps coming from your modem's speaker. These beeps are the same tones a touch-tone phone system uses to dial the number previously displayed in your Cardfile window. A few seconds later, you hear the sound of your friend's voice on the phone.

Tip: If Windows is not configured to recognize and use your modem automatically, you can specify the modem setting for the current call by choosing the **S**etup button in the Autodial dialog box.

Note: If you're used to more sophisticated telecommunications programs than Cardfile, you might be thinking you have to issue some command to "hang up," but Cardfile cuts the connection automatically when you hang up. All Cardfile does is dial the phone number.

Deleting Records from a Cardfile Database

Now that we're finished with the special card we created to test the Autodial command, let's get rid of it. Deleting a record from a Cardfile database is a simple two-step operation.

1. Using a **Go To** or **Find** command, bring the card containing the record you want to delete to the front of the Cardfile window.
2. Select the **Delete** option from the pull-down Card menu.

 Note: Because your friend's record was displayed in the Cardfile window, you needed to perform only the second step listed previously.

201

Q To Delete a Cardfile Record

1. Choose **Card** from the Cardfile menu bar.

   Cardfile displays its pull-down Card menu.

2. Choose **Delete**.

   Cardfile displays a prompt box asking you to verify the Delete operation (see Figure 7.10)

3. Choose OK.

   Cardfile deletes the selected record and returns you to the current file. □

Cardfile displays the option box shown in Figure 7.10, asking you to verify that you do indeed want to delete the current record. Notice that the default option in this box is Cancel. Choosing Cancel aborts the Delete operation and leaves the current record within your database.

Figure 7.10. Windows guards against accidentally deleting records in a Cardfile database.

Quitting Cardfile

Let's go ahead and quit the Cardfile application. We'll return to Cardfile in Chapter 12, "Putting It All Together."

 To Quit Cardfile

1. Prior to quitting Cardfile, save your file.

2. Choose File from the Cardfile menu bar.

   Cardfile displays its pull-down File menu.

3. Choose Exit.

   This closes the Cardfile window and returns you to Program Manager. □

Because you modified the contents of this database and it was saved earlier in this chapter, Cardfile asks whether your changes to that file should be saved to the PRACTICE.CRD file before closing the current window. To save these changes, choose Yes.

Cardfile updates the PRACTICE.CRD file and returns you to Program Manager, from which you can select more Windows programs. That's exactly what we'll do in the next chapter, when we look at another Windows accessory, Calendar.

What You Have Learned

▶ Database management is an extremely powerful PC application. Using database management, you can keep track of large amounts of information quickly and efficiently, drawing on those types of operations computers perform best.

▶ Cardfile is the Windows database manager. You can use Cardfile to record, manage, and analyze virtually any type of information, on any subject. Furthermore, Windows' pull-down menus make using even the most advanced features of Cardfile, like the ability to find records based on their contents, easy to learn and use.

▶ Anyone with a Windows-compatible modem automatically can dial phone numbers stored in a Cardfile database using the Autodial command.

Calendar

In This Chapter

▶ *How to keep track of important dates and appointments with the Windows Calendar*

▶ *How to set a Calendar alarm*

As its name implies, Calendar is Windows' electronic answer to the traditional appointment calendar. Like its paper predecessor, the Windows Calendar can be used to record appointments, remind you of upcoming commitments, and even jot down a quick note to make sure you don't forget important events like your mother-in-law's birthday or your anniversary (Name a haggard husband or woeful wife who hasn't let this slip by at some time or another through the years). Furthermore, Windows enhances your ability to track such information by integrating Calendar into the total Desktop environment, thus making its advanced time-management features available to you at the push of a key or click of a mouse button, anytime during a Windows session.

Calendar Features

Features of the Windows Calendar accessory include

▶ The capability to view and analyze your scheduled appointments on a daily or monthly basis.

▶ Appointment entries that can be edited easily to reflect changes in your schedule.

▶ A built-in alarm that reminds you of planned events and appointments before they happen.

▶ The capability to incorporate notes about your appointments into the Calendar display using an on-screen scratch pad.

▶ A Mark option so that you quickly can mark special days in Calendar's Monthly view.

As you can see, using the Windows Calendar application can give an entirely new meaning to the old phrase "time on your hands." Let's start using Calendar.

Adding Calendar to the Book Exercises Program Group

As you probably have noticed, Calendar has not been added to your Book Exercises program group. Let's correct that oversight now. When adding Calendar to the program group, we'll look at still another example of the flexibility of the Windows GUI.

Minimizing a Program Group Window

To prepare for this exercise, let's temporarily close the Book Exercises program group and minimize it to a group icon. There are two ways to minimize an individual window in your Windows workspace:

1. By selecting the Minimize option from a window's Control menu.

2. By clicking a window's Minimize box, the window becomes a small icon on your workspace.

We'll use the first method described here to familiarize you with the Control menu options associated with individual windows.

 To Minimize the Program Group to a Group Icon

1. Click the Control menu. This is the menu box on the far left of the active group's title bar.

    This displays the Control menu for the active window.

2. Choose Minimize.

    Windows shrinks the active window down to a group icon. □

Step 1 displays the pull-down menu shown in Figure 8.1. You use a window's Control menu to specify operations you want performed on that window only, rather than your total Windows environment.

205

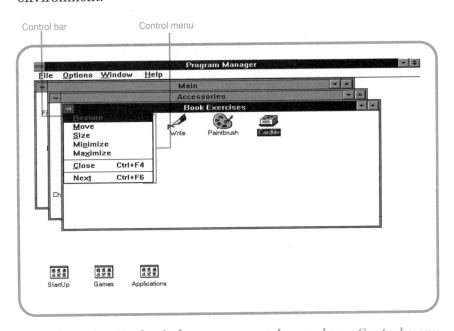

Figure 8.1. Each window on your workspace has a Control menu from which you can select commands that affect only that window.

Step 2 shrinks the Book Exercises program group to a group icon, which Windows positions with the other inactive icons across the bottom of your Windows workspace.

Copying an Accessory to a Group Icon

Previously, we only have copied accessories into open windows—as was the case when we first created our Book Exercises program group in Chapter 5, "Managing a Windows Program." A program group does not have to be open, however, for you to modify it. To demonstrate this, let's copy the Calendar application into our Book Exercises group icon.

1. Click the Accessories window.
2. Position the mouse cursor over the Calendar icon in the Accessories program group.
3. Press the left mouse button.
4. Press and hold down the Ctrl key.
5. Drag the mouse until the duplicate Calendar icon is sitting over the Book Exercises group icon.
6. Release the left mouse button and the Ctrl key.

It doesn't really look like much happened, does it? Don't worry. Something did. We'll reopen the Book Exercises program group to see what. Rather than simply double-clicking the Book Exercises group icon, which would work, let's try something else. This time, let's use the **Restore** command to return that program group to its previous full-screen display.

Restoring a Group Icon

You might be wondering how to specify a **Restore** command, which is located on the **C**ontrol menu, when the Book Exercises program group's Control menu box is not visible. I'm glad you asked.

Clicking a group icon has the same effect as choosing the Control menu box when that group is displayed in a window—that is, the click calls the Control menu, as illustrated in Figure 8.2. Notice that the **R**estore option on this menu is displayed in clear print, indicating it can be selected.

 To Restore a Group Using Control Menu

1. Click the group icon.   This displays the Control
                                  menu for the selected Group
                                  icon.

2. Choose Restore.   ☐

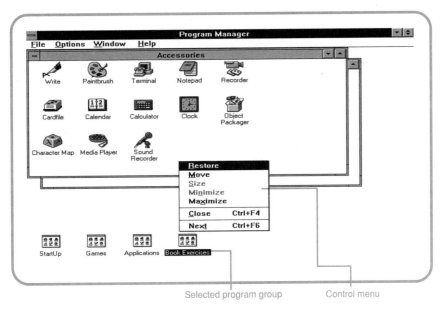

Figure 8.2. Clicking a group icon displays that group's Control menu.

The **Restore** command returns a program group to its previous size and location—it restores that program group to the way it was before you issued the most recent **Minimize** command. In this case, the Book Exercises program group was restored to the Windows workspace, as illustrated in Figure 8.3. And guess what? The Calendar accessory now is included in this group.

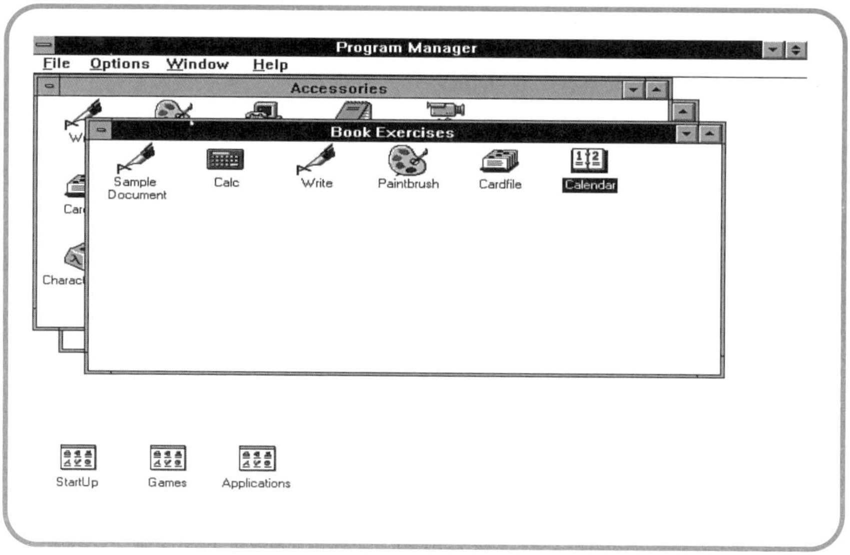

208

Figure 8.3. The Restore command restores a program group exactly as it was displayed before you issued the previous Minimize command.

Starting Calendar

Q **To Start the Calendar Accessory**

Double-click the Calendar
icon.

Windows starts the Calendar Accessory.   □

After a few seconds you'll see the Calendar display, shown in Figure 8.4. The first time you start Calendar, it displays a window resembling a typical page from a more traditional daily appointment book.

 Note: Your display shows a different date, the current date, which Calendar reads from your system clock.

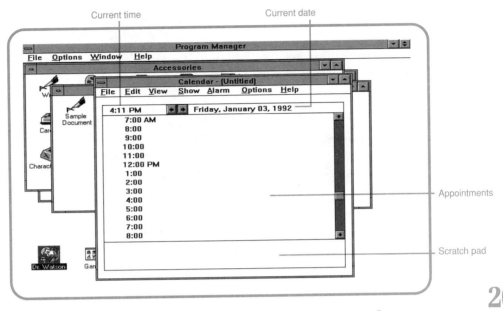

Figure 8.4. Calendar's initial display resembles a page from a daily appointment book.

Notice that, as was true with Write and Cardfile, Calendar creates an Untitled file the first time you start it. We'll name our new Calendar file in a few minutes. Before we do, though, let's take a look at some rudimentary Calendar operations.

Displaying Calendar's Monthly View

Calendar offers an alternative to the appointment book display shown in Figure 8.4. You can examine your schedule over a longer period of time than would be convenient with Calendar's Daily display by selecting Calendar's second display option, Month view.

 To Switch Calendar to a Month View

1. Choose View from the Calendar menu bar.

Calendar displays its pull-
down View menu.

2. Choose Month.
Calendar changes its display to the **M**onth view.   □

Calendar changes its display to the **M**onth view, as illustrated in Figure 8.5.

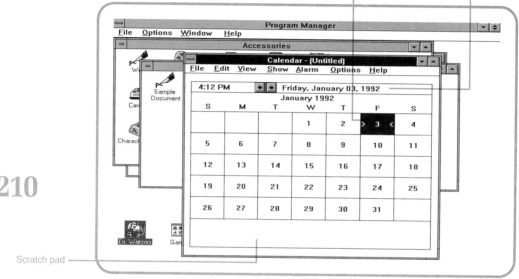

Figure 8.5. Use Calendar to analyze more than a single day's schedule with the Month view option.

Tip: If you're working at the keyboard and need to quickly change the Calendar view, you can do so by pressing F8 (Day) or F9 (Month).

Calendar makes it easy to determine certain information with a quick glance when Calendar is displayed in its Month view:

▶ Notice that one date is highlighted. This indicates the active date. When you first start Calendar, it automatically makes the current date active (January 3, 1992, in Figure 8.5)— providing, of course, your system clock is set correctly. You can change the active date, as you will see later in this chapter.

▶ Use the two horizontal scroll buttons located at the top of the Calendar display to thumb through different months sequentially, a procedure not unlike turning the pages of a traditional calendar. Mouse users can access this feature by clicking the appropriate action button. The corresponding keyboard commands are PgUp (the previous month) and PgDn (the next month).

▶ Calendar includes the familiar Windows menu bar across the top of its display window.

Because we're in Month view, let's examine the various Calendar features there.

Marking a Date

Remember how I told you Calendar could guarantee that you never again forget your wedding anniversary (or, for my unmarried readers, any other important annual event)? We'll start by adding a subtle reminder on June 15 to our sample Calendar. In Calendar's terminology, this would involve *marking a date* in the current file. Marking a date is a two-step process:

1. Change the active date to the date you want to mark.
2. Use the Mark command in the **O**ptions menu to attach a mark to that date.

Q To Change an Active Date

1. Choose **S**how from the Calendar menu bar.

Calendar displays its pulldown **S**how menu.

2. Choose **D**ate from the pulldown Show menu.

This displays the Show Date dialog box, as shown in Figure 8.6.

3. Type the date you want to switch to and press Enter. Use the format mm/dd/yy.

Calendar highlights the specified date.

Use the previous Quick Step to change the active date to June 15. Now that June 15 is the active date, we can mark it as a special occasion.

211

Show Date

Show Date: ☐   OK

Cancel

Figure 8.6. Use the Show Date dialog box to enter the date you want to make active in the current Calendar display.

 Recording an Event with Calendar

1. Make the date on which this event occurs the active date in your Calendar file.

2. Choose Options from the Calendar menu bar.

   Calendar displays the pull-down Options menu.

3. Choose Mark.

   Calendar displays the Day Marking options box.

4. Click the symbol you want displayed with this date and choose OK.

   This associates the specified date with the selected symbol.

5. If necessary, use the View menu to switch to the **D**ay view for the active date.

   This switches you to the **D**ay view to enter specific information about the event.

6. Enter any text you want associated with this event into either the time or the text entry box at the bottom of the Day window.   ☐

Step 3 displays the Day Markings option box shown in Figure 8.7. Use this option box to specify which of five symbols you want assigned to the active date. You can organize your Calendar files so that a quick scan of a month gives you an idea of your schedule for that month by associating a different symbol with different types of special events. You could, for example, use Symbol 1 for personal events, Symbol 2 for business meetings, Symbol 3 for project deadlines, and so on. In this case, we'll choose Symbol 4.

Use Steps 1 through 4 in the previous Quick Step to assign symbol 4 to June 15. Calendar returns you to the **M**onth view of the currently active month. Notice, however, that a small x (Symbol 4) has been placed in the date box for June 15.

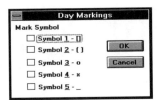

Figure 8.7. You can organize your Calendar files by assigning different symbols to different types of special events.

Adding Notes to a Calendar File

Admittedly, a small x in a date box doesn't tell you much, but it doesn't have to. Remember, that mark only serves as a reminder of some important event. To specify what that event is, you'll probably want to attach a note to its daily view.

Switching from a Month to a Day View

Earlier we accessed the **View** menu on the Calendar menu bar to switch between the **Month** and **D**ay view. There is a simpler way to call a Day view of June 15.

To Toggle Between Views for a Specific Day

Double-click the status line for the specified day.

This toggles Calendar between the **Month** and **D**ay view.

Tip: Double-clicking the status bar anywhere to the right of the scroll bars switches back to a Month view from a daily appointment book display.

Using Calendar's Scratch Pad

You can use the scratch pad to hold reminders about specific events and appointments recorded in your Calendar file. Let's use the Calendar scratch pad to attach a reminder of our imaginary wedding anniversary to the daily calendar for June 15.

 To Add a Reminder to an Active Date on the Scratch Pad

1. Position the mouse cursor anywhere in the blank box at the bottom of the Calendar window.

2. Click the left mouse button.   This places the cursor in the scratch pad for the current date.

3. Type the reminder you want.   □

Use the previous Quick Step to enter a reminder for "Wedding Anniversary" into the scratch pad for June 15. That takes care of our general reminder. Next, let's enter an individual appointment in our June 15 daily calendar—lunch reservations arranged to celebrate this special day.

Recording Individual Appointments in a Daily Calendar

Let's assume that you've arranged to meet your spouse for lunch at 12:45. Rather than appending this information to that day's scratch pad, it makes more sense to record this appointment for the actual time it's scheduled to take place. There's only one problem. Calendar's default daily display divides the day into 60-minute increments. To record an 11:45 appointment, therefore, you'll first need to insert a special line into June 15 for that time.

Specifying a Special Time

You can specify an appointment for a time other than Calendar's default values by using the Special Time command.

To Specify an Appointment for a Special Time on the Current Day

1. Choose Options from the Calendar menu bar.

   Cardfile displays its pull-down menu.

2. Choose Special Time.

   Cardfile displays the **Special Time** dialog box (see Figure 8.8).

3. Type the time for which you want to insert an appointment.

4. Indicate AM or PM.

5. Press Enter or choose Insert.

   Cardfile adds a line to the **D**ay view for the specified time.

6. Type information about this appointment in its time slot.

   Step 2 displays the **Special Time** dialog box, shown in Figure 8.8, which you use to insert an appointment line for times other than the Calendar default values. For this exercise, enter **11:45** and **Anniversary Luncheon Date** when you reach Step 5 of the previous Quick Step. □

215

Figure 8.8. You can specify special times for your appointments using Calendar's Special Time command.

At Step 4, Calendar inserts a new line for the specified time and returns you to its daily view. Now that this line exists, you can use it to record your special anniversary plans.

After Step 5, your Calendar display should resemble Figure 8.9, which shows both the scratch pad note and the individual appointment added to the June 15 record.

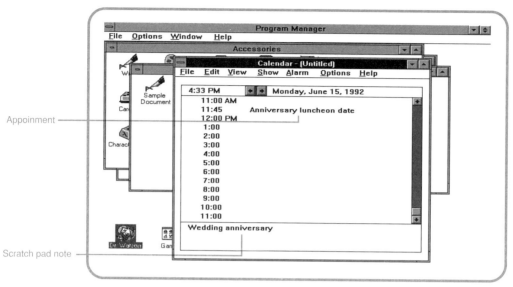

Appoinment

Scratch pad note

Figure 8.9. In this screen, both the scratch pad note and appointment record remind you of this special day.

For many people, this might be enough to ensure continued marital bliss. Others might need a little extra reminder (I know myself too well). I'll take all the help Calendar can give me. Luckily for me, and others like me, Calendar still has one more trick up its electronic sleeve.

The Calendar Alarm Feature

Setting an alarm is a logical and effective way to make certain you don't forget appointments recorded in your Calendar file.

Setting an Alarm

This feature is so simple, we're going to breeze right through it. Use the following Quick Step to set an alarm for the luncheon date.

Setting Alarms and the Alarm Timer with Calendar

1. Make the day for which you want to specify an alarm the active date.

2. If necessary, switch to the **D**ay view.

3. Position the cursor in the time period for which you want to set an alarm.

4. Press F5 or choose the **S**et option on the **A**larm menu.
   A stylized alarm bell appears to the left of the selected time.

5. Choose **A**larm from the Calendar menu bar.
   The pull-down Alarm menu appears.

6. Choose **C**ontrols.
   The Alarm Controls dialog box appears.

217

7. Specify the number of minutes (0-10) before the selected time that you want an alarm to sound.

Note: In Step 4 of the previous Quick Step, F5 and the **S**et option on the Alarm menu accomplish the same thing. Why perform two mouse operations when a single keystroke accomplishes the same thing? As good as a graphical interface is, there are times when nothing beats the reliable old PC keyboard.

This places a small bell icon next to the current appointment line. Now, you might imagine that anyone would feel fairly secure in their ability to remember this luncheon date. Secure maybe, but quite possibly, still not positive.

Setting an Alarm to Ring Early

You want positive? I'll give you positive—by showing you how to set this alarm to ring 10 minutes early.

√ To Set Your Alarm to Ring Early

▶ Choose **A**larm from the Calendar menu bar.

▶ Choose **C**ontrols.

▶ Type **10**.

▶ Choose OK or press Enter.

The second step displays the **A**larm Controls dialog box, as shown in Figure 8.10. The number you enter into the **Early Ring** field determines how long prior to a recorded appointment Calendar will begin sounding its alarm.

Figure 8.10. Setting the alarm to alert you before your appointment.

218

As these few examples illustrate, Calendar provides some impressive time-management tools. And all these features come bundled with the basic Windows package. Before we end our discussion of Calendar, let me point out one more advantage of organizing your schedule electronically, rather than depending on more traditional methods.

Creating a Personal Calendar File

I don't know how it is with your family, but here at Chez Nims everyone uses the same calendar—a free gift from the local pharmacy that's magnetically clamped to the side of our refrigerator—to keep track of important events. Consequently, by the time the last day of a given month rolls around, the calendar page contains more notes, reminders, quickly scribbled phone numbers, and more general graffiti than a New York subway train. By creating and managing multiple Calendar files, this problem is solved. Therefore, each person with access to your Windows environment can set up a different Calendar on which to keep track of his or her schedule.

To Create a Personal Calendar File

1. Choose File from the Calendar menu bar.	Calendar displays its pull-down **F**ile menu.
2. Choose Save As.	Calendar displays its Save **A**s dialog box.
3. Specify a name and location (directory) for your file.	
4. Click OK.	This saves the file under the name you specified and returns you to the current window (note the file name change). ☐

Use the previous Quick Step to save the file with the name MYTIME in the WINBOOK directory. Calendar displays a Save **A**s dialog box virtually identical to the ones you already have seen in Write and Cardfile. Use this dialog box to assign a name to your new Calendar file.

Calendar creates the new file. Notice that the top line of the Calendar display now contains the name you entered into the Save **A**s Name dialog box, MYTIME. Calendar automatically adds the .CAL extension to this file name (The MYTIME.CAL name replaces the previously Untitled Calendar legend). Now that we have created our personal appointment file and saved it to disk, let's end this Calendar session.

219

Quitting Calendar

 To Quit Calendar

1. Choose File from the Calendar menu bar.	Calendar displays its **F**ile menu.
2. Choose Exit.	Windows closes Calendar and returns you to the Program Manager. ☐

Because you just saved your most recent activity to a disk file, Calendar bypasses the cautionary prompt box encountered in earlier chapters and immediately returns you to the Calendar Program Manager.

What You Have Learned

▶ The Windows Calendar accessory helps you organize and manage time, perhaps your most precious resource. You can record planned activities and then review your schedule by day or month using Calendar.

▶ Calendar recognizes two distinct types of activities: date-related events and appointments assigned to specific times. You mark dates to remind you of special days, such as birthdays and anniversaries. Individual appointments represent activities planned within a specific date, such as business meetings and luncheon dates.

▶ After an event is recorded in Calendar, you can use that program's Alarm feature to make certain you don't forget the event.

Paintbrush

In This Chapter

▶ *A definition of Paintbrush and what it does*
▶ *How to start Paintbrush*
▶ *How to access and use the Paintbrush Toolbox*
▶ *How to include text in a graphic file*
▶ *How to mix text and graphics with Paintbrush*

What Is Paintbrush?

Paintbrush is the Windows graphics program. Based on the popular PC Paintbrush program from ZSoft Corporation, Paintbrush easily enables you to create a variety of graphic images. Having Paintbrush installed in your Windows environment is like having an electronic Etch-A-Sketch sitting on your desktop, ready to use. Doodlers love Paintbrush.

Paintbrush is useful for more than mere doodling, however. A well-designed graphic can enhance the appearance of virtually any document, including something as potentially boring as a form letter announcing an upcoming reduction of the purchase price of widgets. Let's put Paintbrush through its paces by designing a stationery logo for Wonderful Widgets, Inc.

> **Note:** In addition to adding an element of fun to our examination of the Windows environment, this chapter provides you with your first taste of how the various Windows accessories complement one another, thus creating a total work environment where the output of your PC activities can be greater than the sum of its parts.

Starting Paintbrush

You run Paintbrush by double-clicking its screen icon, a stylized artist's palette and paintbrush. Because Paintbrush exists in our Book Exercises program group, let's start it from there.

 To Start the Paintbrush Accessory

Double-click the Paintbrush icon.	Windows opens a Paintbrush window. □

This loads Paintbrush and displays its opening screen. For convenience, click the maximize box to expand Paintbrush to full-screen size. Your display should now resemble Figure 9.1.

It's not much to look at, is it? The initial Paintbrush screen shouldn't be anything fancy.

Think of your Paintbrush display as being the electronic analog of an artist's canvas. If you think about it, even the greatest masterpiece ever painted began its life as an empty canvas. Over time, however, the artist transformed this emptiness into meaningful images. That's exactly what you do with Paintbrush. Recognizing that an artist requires special implements to create his or her art (a palette, paint, paintbrushes, and the like), Paintbrush provides a number of tools to simplify life for the budding PC Picasso—tools you learn about as this chapter progresses. First, a word about everyone's favorite electronic rodent, the mouse.

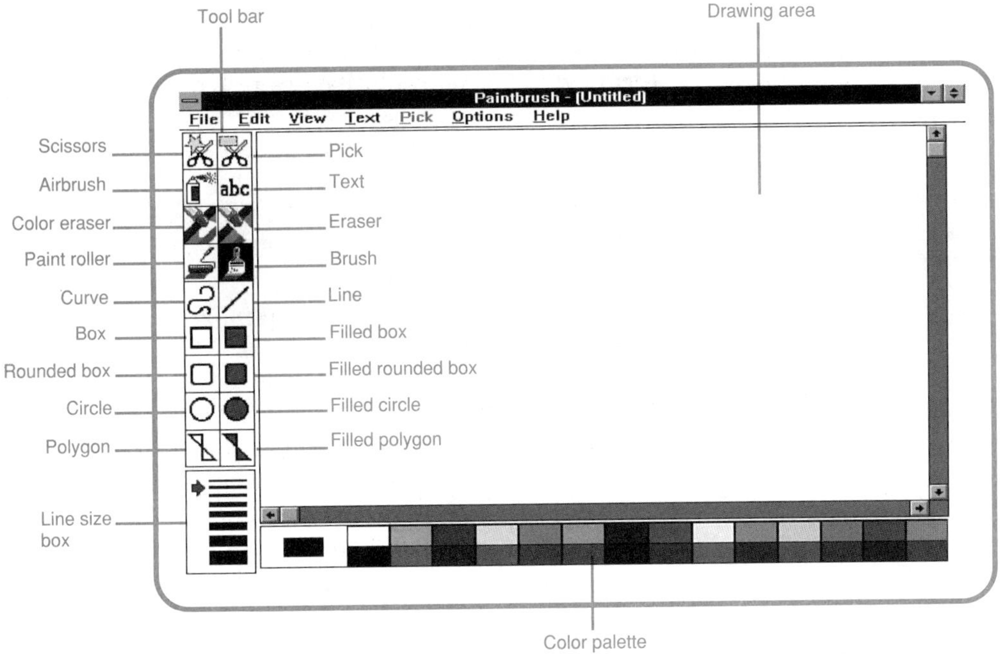
Tool bar
Drawing area
Paintbrush - (Untitled)
File Edit View Text Pick Options Help
Scissors
Airbrush
Color eraser
Paint roller
Curve
Box
Rounded box
Circle
Polygon
Line size box
Pick
Text
Eraser
Brush
Line
Filled box
Filled rounded box
Filled circle
Filled polygon
Color palette

Figure 9.1. The opening Paintbrush screen.

Paintbrush is the one Windows accessory in which using a mouse represents more than mere convenience. In addition to serving as a pointing device, as it does in all other Windows accessories, the mouse assumes the role of paintbrush after you begin filling in your electronic canvas. Although it might be possible to run Paintbrush without a mouse, I don't recommend it. A paintbrush simplifies creating artistic masterpieces; a mouse simplifies working in the Windows Paintbrush accessory. It's as simple as that.

The Paintbrush Tools

The drawing tools are accessed from the set of icons running down the left side of the Paintbrush display, the area of the screen referred to as the Toolbox. Each tool serves a different function, and you can use the tools to create and edit your Paintbrush images.

These tools are listed in the order of their appearance, from left to right and from top to bottom of the Paintbrush display. The functions that you can perform using these tools also are noted.

Scissors	Selects an irregularly shaped area of your picture, which you can then manipulate with the various Paintbrush commands located in the **E**dit and **A**ction menus.
Pick	Selects a square or rectangular shaped area of your picture, which you can then manipulate using your mouse or the various Paintbrush commands located in the **E**dit and **A**ction menus.
Airbrush	Produces a circular pattern of dots in the current foreground color.
Text Tool	Adds text, using several different fonts and type sizes, to your Paintbrush pictures.
Color Eraser	Changes selected foreground colors under the Eraser icon to a background color or, alternately, automatically changes every occurrence of one color in the drawing area to another.
Eraser	Changes any areas it touches into the currently selected background color.
Paint Roller	Automatically fills colors or patterns within any closed shapes you create.
Brush	Adds freehand sketch elements to your Paintbrush pictures.
Curve	Generates curved lines, resembling portions of a circle or other rounded object.
Line	Draws a straight line between two specified points.
Box	Draws squares and rectangles outlined in the foreground color.

Filled Box	Draws squares and rectangles that are filled with the foreground color.
Rounded Box	Draws squares and rectangles having rounded corners and outlined in the foreground color.
Filled Rounded Box	Draws squares and rectangles with rounded corners that are filled with the foreground color.
Circle	Draws circles and other rounded (or elliptical) shapes outlined in the foreground color.
Filled Circle	Draws circles and other rounded (or elliptical) shapes that are filled with the foreground color.
Polygon	Generates triangles or other multisided, irregularly shaped (polygonal) objects outlined in the foreground color.
Filled Polygon	Generates triangles or other multisided, irregularly shaped (polygonal) objects that are filled with the foreground color.

225

Now that you know what each Paintbrush tool is designed to accomplish, let's see how they can be used.

Selecting a Paintbrush Tool

You activate a Paintbrush tool by clicking its corresponding icon. Let's see how this works by selecting the Filled Circle tool.

 To Select a Tool from the Palette

1. Move your mouse until the mouse cursor is pointing to the tool you want to select.

2. Click the left mouse button.   This selects the tool.   □

Use the previous Quick Step to select the Filled Circle tool (see Figure 9.1) This highlights the Filled Circle icon within the Toolbox, identifying it as the currently active tool. After a tool is active, you can use it to create or modify elements within the drawing area, that currently blank portion of the Paintbrush display in which you create your pictures and graphic images.

Before we begin creating our letterhead logo, however, let's add one element to the Paintbrush display that makes it easier for you to coordinate the following exercise.

Displaying Cursor Coordinates

As you perform operations within the Paintbrush drawing area, you actually are manipulating the individual picture elements (or *pixels*, the dots on the video screen) your PC uses to generate its display. You can use the **C**ursor Position command, located on the **V**iew menu, to tell Paintbrush to display coordinates indicating the current position of the mouse cursor within its drawing area. Doing so simplifies such activities as arranging objects in a line, drawing straight lines, and so on.

 To Display the Cursor Coordinates

1. Choose View from the Paint-brush menu bar.

   Paintbrush displays its View menu.

2. Choose Cursor Position.

   This causes your cursor coordinates to be displayed in the Paintbrush window. □

Your screen now resembles Figure 9.2. Notice that the current cursor coordinates appear in a small box near the top-right corner of the Paintbrush display. In the following figure, the cursor is located 63 pixels in and 61 pixels down from the left and top borders of the Paintbrush drawing area, respectively. The actual numbers shown on your screen might be different.

Go ahead and move the mouse cursor around the drawing area for a few seconds. As you do, notice how the coordinates listed in the cursor position box change to reflect this movement.

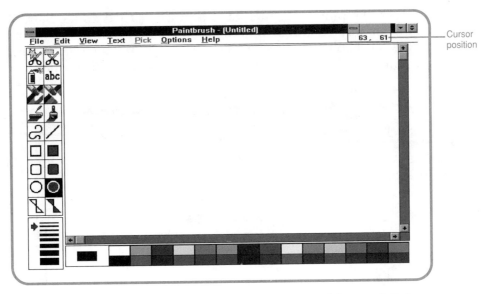

Figure 9.2. *Displaying the cursor position simplifies such Paint-brush activities as aligning objects and drawing straight lines.*

Using a Drawing Tool

Now that we can establish common reference points for the mouse cursor, let's draw a filled circle.

 To Draw a Filled Circle

1. Select the Filled Circle tool.

2. Position the mouse cursor at the starting point.

3. Press and hold the left mouse button.

4. Drag the mouse down and to the right until the circle outline matches the shape you want.

   As you drag your mouse, Paintbrush displays an outline of the circle you're creating.

5. Release the left mouse button.

   Paintbrush creates a filled circle at the specified location. □

Use the previous Quick Step to draw a filled circle. Start at approxiamtely 265, 125. Drag approximately to coordinates 350, 200. Your display now resembles Figure 9.3, in which Paintbrush has drawn a filled circle, using the specified cursor coordinates.

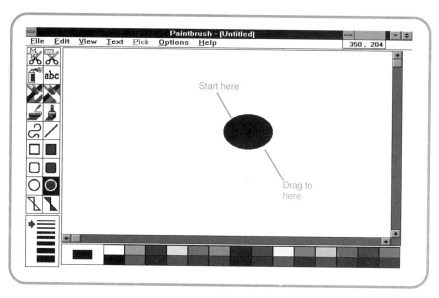

Figure 9.3. Dragging your mouse with an activated tool automatically creates the shape associated with that tool within the Paintbrush drawing area.

> **Note:** Depending on the type of monitor you use, this circle might appear slightly more elliptical, or elongated, on your display.

All of the Paintbrush tools operate in basically the same manner. That is, you use the mouse to activate the tool you want to use, then move the mouse cursor into the Paintbrush drawing area and perform the operation associated with whatever tool you selected.

Using the Paintbrush Drawing Tools

1. Click the desired drawing tool in the two columns of Tool icons running down the left side of the Paintbrush window.

    Paintbrush highlights the selected tool.

2. Position the mouse cursor on the Paintbrush workspace where you want the selected shape to begin.

3. Press and hold down the left mouse button.

4. Drag your mouse to the position you want the selected shape to end.

    As you drag the mouse, an outline defining the selected shape for the current cursor location appears.

5. Release the left mouse button.

    Paintbrush draws the requested shape at the specified location. □

229

You see several examples of what specific tools accomplish later in this chapter, as we go about the task of creating a corporate logo for our imaginary company, Wonderful Widgets, Inc. Before beginning this project, however, let's get rid of the filled circle we drew in the previous exercise.

The easiest way to erase an object is to use the Eraser tool to change that object to the background color. This is similar to using an eraser to eliminate pencil marks and return a page to the color of the paper underneath.

 To Activate the Eraser Tool

1. Move your mouse until the mouse cursor points to the Eraser icon (the third icon from the top in the right column of the Toolbox).

2. Click the left mouse button to activate the Eraser tool.

3. Move the mouse cursor back into the drawing area.

A small white square appears representing the size of the area that will be erased each time you press the mouse button or, alternately, drag the mouse over a portion of the Paintbrush display. ☐

The operative word here is small. That's a small square, and we have a big circle to erase. We can, however, change the size of the square so we can erase the circle quickly.

Changing the Drawing Width

Use the Line size box, located in the bottom-left corner of the Paintbrush display, to change the size of the area affected by a Paintbrush tool or, alternately, the thickness of the border around any objects you draw. Selecting a larger line size, for example, would increase the area affected by the Eraser tool, something that comes in handy as we erase the circle.

 To Increase the Line Size

1. Move your mouse until the mouse cursor is pointing to the appropriately sized line in the Line size box.

2. Click the left mouse button.

This makes the selected width the current line size. ☐

Now move the mouse cursor back into the drawing area. This time you should see a much bigger square representing the size of your eraser. In addition, notice that the arrow that previously indicated the thinner line size now points to the one you just selected. It should be big enough, in fact, to make erasing the circle an easy task.

Using the Eraser

To use the Eraser tool, press and hold the left mouse button, then drag the Eraser icon (the white square) across the area to be eliminated.

 To Use the Eraser

1. Activate the Eraser tool.

   This activates Paintbrush's electronic eraser.

2. Move the eraser icon until it partially obscures the object.

3. Press and hold down the left mouse button.

4. Drag the mouse back and forth over the object until it has all been erased.

   Paintbrush replaces areas it erases with the background color. □

Voilà! We have a blank screen. So, let's take advantage of this blank screen and get down to the nitty-gritty of designing our Wonderful Widgets corporate logo, checking out some additional features of Paintbrush on our way.

Adding Text to a Picture

Even admitting the validity of the adage that a picture is worth a thousand words, there are times when only words suffice. For example, it doesn't make sense to design a company letterhead that does not include your company's name. Ideally, then, we'd want to incorporate "Wonderful Widget, Inc." into the Paintbrush file we are creating. As luck would have it, we can accomplish this using Paintbrush's Text tool.

231

To Enter Text in the Drawing Area

1. Position the mouse cursor over the Text icon (the second icon from the top in the right column of the Toolbox).

2. Click the left mouse button.   This activates the Paint-brush Text tool.

3. Position the mouse cursor at the coordinates you want the text to start.

4. Click the left mouse button.   This places a text cursor at the specified location.

5. Type the text.   ☐

Use the previous Quick Step to type **Wonderful Widgets, Inc.** approximately at coordinates 150, 80. Don't click the left mouse button at this point. I will explain the reasons behind issuing this caution shortly. Your screen now resembles Figure 9.4, which shows the text you typed added to the Paintbrush drawing area.

232

Changing Text Attributes

The company's name is there, to be sure. But it's not very dramatic, is it? I can't imagine many people going out of their way to read a piece of paper topped by such a mundane letterhead. Let's add a little spice to our corporate name by using a different kind of lettering. We'll begin by making our text a little larger.

 Selecting Typestyle Attributes.

1. Select Text from the Paint-brush menu.   Paintbrush displays a pull-down menu listing the various text attributes you can apply to your text.

2. Select Fonts from the Text bar.   Paintbrush displays the Font options box (see Figure 9.5).

3. Select the font attributes
   you want.

4. Choose OK.

Any text you enter at this
point reflects the attributes
chosen in the previous
steps. □

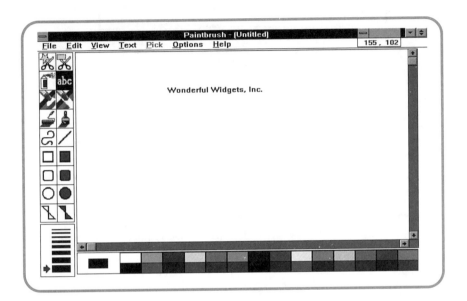

*Figure 9.4. Use the Text tool to include text in a Paintbrush
graphic.*

Let's use the Font options to enhance the appearance of our
corporate logo. First, change the font size to 24. The larger type is
more apt to attract someone's attention. Let's also try using a
different *font*, or lettering design, for the company's name.

Change the font to Roman. Now we're getting close. The Roman
font is certainly fancier than Paintbrush's default System lettering.
The Roman font adds a little class to our letterhead.

Font   Style

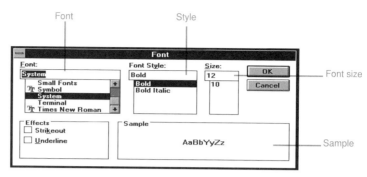

Figure 9.5. You can enhance the appearance of text in a Paintbrush file with the Font options.

Finally, use the Font dialog box to change the logo to Bold, Italic, and Underline. Choose OK. Your display now resembles Figure 9.6, which shows how Paintbrush has modified the appearance of the company logo, based on the Style options you specified. Now we have the beginnings of an attractive letterhead.

234

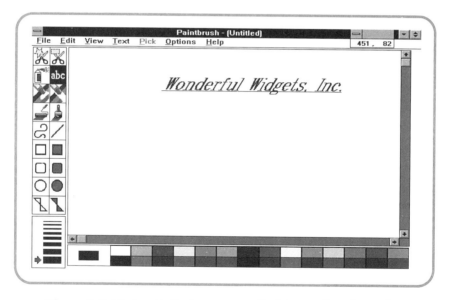

Figure 9.6. Style attributes are applied immediately to the current text.

Caution: Changing size, font, and style attributes affects only the current text, which Paintbrush defines as any letters entered prior to the last time you used the mouse cursor to select a text input location. If you had clicked the left mouse button earlier, the new values we've selected here would not have been applied to our Wonderful Widgets logo.

Any subsequent text you enter at this time will be printed in the current type style, until you use the various Paintbrush menu options to modify the font attributes again. Before we go further, let's return the Size, Font, and **S**tyle options back to some settings that are less showy.

1. Click the left mouse button to deactivate the current text.
2. Choose the Font option from Paintbrush Text menu.
3. Set Size to 12.
4. Choose System **F**ont.
5. Select the Bold font style.
6. Turn off Underline.

235

Now that we're on a roll, let's complete the address that we want to include in the company letterhead.

1. Position the mouse cursor approximately at coordinates 215, 105.
2. Click the left mouse button.
3. Type **4321 Corporate Drive** and press Enter.
4. Type **New York, NY 10012** and press Enter.
5. Press the space bar five times.
6. Type **(212) 555-1234** and press Enter.

When you've finished, your display resembles Figure 9.7, which shows address information added to the previous screen. The only element missing from our letterhead now is some type of graphic that draws the reader's attention to the stationery and, therefore, whatever message it contains. Before doing so, however, let's relocate our letterhead address to make room for this graphic.

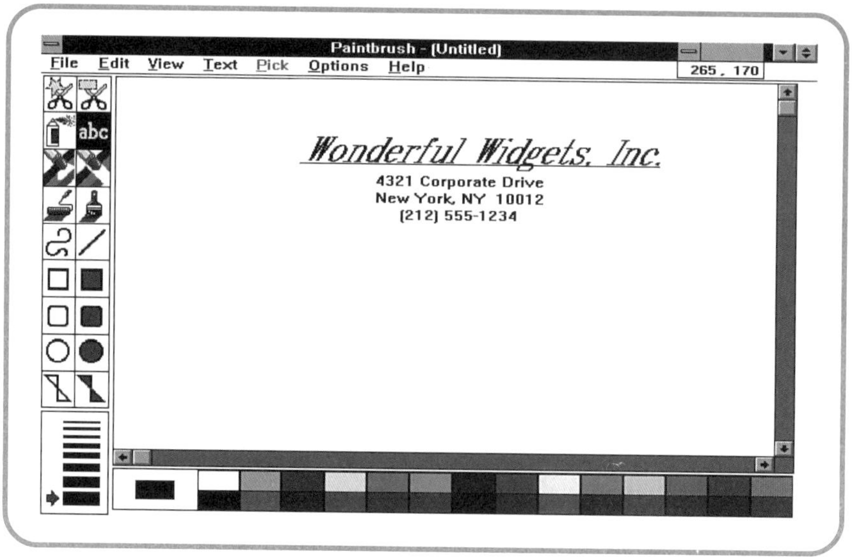

Figure 9.7. Paintbrush's System font works well for standard text.

236

Using the Cutout Tools

Use the Paintbrush cutout tools to select a segment of the drawing area for additional processing. The two available cutout tools include:

Scissors   Selects an irregularly shaped section of the Paintbrush display.

Pick   Selects a square or rectangular shaped section of the Paintbrush display.

After defining a cutout, you can use commands from the **E**dit menu to Cut, **C**opy, **P**aste, and **S**ave the cutout section. Options in the **P**ick menu also can be applied to cutout sections. We won't be doing anything quite this fancy. Instead, we use the **P**ick tool to select and then move our address information to a different location within the drawing area.

To Move an Object

1. Position the mouse cursor over the Pick icon (the first icon on the right column of the Toolbox).

2. Click the left mouse button.   This activates the Pick tool.

3. Position the cross hair to a location that defines a corner of the section you want to move (at the approximate coordinates 135, 60).

4. Press and hold down the left mouse button.   This defines an anchor point for the Pick tool.

5. Drag the mouse until the area you want to move is entirely surrounded by a dotted line.

6. Release the left mouse button.   This "picks" the enclosed area.

7. Position the mouse cursor within the selected area.

8. Press and hold down the left mouse button.

9. Drag the mouse cursor to the new location where you want to position the selected area.

10. Release the left mouse button.   Paintbrush moves the selected area to the specified location. ☐

237

Now, let's use the Pick tool to select and move our address information to a different location within the drawing area.

✓ **To Move the Address Information**

▶ Position the mouse cursor over the Pick icon (the first icon on the right column of the Toolbox).

▶ Click the left mouse button to activate the Pick tool.

▶ Position the cross hair just above and to the left of your address block (at about coordinates 135, 45).

▶ Press and hold down the left mouse button.

▶ Drag diagonally across the address until it is entirely surrounded by a dotted line.

▶ Position the mouse cursor in the upper-left corner of the address block.

▶ Press and hold down the left mouse button.

▶ Drag the mouse cursor to coordinates 145, 200.

▶ Release the left mouse button.

This moves the selected cutout to a new location, lower on the screen. The top of our address information now has free space for a graphic image.

Mixing Text and Graphics

Because no one really knows what a widget looks like, I can design and draw any graphic I please to complement the letterhead address. I plan to keep this simple. Before starting, let's do two things:

▶ Reduce the line size back to a more manageable width. (Choose second line size.)

▶ Save the address information to a Paintbrush file to protect the work we've done so far. (Use filename LOGO.)

✓ To Decrease the Linesize

▶ Move your mouse until the mouse cursor is pointing to a thinner line in the line size box.

▶ Click the left mouse button to select the thinner line size.

✓ To Save the Address Information to a Disk File

▶ Choose **File** from the Paintbrush menu bar.

▶ Choose Save **As**.

▶ At the Save **As** dialog box, type LOGO.

▶ Double-click the WINBOOK file folder.

▶ Choose OK.

Now we're ready to create our graphic—a nice, simple image, the primary purpose of which is to represent our imaginary widget.

1. Position the mouse cursor over the Filled Rounded Box icon (the third icon from the bottom in the right column of the Toolbox).
2. Click the left mouse button to activate the Filled Rounded Box tool.
3. Position the mouse cursor at coordinates 250, 130.
4. Press and hold down the left mouse button.
5. Drag the mouse cursor to coordinates 340, 180.
6. Release the mouse button.
7. Position the mouse cursor over the Line icon (the fifth icon from the top in the right column of the Toolbox).
8. Click the left mouse button to activate the Line tool.
9. Position the mouse cursor at coordinates 235, 185.
10. Press and hold down the left mouse button.
11. Drag the mouse cursor to coordinates 350, 185.
12. Release the mouse button.

239

When you've completed these steps, your screen resembles Figure 9.8, which now contains an admittedly primitive image of a widget above our address information.

That's all there is to it. We've now designed a corporate logo and company letterhead for the Wonderful Widgets Company. Before quitting Paintbrush, you'll want to save this image because we'll be using it in a later chapter.

 To Save the Current Image

1. Choose **File** from the Paint-brush menu bar.	Paintbrush displays its File menu.
2. Choose **Save**.	Paintbrush saves your image, using the current filename. □

Now we're ready to close down Paintbrush and end this chapter.

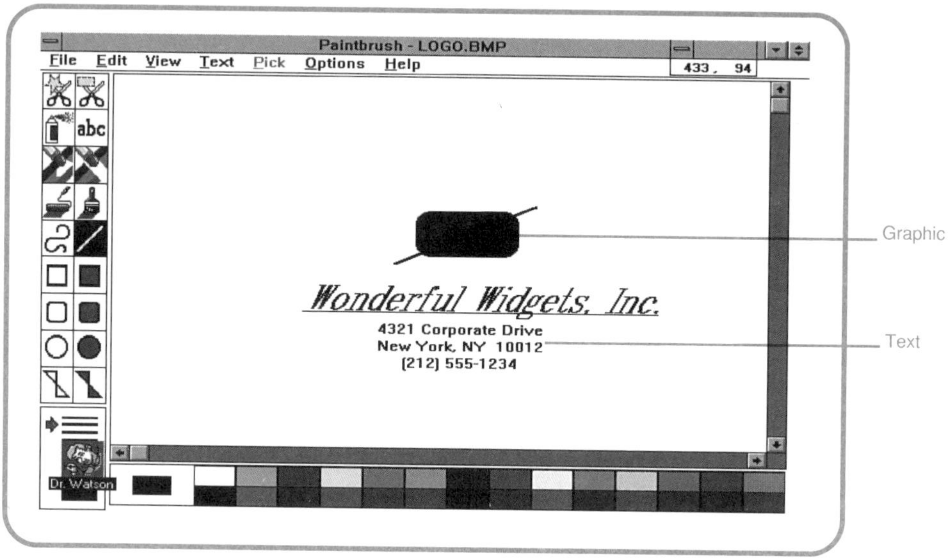

Figure 9.8. You can use the various Paintbrush tools to create graphic images as simple or complex as the situation demands.

240

Quitting Paintbrush

Q **To Quit Paintbrush**

1. Choose File from the Paintbrush menu bar.

   Paintbrush displays its **File** menu.

2. Choose Exit.

   Windows exits Paintbrush and returns you to the Program Manager.   □

Because you just saved your most recent activity to a disk file, Paintbrush bypasses the cautionary prompt box encountered in earlier chapters and immediately returns you to the Windows Program Manager.

What You Have Learned

▶ Paintbrush is the Windows graphics program. Using Paintbrush, you can create pictures consisting of geometric shapes, freehand drawings, and other graphic images.

▶ Paintbrush provides several drawing tools to simplify the process of designing and creating your graphic images. With these tools you can quickly draw circles, boxes, rectangles, and even irregular polygons, all with a few simple mouse movements. These geometric shapes—or tools, as they are called in the Paintbrush vernacular—can then be enhanced using additional Paintbrush features such as color and fill patterns.

▶ You can enter text in the drawing area using the Text tool included in Paintbrush. These text passages can be printed in a variety of type sizes and font attributes to add emphasis to your Paintbrush graphics.

241

Terminal

In This Chapter

- ▶ *A definition of telecommunications*
- ▶ *How to configure the Windows Terminal application to run properly on your PC system*
- ▶ *How to use Terminal*

What Is Telecommunications?

I'm not going to let this discussion get very complex. Several well-written books explain telecommunications in more detail than I have the luxury of going into here. Consequently, I'll keep this overview of telecommunications relatively simple.

Specifically, telecommunications is the process of using your personal computer, a modem, and special software to communicate with another similarly equipped computer over standard telephone lines. Get it? Telephone communications between two computers—telecommunications.

Beyond this simple definition, many technical considerations come into play if you decide to use your PC to access another computer in a different location. (As you'll soon see, however, the Windows Terminal accessory virtually eliminates the need to worry about such minutia.) That explains what telecommunications is. Next, let's address how telecommunications does this. To understand that, you need to know a little about one specific piece of PC hardware: a *modem.*

The word *modem* is derived from the expression modulate/demodulate, which is precisely what a modem does. At one end of the telecommunications link, it *modulates* the digital signals a computer generates into analog tones compatible with a standard telephone line. Conversely, on the other end of this link, a modem *demodulates* the analog tones transmitted over a standard telephone line into the digital signals your computer requires to work properly. The electronic principles governing how this occurs are complex and, within the parameters of our current discussion, unimportant. What is significant is that this series of events must happen, if two computers are to communicate successfully with one another over a telephone hookup. You must have a modem to use the Windows Terminal application. If you don't own a modem, you might want to skip ahead to the next chapter. If your personal computer system includes a modem, however, read on. The next thing you learn is what that modem—and by extension, the telecommunications capabilities that the modem supports—enable you to do.

Sending and receiving electronic mail, transferring files, researching arcane information, conferring with other personal computer users who share your interests, shopping for a new car or computer, even playing games—these represent but a few of the activities you can participate in after you've learned to use Terminal. You can pursue these activities at your convenience, any time of the day or night. You see, your computer is as ignorant of minutes as it is of miles. I've run across European callers using the various on-line services to which I subscribe at three or four o'clock in the morning, my time—which only makes sense, because it is late afternoon or early evening in their part of the world. From this perspective, telecommunications has helped shrink the world, to bring us all a little closer.

That, in a nutshell, is what telecommunicating is all about. And Terminal, the Windows' application that we concentrate on during the remainder of this chapter, is designed to help you telecommunicate. Let's get started. After all, there's a whole world out there waiting for you.

Starting Terminal

I knew we wouldn't be combining your on-line activities with any other exercises in this book, so I did not have you incorporate Terminal into the Book Exercises program group. Consequently, you need to access the Accessories program group before you can start Terminal.

 Switch to the Accessories Window

1. Position the mouse cursor on any visible portion of the Accessories window.
2. Click the left mouse button.

The Terminal icon, a picture of a personal computer with a telephone in front of it, will be visible within the Accessories window.

245

 To Start Terminal

Double-click the Terminal icon.	Windows runs Terminal in its own window. □

If this is the first time you've started Terminal, Windows needs to request a critical piece of information about how your hardware is configured for telecommunications. Specifically, Windows needs to know the serial port (COM port) to which your modem is attached, as shown in Figure 10.1.

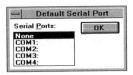

Figure 10.1. The first time you start Terminal, you need to tell Windows about your hardware setup.

To Specify a Serial Port for Your Modem Operations

1. Start the Terminal program. The Default Serial Port dialog box is displayed.

2. Choose the COM number
corresponding to the
serial port your modem is
attached to.

3. Choose OK or press Enter.   Terminal automatically
configures to use the
specified COM port.   □

> **Tip:** Unless you know differently, it's safe to assume your
> modem is attached to COM1, the first serial port installed
> on your PC. If you are unsure of your modem port, take the
> necessary steps to find out. Terminal will not work properly if
> you specify an incorrect COM port.

After specifying your modem port, you are advanced to the
main Terminal screen, shown in Figure 10.2.

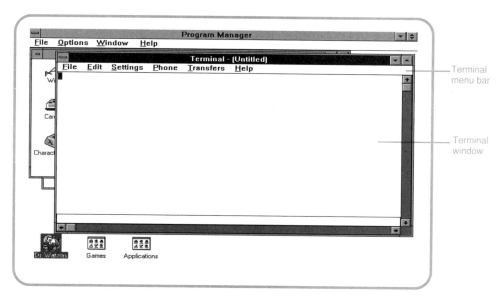

Figure 10.2. The main Terminal screen.

Before outlining the steps required to have Terminal connect
your PC to another computer, we need to discuss how you set up
Terminal for a given on-line session, beginning with how the two
computers involved communicate with one another.

Setting Communication Parameters with Terminal

For telecommunications to be successful, both computers involved in an on-line session must speak the same language. Think of this as resembling normal human conversations, wherein two people generally use a single language (for example, English) to communicate with one another. When working with a modem, this language consists of several special settings called *communication parameters.* Communication parameters determine how Terminal formats your data prior to transmitting it across the phone line.

 Setting Communication Parameters

1. Choose **S**ettings from the Terminal menu bar.

   Terminal displays its Settings options.

2. Select **C**ommunications.

   The Communications dialog box appears, containing the various parameter settings available in Terminal.

3. Specify the settings appropriate for the current communications session, including Baud Rate, Parity, Flow Control, and COM port selection.

4. Click OK or press Enter.

   This configures Terminal for the specified settings and returns you to the main Terminal window. □

247

Some terms that follow might seem somewhat confusing at this point in your telecommunications career. (In truth, several of them do represent fairly technical concepts.) Don't worry about this. Although understanding precisely what each setting accomplishes helps you comprehend exactly how telecommunications works, it's not a prerequisite to using Terminal. What is critical is realizing that these settings must be configured properly for your personal computer to communicate with another computer.

The communication parameters you must be aware of to configure Terminal properly for telecommunications include

Baud Rate	This is the transmission rate at which your computer sends and receives information during a Terminal session. You can set Terminal to operate at any of several popular baud rates, including 110, 300, 600, 1200, 2400, 4800, 9600, and 19,200 baud. The type of modem you have determines which baud rates you can use.
Data Bits	This setting represents the number of *bits* (BInary digITS, the individual 0 and 1 settings stored in memory) used to send a single character during a Terminal session. Terminal supports five word-length settings, ranging from 4 to 8 bits.
Stop Bits	This setting specifies the number of bits Terminal appends to the end of each character to indicate that the entire character has been transmitted. You can choose between 1, 1.5, or 2 stop bits.
Parity	This determines how the receiving computer verifies the accuracy of any data you transmit during a Terminal session. Available parity settings supported by Terminal include None, Odd, Even, Mark, and Space.
Flow Control	This setting determines how your PC and the remote computer will coordinate data transfers; that is, how one computer will know when the other computer is waiting for data and vice versa.
Parity Check	Activate this setting if you want Terminal to display the byte in which any parity check errors are encountered. Usually, you leave the **P**arity Check option inactive.

248

Carrier Detect How you set this option depends largely on what type of modem you have. If your modem is 100 percent Hayes-compatible—that is, fully emulates modems manufactured by the Hayes Corporation, the closest thing to a modem standard in the PC marketplace—you should turn Carrier Detect (CD) on. This tells Terminal to use your modem's internal electronics to determine when a connection is made. If you have trouble making connections and have checked to see that all other Terminal settings are correct, try disabling CD. This tells Terminal to bypass a modem's CD circuitry and use its own internal methods for detecting a carrier signal.

249

Individual settings for these parameters can vary, depending on the remote system you plan to contact during a given on-line session. The best rule of thumb I can give you as to how these settings should be configured for a specific on-line session is that they should match the parameters the computer you are connecting with uses to establish a connection over the telephone line.

Use the Communications dialog box to set the proper parameters for an on-line session.

√ **To Set Proper Communications Parameters**

▶ Choose **S**ettings from the **T**erminal menu bar.

▶ Choose **C**ommunications.

▶ Enter correct parameters.

▶ Press Enter or choose OK.

Step 2 displays the Communications dialog box shown in Figure 10.3. The various options in this dialog box correspond to the parameter setting outlined in the previous section. Use the Communications dialog box to specify the appropriate parameters for the remote system you will be contacting with Terminal.

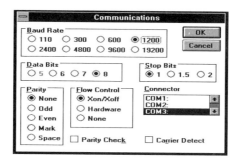

Figure 10.3. The Communications dialog box.

Setting Terminal Preferences

The parameters set in the previous section define how Terminal communicates with the outside world—that is, to whatever remote system you are connected. You also can specify the internal procedures Terminal is to use during a communication session, how Terminal itself is to handle any data exchanged between it and another computer during a remote session. In the Windows vernacular, these settings are called your *Terminal preferences.*

Terminal preferences you can specify include

Line Wrap	Activating Line Wrap causes Terminal to format incoming data automatically to fit within the column width of your Terminal configuration (see columns below).
Local Echo	This setting tells Terminal whether it should send any characters you type directly to your display monitor or enable the remote system to echo these characters back over the phone line after it has received them.
Sound	This setting activates or deactivates the system bell (or more likely, beep) for the remote system.
Columns	This setting lets you specify whether Terminal should format your data for an 80- or 132-column display.

Terminal Font	This setting lets you select the display font Terminal should use. You can select any font or font size that has been installed in your Windows environment.
Show Scroll Bars	This setting lets you tell Terminal whether it should display scroll bars. Displaying scroll bars simplifies the process of reviewing data that has scrolled out of the Terminal display window.
CR to CR/LF	This setting tells Terminal whether it should add a line feed to each carriage return received from the remote system.
Cursor	Use this option to tell Windows what style of cursor you want displayed in your Terminal window.
Translation	You need to use this option only if you plan to have Terminal connect with a remote system that uses a foreign language.
Buffer	Terminal uses a temporary storage area called a *buffer* to store incoming data. You can specify a size for this buffer, ranging from 25 to 400 lines of information using the Buffer option. If you specify a buffer amount exceeding the amount of available memory, Terminal automatically reduces its buffer to an appropriate size.

251

Use the Terminal Preferences dialog box to specify settings for these items.

 Setting Terminal Preferences

1. Choose Settings from the Terminal menu bar.

Terminal displays its Settings options.

2. Select Terminal Preferences.

The Terminal Preferences dialog box appears, containing the various options available for configuring your terminal display.

3. Select the settings you want for your Terminal display.

4. Click OK or press Enter.

Windows makes the necessary changes to your communications environment and returns you to the Terminal window.   □

Step 2 displays the Terminal Preferences dialog box shown in Figure 10.4. The various options in this dialog box correspond to the parameter setting outlined in the previous section.

252

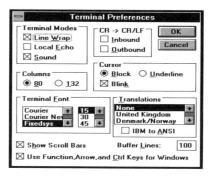

Figure 10.4. The Terminal Preferences dialog box.

Specifying Terminal Emulation

All computers are not created equal. Not only are computers not equal, they also are not the same. Different systems use different standards to communicate with the outside world. I'm not discussing telecommunications between two computers here. Rather, I'm talking about the procedures a single computer employs to transmit instructions from users to its central processing unit. Without getting too technical, this boils down to the type of terminal settings a specific computer recognizes.

Note: In this context, the word *terminal* indicates the type of keyboard and display monitor a specific computer uses, as opposed to the Windows Terminal program.

For your PC to communicate successfully with another system, it must have the capability of emulating the type of terminal that the other system recognizes. Terminal (the Windows accessory) provides a simple method for specifying the type of terminal emulation you want in effect during an on-line session.

Q To Specify Terminal Emulation

1. Choose **S**ettings from the Terminal menu bar.	Terminal displays its **S**ettings option.
2. Choose Terminal Emulation.	Terminal displays the Terminal Emulation dialog box.
3. Select the appropriate Terminal Emulation.	
4. Press Enter or choose OK.	Windows adjusts your communication environment and returns you to the Terminal window. □

253

Step 2 displays the Terminal Emulation dialog box shown in Figure 10.5. Use this dialog box to specify the type of terminal (keyboard/display) Terminal (the Windows accessory) should emulate for a given system.

Figure 10.5. The Terminal Emulation dialog box.

 Tip: You have an emulation mismatch if the remote system does not respond to commands issued from your PC. As a rule, you should use DEC VT-100 (ANSI) emulation when connecting to a commercial on-line service or another PC. Many mainframe computers, on the other hand, use DEC VT-52 terminals. If all else fails, try TTY, the most generic emulation Terminal supports.

Specifying a Phone Number

Of course, before Terminal can call a remote system, it needs to know the telephone number at which that system can be reached.

 To Specify the Telephone Number of a Remote System

1. Choose **S**ettings from the Terminal menu bar.

   Terminal displays its **S**ettings option.

2. Choose Phone Number.

   Terminal displays its Phone Number dialog box.

3. Enter the appropriate information for your call.

4. Press Enter or choose OK.

   Terminal records the information entered into the Phone Number dialog box. □

Step 2 displays the Phone Number dialog box shown in Figure 10.6. Use this dialog box to specify the phone number Terminal should use to connect with the remote system you want to call.

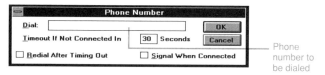

Figure 10.6. The Phone Number dialog box.

Additional information you can specify with the Phone Number dialog box includes

Timeout
: Use this field to specify the number of seconds you want Terminal to wait for a connection to be made successfully with the remote system.

Redial
: Use this option to tell Terminal that, if no connection is made within the number of seconds specified in the Timeout field, it should try automatically to redial the number.

Signal When Connected   Activating this option tells
                         Terminal to sound an audible
                         tone after a connection is
                         established.

Saving a Terminal Configuration

The good news is that after your parameters and terminal options are set properly, you're ready to have Terminal call a remote system. The better news is that you don't need to repeat all these steps each time you want to make an on-line connection. You can save the current settings to a disk file with Windows. When this file exists, loading it back into memory automatically prepares Terminal to contact any system that uses the settings it contains.

255

 To Save Your Current Terminal Settings to a Disk File

1. Choose **File** from the   Terminal displays its
   Terminal menu bar.   File option.

2. Choose Save **As**.   Terminal displays its Save
                                    As dialog box.

3. Enter the name you want
   assigned to the current
   settings.

4. Choose OK or press Enter.   The current settings are
                                    saved under the specified
                                    filename and you're re-
                                    turned to the Terminal
                                    window.   ☐

Tip: Whenever possible, select a filename that indicates the task for which specific file settings are used. You might, for example, assign the filename CSERVE to a Terminal file containing the correct settings for connecting with CompuServe. Unless you specify a different file extension during the Save operations, Windows automatically assigns a .TRM file extension to Terminal files.

Making a Connection with Terminal

After you specify the proper settings for a given session—or alternately, use the **File Open** command to load a disk file containing the appropriate settings into RAM—you're ready to begin telecommunicating. Do that by telling Terminal to dial the remote system.

 To Dial a Remote System

1. Choose **P**hone from the Terminal menu bar.

   Terminal displays its Phone options.

2. Choose **D**ial.

   The Phone Number dialog box is displayed.

3. Enter the phone number you want to dial and press Enter.

   Terminal dials the specified number, using the current communications settings. Notice that as Terminal performs the steps required to make this connection, the commands associated with those steps are displayed within the Terminal display, as illustrated in Figure 10.7. ☐

What happens after Terminal makes a connection depends on the specific remote system you have called. Figure 10.7, for example, shows the sign-on prompt you see when you call a PC that is running Procomm Plus in Host mode.

Each remote system you access with Terminal uses different procedures. For this reason, I'm not going to go any further on the system I called than this opening prompt. Instead, we'll use the **H**angup command to drop this connection and return to the main Terminal display.

 To Disconnect Terminal from a Remote System

1. Choose **P**hone.

   Terminal displays its Phone options.

2. Choose Hangup.

This causes Terminal to send a hangup string to your modem. As a result, Terminal drops the previous connection and returns to its standard display. □

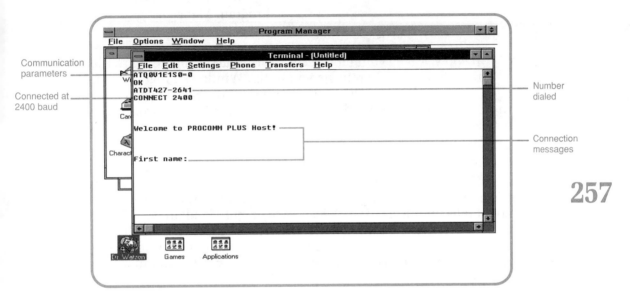

Communication parameters

Connected at 2400 baud

Number dialed

Connection messages

Figure 10.7. Terminal automatically performs all steps required to call the remote system.

Caution: With certain on-line services, you must first sign off that system (using an Exit, Goodbye or some other command) before disconnecting the Terminal line, or the service continues to bill you for on-line time. Check to see whether this is true of any services you use before you issue a Hangup command to end a remote session.

Quitting Terminal

Now we're ready to quit Terminal and return to the Windows Program Manager.

To Quit Terminal

1. Choose File from the Terminal menu bar.

   Terminal displays its File
   options.

2. Choose Exit.

   Windows closes Terminal
   and returns you to the
   Program Manager.

3. Choose Yes or press Enter.   □

If you've saved your most recent Terminal settings to a disk file,
Terminal immediately returns you to the Windows Program Manager. If your telecommunications configuration has changed since
the last Save operation, Windows displays a cautionary prompt box
asking whether you want to save the current settings before exiting
Terminal.

This concludes our tour of the Windows Terminal accessory.
Admittedly, we've only mentioned a few of Terminal's assets. The
program includes enough features and functions to keep you excited
about telecommunications for years to come. My main hope is that
this chapter has communicated some of the reasons I personally find
telecommunications to be such an exciting activity. Additionally,
it's given you enough information to see how easy telecommunicating
with Terminal can be.

Note: In a tip of the cap to crass commercialism, I'm going
to suggest you pick up a copy of "The First Book of
Modem Communications" authored by myself and published
by SAMS.

What You Have Learned

▶ Telecommunications is the process of using your PC, a
  modem and special software to communicate with another
  similarly equipped computer over standard telephone lines.
  Terminal is the Windows telecommunications accessory.

▶ You use interactive dialog boxes to configure Terminal to run properly with your PC hardware—specifically, your computer and modem. You can use additional dialog boxes to set up Terminal to connect with a remote system using the communication parameters that system requires to telecommunicate successfully.

▶ Using Terminal you can further simplify telecommunications by saving specific communication settings to a disk file, which then can be reloaded into memory each time you want to contact the remote system to which those settings apply.

259

Additional Windows Accessories

In This Chapter

▶ *A discussion of the remaining Windows accessories and how they are used*

▶ *How Recorder can be used to automate your Windows operations*

The Remaining Windows Accessories

We've accomplished much over the past few chapters. We've composed a letter with Write, started organizing an address file with Cardfile, created the beginnings of a time-management system with Calendar, designed a corporate logo with Paintbrush, and learned to put your PC in touch with the rest of the world with Terminal. Certainly, the capability to do all this, plus the advantages associated with working in a graphics-based operating environment, more than justify adding Windows to your PC arsenal, and we're not done yet!

Although you do most of your work with Write, Cardfile, Calendar, Paintbrush, and Terminal, Microsoft includes several other less powerful accessories in the basic Windows package. Call these additional items miniaccessories. The remaining Windows accessories include

► Calculator

► Clock

► Notepad

► Recorder

► Object Packager

► Character Map

► Media Player

► Sound Recorder

In this chapter, we look briefly at each of these remaining accessories and see how each works within the total Windows environment.

Calculator

As its name implies, the Windows Calculator is similar to the hand-held calculator many of us keep within arm's reach throughout the workday. Although hardly appropriate for pulling together an annual budget, the Windows Calculator is ideal for those types of quick-and-dirty calculations all of us have to perform with surprising regularity. (My own battery-powered, manual calculator—which I picked up for $6 at a local yard sale several years ago—has had so much use, half its keys are worn down to bare plastic.) Furthermore, because it's an integrated part of your Windows workspace, Calculator is always available—literally a keystroke away—during a Windows session. Finally, you can use the Windows Clipboard Viewer to transfer the results of your calculations into other Windows applications.

Starting Calculator

Because we're currently in the Accessories window, let's start Calculator from there.

To Start Calculator

Double-click the Calculator icon.

Windows opens a Calculator window. □

This displays the Windows Calculator, as shown in Figure 11.1. As you can see, the Windows Calculator resembles a credit card-sized calculator. Not surprisingly, it also works in much the same way.

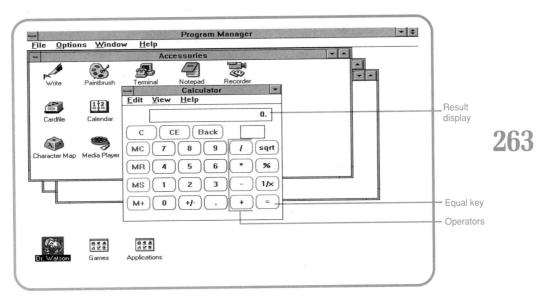

Figure 11.1. The Windows Calculator.

263

Using Calculator

To push a Calculator button, position the mouse cursor over that button and press the left mouse button. Calculator entries also can be made using either the row of number keys running horizontally across the top of your keyboard or the numeric keypad, probably located to the far right of your keyboard.

> **Note:** If you plan to use your PC's numeric keypad, you first must activate Num Lock. Depending on what type of keyboard you have, this might be the default setting following system startup. Pressing a special key marked Num Lock toggles the keypad between its usual cursor control functions (the arrow keys, PgUp, PgDn, and so on) and the ability to enter numeric values and perform mathematical operations (using 0–9, +, and –).

Calculator Functions

Calculator supports seven mathematical functions, listed in Table 11.1.

Table 11.1. Calculator's mathematical functions.

Function	Key
Addition	+
Subtraction	[–]
Multiplication	* or x
Division	/
Square root	sqrt
Percentages	%
Reciprocal	1/x

Note: The keys for square root (sqrt) are typed sequentially.

Additionally, Calculator supports four memory functions, shown in Table 11.2.

Table 11.2. Calculator's memory functions.

Funtion	Key
Clear memory	MC
Display the current content of memory	MR
Store the current value in memory	MS
Add the current contents of memory	M+

There are four remaining Calculator operations, each of which is performed by pressing the corresponding key icon on the Calculator display, shown in Table 11.3.

Table 11.3. Additional keys for Calculator.

Function	Key
Clear the current calculation	C
Clear the current entry	CE
Clear the rightmost digit of the current number	Back
Change the sign of the currently displayed number	+/-

A Sample Calculator Session

Using Calculator is so straightforward, it really doesn't require any extensive explanation. To get your feet wet, however, let's calculate 12 percent of 260.

✔ **To Find a Percentage**

▶ Type **260** (or, alternately, press these buttons with the mouse cursor).

▶ Choose – (the minus sign).

▶ Type **12** (or alternately, press these buttons with the mouse cursor).

▶ Choose **%** (the percent sign).

▶ Press = (the equal sign).

When you have completed this simple calculation (260 minus 12 percent of 260), your screen resembles Figure 11.2, which shows a result of 228.8 in the Calculator display. Using Calculator really is this easy; there's not much to it unless you want more power.

Accessing the Scientific Calculator

In addition to simplifying the kinds of rudimentary mathematical operations listed earlier, Windows also responds to the needs of those people who look for real clout when performing calculations. It's hard to imagine a situation that could not be accommodated by Windows scientific calculator.

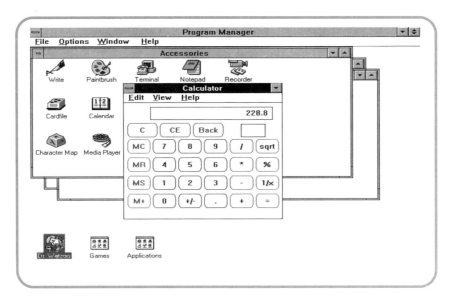

Figure 11.2. The Windows Calculator works much like a standard calculator.

 To Access the Scientific Calculator

1. Choose View from the   Calculator displays its
   Calculator menu bar.   View menu.
2. Choose Scientific.   Windows displays its
                                  Scientific calculator.   □

Selecting the Scientific view calls the Windows scientific calculator, as shown in Figure 11.3.

If you don't understand how a scientific calculator works, don't use it. If you do understand scientific calculations, on the other hand, you certainly don't need any help from little, ol' math-anxiety-ridden me, so let's get back to the standard calculator.

 To Return to the Standard Calculator

1. Choose View from the   Calculator displays its
   Calculator menu bar.   View menu.
2. Choose Standard.   Windows displays its
                                  Standard calculator.   □

Windows preserves your previous calculations whenever you change calculator views, as a quick glance at Figure 11.3 discloses.

Now that I've diplomatically avoided having to reveal my total lack of math skills, let's tuck Calculator away and move on.

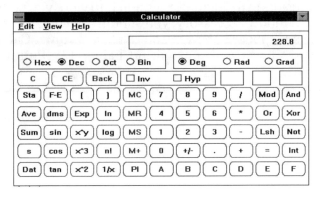

Figure 11.3. The Windows scientific calculator places true math power at your fingertips.

267

Exiting Calculator

You might have noticed there is no File option on the Calculator menu bar. Until now, we've always used an **E**xit command within the **F**ile menu to close the Windows accessories. Are you stuck in Calculator? Of course not.

 To Exit Calculator

1. Position the mouse cursor over the Control box in the top-left corner of the Calculator window.

2. Click the left mouse button.   This displays the Calculator Control menu.

3. Choose Close.   Windows closes the Calculator and returns you to Program Manager.

> **Tip:** Exiting the Windows Calculator accessory is like turning off a traditional hand-held calculator. All previous work, including any values or calculations stored with the Calculator memory functions, are lost. If you plan to incorporate the results of a Calculator session into work you perform in another Windows accessory, you should save that result to the Windows Clipboard Viewer before closing down Calculator. Clipboard Viewer is discussed in Chapter 12, "Putting It All Together."

Clock

The Windows Clock accessory is...well...a clock. That really says it all. Let me show you what I mean.

 To Display the Windows Clock

Double-click the Clock icon.	Windows displays its on-screen clock. ☐

The first time you start Clock, it uses the digital display format shown in Figure 11.4. About the only other feature associated with Clock is the option to change this display to a more traditional analog format.

To Switch Clock to an Analog Display

1. Choose Settings from the Clock menu bar.   Clock displays its Settings menu.
2. Choose Analog.   Clock changes to an Analog display. ☐

The Clock display changes to an analog format, as shown in Figure 11.5.

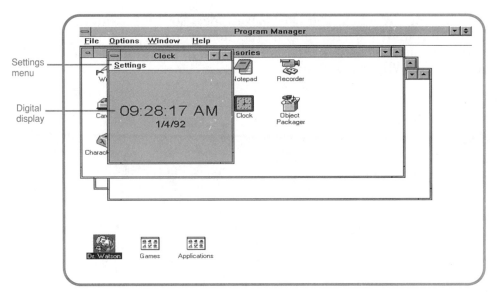

Settings menu

Digital display

Figure 11.4. The first time you open Clock, it uses a digital display.

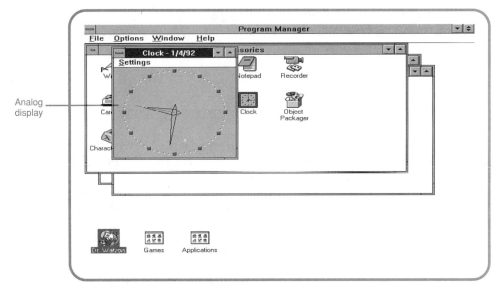

Analog display

Figure 11.5. You can change your Clock display to an analog format.

Like any window, you can resize Clock, so it takes minimal space on your display. If you want, therefore, you can place a small display containing Clock in a corner of your workspace for reference during your Windows session.

 To Exit Clock

1. Position the mouse cursor over the Control menu in the top-left corner of the Clock window.

2. Click the left mouse button.   This displays the Clock Control menu.

3. Choose Close.   Windows exits Clock and returns you to the Program Manager.   □

 Note: Windows remembers the last Clock display option used. If you restart the Clock accessory now, for example, it would open automatically in digital mode.

Notepad

You should think of Notepad as resembling a "baby" Write. If you keep this comparison in mind, you will have no trouble understanding what Notepad is and how it's used. (For example, Notepad supports none of the advanced formatting features found in Write. You can't specify justification or use multiple fonts in a Notepad file.)

Like Clock, Notepad is exactly what its name implies—a simple notepad. This doesn't mean, however, that Notepad suffers from a lack of empirical uses. Whereas Write is appropriate for documents of almost any size, Notepad is more useful for jotting down short notes. Another task for which Notepad is ideally suited is creating and editing ASCII files, such as your CONFIG.SYS file and batch files. There is one task at which Notepad excels, as you see a little later in this section. Right now, though, let's get Notepad running in your Windows workspace.

Starting Notepad

 To Start Notepad

Double-click the Notepad icon.

Windows opens a Notepad window.

This calls the opening Notepad screen shown in Figure 11.6. As was true in Write, Notepad initially presents you with an empty window, the electronic equivalent of a blank piece of paper.

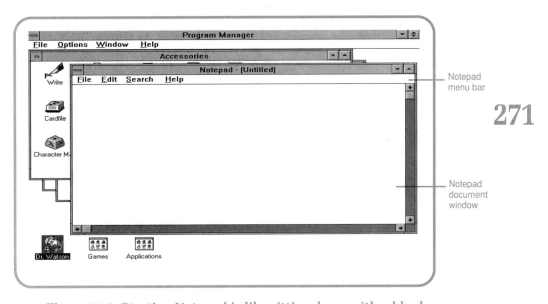

271

Figure 11.6. Starting Notepad is like sitting down with a blank piece of paper.

Although admittedly less powerful than Write, Notepad supports several useful features. For starters, when you activate its Word Wrap feature, Notepad can automatically take words that don't fit within its document margins and move them down to the next line. Notepad also supports full search capabilities, but it does not include a find-and-replace feature. In addition to supporting the normal methods for marking text, you quickly can mark an entire Notepad document for additional processing using the Select All command. This last feature is especially useful when copying a

Notepad document to the Windows Clipboard Viewer for subsequent transfer to another application. There's also that task I mentioned earlier, the one at which Notepad excels—its capability of maintaining automatically a log file of your activities.

Creating a Log File with Notepad

You can use Notepad to create a file that, each time it is opened, automatically appends the current time and date to its contents. Used properly, this file represents the perfect tool for keeping track of what you are doing and when you are doing it.

 To Create a Notepad Log File

1. Start Notepad.
2. Type .**Log** and press Enter.   This identifies the current file as a LOG file.
3. Save the new file and exit Notepad.   Each time you open this file, Windows automatically places a date and time startup in it.   □

 Note: You must type .LOG in capital letters for Notepad to recognize this as a time-log file.

Now, try the following experiment:

1. Type .**LOG** and press Enter twice.
2. Choose **File** from the Notepad menu bar.
3. Choose **Exit.** Because you have not saved the current Notepad file to disk, Windows displays a prompt box asking whether it should save your changes.
4. Press Enter or choose Yes. Windows displays a File Save **As** dialog box.
5. Type **MYLOG.** Double-click the WINBOOK file folder. Choose OK. Windows exits Notepad and returns you to the Accessories program group window.

Now, let's get really fancy.

1. Position the mouse cursor over the Notepad icon in your Accessories program group.
2. Press and hold down the Ctrl key.
3. Press and hold down the left mouse button.
4. Drag the mouse cursor to any visible portion of your Book Exercises program group window.
5. Release Ctrl and the left mouse button. This adds a copy of the Notepad accessory to your Book Exercise program group.
6. Click any visible portion of the Book Exercises program group to make it the active window.
7. Choose **Window**.
8. Choose **Arrange Icons**.
9. Choose the Notepad icon.
10. Choose **File** from the Program Manager menu bar. (Make sure you access the Program Manager **File** menu, not Notebook's **File** option.)
11. Choose **Properties**.

This displays the Program Item Properties dialog box shown in Figure 11.7. You can use this dialog box to customize the text associated with an on-screen icon and the command executed whenever the icon is selected.

✔ To Modify the Properties of the Current Notepad Icon

▶ Press Backspace to erase Notepad from the Description prompt.

▶ Type `Activity Log`.

▶ Position the mouse cursor at the end of NOTEPAD.EXE in the Command Line prompt box.

▶ Press Spacebar.

▶ Type `C:\WIN31\WINBOOK\MYLOG.TXT`.

> **Note:** If you installed Windows in a location other than the WIN31 directory on drive C or are using a different directory for your book exercises, adjust the filename entered into the Command Line prompt accordingly.

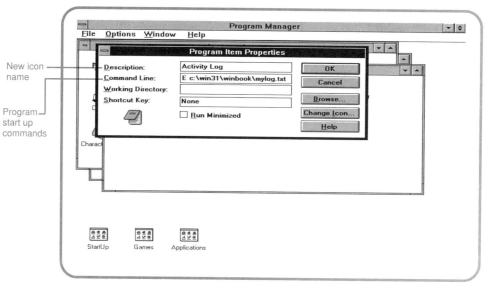

New icon name

Program start up commands

Figure 11.7. The Program Item Properties dialog box.

When you've finished, your screen should resemble Figure 11.8, which shows the specified information entered into the Program Item Properties dialog box.

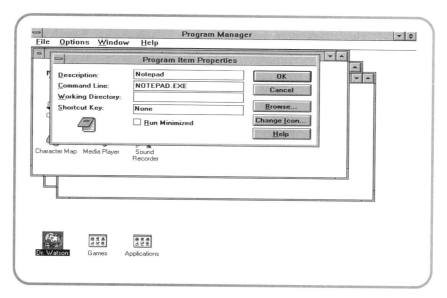

Figure 11.8. Using the Program Item Properties option of the File Properties command, you can customize the way Program Manager treats your on-screen icons.

✓ To Complete This Exercise

▶ Choose OK or press Enter.

Use the following Quick Step as a reference for modifying other icons so that they automatically load a file for you at startup.

To Automatically Load a File with a Program

1. Choose the icon for the application you plan to associate with a specific file.	The selected icon is highlighted.
2. Choose File from the Program Manager menu bar.	This displays the Program Manager File menu.
3. Choose Properties.	This displays the Properties dialog box.
4. Enter a new name for this icon in the Description field.	
5. Enter the command you want executed when you select this icon in the Command Line field.	
6. Click OK or press Enter.	Windows records the new instructions for this icon and returns you to the Program Manager. □

275

> **Note:** If you installed Windows in a location other than the WIN3 directory on drive C or are using a different directory for your book exercises, adjust the filename entered into the Command Line prompt accordingly.

Start Notepad by using the modified Notepad icon from your Book Exercises program group. Since you have modified your Notepad icon, Windows starts Notepad and automatically opens your MYLOG file. Furthermore, because the MYLOG file begins with the LOG command, Notepad appends the current time and date to the end of this file, as illustrated in Figure 11.9. Type an entry into MYLOG identifying whatever you were doing at the time it was opened and, voilà, you have an instant activity log.

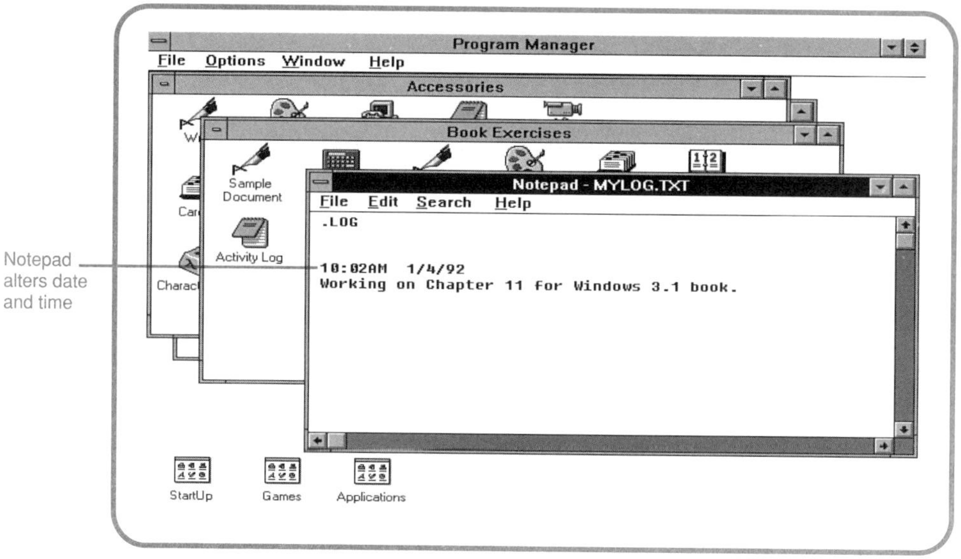

Notepad
alters date
and time

*Figure 11.9. The LOG command tells Notepad to enter the date
and time in a file each time that file is opened.*

> **Note:** Notepad reads the time and date from your system
> clock.

✓ To Close Your Time-Log File After Making an Activity Entry

▶ Choose **F**ile from the Activity Log menu bar.

▶ Choose **E**xit.

▶ Choose Yes or press Enter when the Save current changes
prompt appears.

Using Notepad in this way automates the process of keeping
track of your activities, an especially useful feature for anyone who
needs to document their time for customer billing, tax records, and
so on. Windows, however, can automate much more than a time log.
In a modern twist on the old injunction, "Physician, heal thyself,"
you can tell Windows to automate virtually any of its operations
using another accessory, the Windows Macro Recorder.

Macro Recorder

In computer jargon, a *macro* is a series of keystrokes that has been assigned to a single command, keystroke, or key combination.

You can record a sequence of keystrokes and mouse actions for future use with the Windows Macro Recorder. After a macro is recorded, it can be *played back*—that is, the keystrokes and commands it contains can be re-executed—at virtually any time during a Windows session. In this section, you create a simple macro just to get a feel for how the Windows Recorder accessory works.

 Recording a Macro

1. Open the Accessories window.   A Recorder window opens.

2. Double-click the Recorder icon.

3. Choose **M**acro from the Recorder menu bar.

   The **M**acro menu is displayed.

4. Choose the Re**c**ord option.

   The Record Macro dialog box appears. You use this box to specify information about the new macro, including its name, the type of commands to be recorded, and an optional Shortcut Key.

5. Choose **S**tart.

   The Record Macro dialog box disappears, and you are returned to the regular Windows environment.

6. Perform the steps and commands you want included in the new macro.

7. When all the desired steps have been completed, press Ctrl+Break to stop the Macro Recorder.

   Windows displays its Recorder prompt box.

8. Click **S**ave Macro.

   Windows saves your macro instructions for future use.

9. Click OK.

277

Starting Recorder

To record a macro for later playback, you first need to open the Recorder accessory.

✓ To Start the Recorder Accessory

▶ Position the mouse cursor on any visible portion of your Accessories program group.

▶ Click the left mouse button to bring the window forward.

▶ Double-click the Recorder icon.

This opens an untitled Recorder window, as shown in Figure 11.10. Unlike other Windows applications, which display the actual keystrokes you enter, the Recorder window contains only a listing of the macros you create and assign to a given Recorder file.

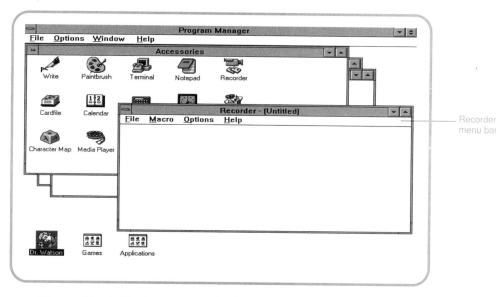

Figure 11.10. The Recorder window is used to display a listing of macros assigned to a given Recorder file.

Before creating a macro, however, let's open a Notepad window. You use this window in a few moments to enter the keystrokes our sample macro contains.

1. Position the mouse cursor on any visible portion of your Accessories program group.

2. Click the left mouse button.

3. Double-click the Notepad icon.

Creating a Macro

After the Notepad accessory is running and a Recorder window has been opened, you can start creating a new macro.

1. Press Alt-Esc until the Recorder window reappears.

2. Choose **M**acro from the Recorder menu bar.

3. Choose **R**ecord.

Whenever you create a new macro, Recorder displays the Record Macro dialog box shown in Figure 11.11. Use this dialog box to enter information about the new macro and how it will work.

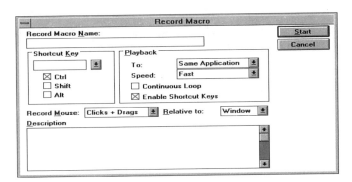

Figure 11.11. The Record Macro dialog box.

✓ To Tell Recorder About the Sample Macro

▶ Type Name/Address and press Tab.

▶ Type Insert.

▶ Choose the down arrow box next to the text Same Application in the **P**layback To: field.

▶ Choose Any Application.

▶ Choose the down arrow box next to the Record Mouse: field.

▶ Choose Ignore Mouse.

▶ Position the mouse cursor in the Description box and click the left mouse button.

▶ Type **automatically enter name and address in any application**.

▶ Choose Start or press Enter.

Windows closes the Recorder window and returns you to the Accessories program group. (Recorder is still running in the background.)

✓ To Enter the Actual Keystrokes That Will Comprise Our Test

▶ Position the mouse cursor on any visible portion of the Notepad window and click the left mouse button. Windows makes the Notepad window active.

▶ Type your name and address, using the format shown in Figure 11.12.

▶ Press Ctrl+Break to tell Windows that it should stop recording the current macro.

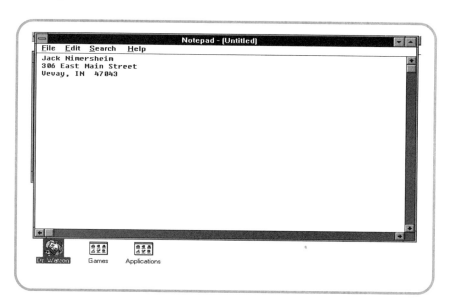

Figure 11.12. Enter your name and address for the sample macro.

Windows displays the Recorder prompt box shown in Figure 11.13. Use this box to tell Windows what you want to do with the current macro.

Figure 11.13. Windows asks what Recorder should do with the current macro keystrokes.

√ To Save Our Test Macro

▶ Choose **S**ave Macro.

▶ Choose OK or press Enter.

Windows stops recording your keystrokes and returns you to the untitled Notepad window. At this point, you can reopen the Recorder window and save this macro to a disk file.

281

√ To Save Our Macro to a Disk File

▶ Double-click the Recorder icon at the bottom of your screen.

▶ Choose **F**ile from the Recorder menu bar.

▶ Choose **S**ave.

▶ When the **S**ave dialog box appears, type **MYMACS** and press Enter.

What happened? To answer that question, let's return to the untitled Notepad window.

1. Position the mouse cursor on any visible portion of the Notepad window and click the left mouse button. Windows makes the Notepad window active.

2. Press Ctrl+Ins (the Shortcut Key you assigned to your new macro).

If all went as planned, Windows automatically entered a second copy of your name and address into the untitled Notepad file. Congratulations! You have just created your first macro.

> **Note:** The Windows macro feature is an extremely powerful tool—too powerful in fact, for me to cover all its capabilities in this book. I simply wanted to introduce you to the Recorder accessory that you use to create macros for your Windows environment. For more information on how Recorder works, refer to the "Windows User's Guide."

Before we move on, let's clean up our cluttered workspace:

1. Close the Untitled Notepad file without saving it.
2. Double-click the Recorder icon to restore it to an on-screen window.
3. Double-click the Recorder Control OK to close Recorder.

This returns you to the Accessories window, which strikes me as a good place to begin our discussion of the remaining four accessories.

Window to the Future

Windows 3.1 includes four new Accessories not found in previous Windows releases. These include

▶ Character Map
▶ Object Packager
▶ Media Player
▶ Sound Recorder

Each of these new Accessories supports relatively advanced functions, designed to be used in highly specialized operations. Using Character Map, for example, you can insert characters not found on most PC keyboards into documents characters—a useful tool for creating technical documents but not a capability you'd require for everyday tasks.

Given their advanced nature, I'm not going to spend a great deal of time discussing these new Windows' Accessories. A basic understanding of what each is and what it does still is in order.

Character Map

As mentioned earlier, you can use Character Map to generate characters not found on most PC keyboards. One example of such characters is the Greek letters and symbols often used in complex mathematical formulas. With Character Map you can select such characters from an on-screen chart, and then use the Windows Clipboard to copy these characters into documents created with other Windows applications.

Object Packager

283

You can create an icon to represent an OLE (Object Linking and Embedding) element within a document using Object Packager. (OLE, a powerful new feature of Windows 3.1, is discussed in the next chapter, "Putting It All Together.") Icons created with Object Packager provide a convenient method to identify those portions of a document that are actually files or portions of files created and controlled by other applications.

Media Player

With Media Player, you can control the activities of various system components and files relating to multimedia presentations. Using Multimedia, you can combine diverse elements—sound, images, animation, and so on—into a single presentation. Devices you can control with Media Player include

- ► CD-ROM drives
- ► Videodisc players
- ► MIDI (Musical Instrumental Digital Interface) Sequencer devices
- ► Sound files
- ► Animation files

Media Player incorporates a graphics-based interface containing controls similar to those found on a VCR or compact disk player. For example, the Media Player display contains buttons marked Play, Pause, Stop, and Eject.

Sound Recorder

Sound Recorder can be used to control sound devices attached to your PC. You can use Sound Recorder to create and manage the disk files that contain audio components of a multimedia presentation. Similar to a traditional tape recorder, Sound Recorder includes the capabilities of playing, rewinding, fast-forwarding, and pausing files during playback.

What You Have Learned

284

- ► Rounding out your Windows package are several mini-accessories that can be used for a variety of special activities within a Windows session.
- ► The Windows Calculator can be used for simple mathematical operations. Alternately, Windows provides a scientific calculator option for complex computations.
- ► Notepad is a simple text editor, less powerful than the Windows Write accessory. One special feature of Notepad is that it can be used to create and maintain a time-log file of your activities.
- ► The Windows Recorder accessory can be used to record keystrokes, commands, and mouse operations for subsequent playback. The Recorder accessory resembles the macro feature included in many PC applications.
- ► Windows 3.1 includes several accessories designed to be used in a multimedia environment. Multimedia is a potentially powerful but evolving PC technology, one for which the Windows' GUI ideally seems suited. Admittedly, Microsoft has its corporate eyes set firmly on the future by including multimedia-oriented elements such as Media Player and Sound Recorder with the Windows 3.1 package. If multimedia proves to be as popular a PC platform as many industry experts believe, however, the company's efforts will be well rewarded.

Putting It All Together

In This Chapter

- ▶ *How to manage multiple windows*
- ▶ *How to use the Windows Task List*
- ▶ *How to use the Windows Clipboard to transfer data between windows*

The Many Faces of Windows

Until now, all our discussions of Windows have involved a single application. We've seen how you compose documents with Write, manage information with Cardfile, create pretty pictures with Paintbrush, and so on. As I stated earlier, however, Windows is more than a gathering of individual programs. It is a total, and totally integrated, operating environment that you can use to link the various Windows parts into a whole greater than the sum of its parts. In this chapter, we examine some tools and features Windows provides to accomplish this.

Working with Multiple Windows

DOS is the operating system PC users love to hate. Although there are literally thousands of DOS programs currently available—programs you can use to do everything from write a simple memo to project the annual operating budget of a multimillion dollar corporation—using DOS, you can't load more than one of these programs into memory concurrently. That's like buying a new house with dozens of big, bright, beautiful windows and then discovering that only one of them can be open at any given time. Under such conditions, your house would start to feel stuffy and cramped very quickly. Millions of DOS users work under similarly cramped conditions almost daily, however. They keep trying to perform the many duties for which they are responsible with single-tasking DOS.

Windows eliminates this conflict by opening stuffy old DOS to true multitasking. With Windows running on your PC, each open window represents a different job that needs to be done and that can be done by running a different application or accessory or performing a different task.

This means you could, for example, prepare a letter announcing an upcoming price reduction in Write and have a Cardfile database containing the names and addresses of your important customers loaded in memory and available for reference only a simple mouse click away. Rather than merely talking about Windows' multitasking capabilities, let's see how they work.

Write Revisited

In Chapter 6, "Windows Write," you composed a letter announcing an upcoming price reduction to the Wonderful Widgets product line. At that time, I purposely omitted an opening section, the part of a letter that usually contains the name and address of the company about to be offered this welcome relief. Finally, six chapters later, it's time to correct this oversight. Begin by reloading Write and loading the sample letter, which we called SAVELET.

1. Click any visible portion of the Book Exercises program group to make it the active window.

2. Double-click the Write icon in the Book Exercises program group.

3. Choose **File** from the Write menu bar.

4. Choose **O**pen.

5. Double-click the \WINBOOK directory in the Directory area of the subsequent **File O**pen dialog box.

6. Double-click SAVELET.WRI when this filename appears in the Files section of the **File O**pen dialog box.

7. If necessary, drag the Write window down toward the bottom of your screen until the title bar of the Program Manager window is visible.

This starts Write and loads the SAVELET letter. Although informative, this letter currently looks pretty boring. Let's dress it up by adding a company logo and mailing address. In essence, we're going to transform our simple page of text into an impressive announcement on official letterhead.

On our way from here to there, we're going to introduce a few of Windows features you've not encountered.

287

Preparing to Multitask

We're going to move quickly now as we open additional accessory windows. To finish setting up your multitasking workspace

1. Click any portion of the Book Exercises program group.

2. Double-click the Paintbrush icon.

3. Choose **File** from the Paintbrush menu bar.

4. Choose **O**pen.

5. Double-click the \WINBOOK directory in the Directory area of the subsequent **File O**pen dialog box.

6. Double-click LOGO.BMP when this filename appears in the Files section of the **File O**pen dialog box.

7. Position your mouse cursor anywhere in the Book Exercise program group.

8. Click the left mouse button.

9. Double-click the Cardfile icon.
10. Choose **F**ile from the Cardfile menu bar.
11. Choose **O**pen.
12. Double-click the \WINBOOK directory in the Directory area of the subsequent **F**ile **O**pen dialog box.
13. Double-click PRACTICE.CRD when this filename appears in the Files section of the **F**ile **O**pen dialog box.

Your workspace now resembles Figure 12.1. Pretty crowded, isn't it—what with three accessory windows and all those icons associated with the Windows Program Manager still there? No problem. We can temporarily set aside the Program Manager window.

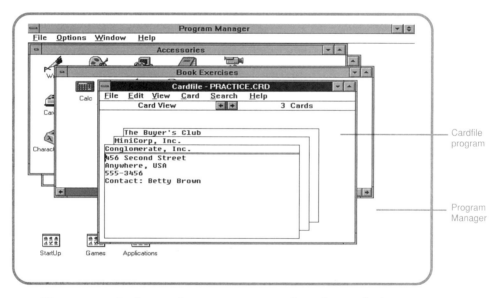

Figure 12.1. A cluttered screen can sometimes be confusing.

Minimizing Program Manager

We've been working almost exclusively in Program Manager since Chapter 5 of this book. Now that we've opened the accessory windows we need, let's temporarily set aside Program Manager by minimizing it to a workspace icon.

To Minimize Program Manager

1. Position your mouse cursor in the Minimize box in the top-right corner of the Program Manager window (the small box with an arrow pointing downward).

2. Click the left mouse button.

Program Manager is reduced to a Group icon located near the bottom of your workspace. □

At this point, your display resembles Figure 12.2 in which the Program Manager window has been reduced to a program icon at the bottom of the Windows workspace. Notice, however, that the individual accessory windows remain accessible. That's good because we're about to access them.

289

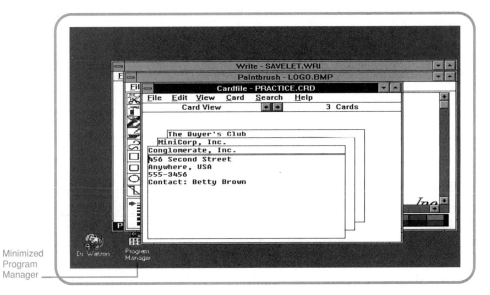

Minimized
Program
Manager

Figure 12.2. Reducing Program Manager to an icon clears the confusion.

The Windows Task List

One problem associated with having multiple windows open concurrently is that some of them might be completely obscured at times. Because the normal procedure for making a window active is to click a visible portion of that window, this could present a problem. It could, but it doesn't. The Windows Task List provides a convenient method for switching between open windows (tasks), regardless of whether they are currently visible within your workspace. To show you what I mean, try the following experiment:

Click the Maximize box of your Write window (the small box with an arrow pointing upward in the right portion of the Write title bar).

This causes your Write window (which through no small coincidence, contains the sample letter we wrote earlier) to fill the entire workspace. How would you access Paintbrush if you needed to? You could reduce the Write window again, but this might be more trouble than it's worth. Instead, why not use the Windows Task List?

 To Access the Windows Task List

1. Click the Control menu box of the active window (the small box on the extreme left of the title bar).

   This displays the Control menu.

2. Choose **S**witch To. ☐

This displays the Task List dialog box shown in Figure 12.3. Notice that this box lists all of the windows (tasks) that are open in the current session. As you've probably guessed, accessing a different window is a simple matter of double-clicking its corresponding task name.

Double-click Paintbrush—LOGO.BMP. This makes the Paintbrush window active and brings it back to the front of your workspace. Now that you're at Paintbrush, start pursuing some of that gestalt I mentioned earlier in this book.

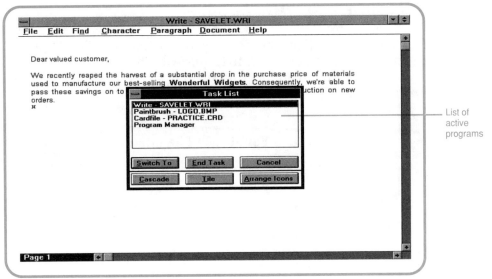

Figure 12.3. The Task List provides a convenient way to switch
between windows in a complex workspace.

Tip: You might have noticed that Ctrl+Esc is listed on the Control menu as an alternate method for accessing the Task List. Depending on what you're doing at the time, you might find this keyboard shortcut even more convenient to use than choosing **S**witch To from the Control menu, as we did in the previous exercise.

Using the Windows Clipboard

If you've ever tried to take data created in one DOS program and transfer it to another DOS program, you quickly learn to love the Windows Clipboard. With Clipboard, exchanging data between two programs running in a Windows session is not only possible, it's virtually painless. In fact, using Clipboard is not that different from using the cut-and-paste feature found in many word processing programs. Again, however, rather than just talking about how easy a Windows feature is to use, let me show you.

Copying Items to the Clipboard

Begin by taking that corporate logo you created in Chapter 9, "Paintbrush," and copying it to Clipboard. Click the Maximize box of your Paintbrush window (the small box with an arrow pointing upward in the right portion of the Paintbrush title bar).

 To Copy Part of a Paintbrush File into the Clipboard

1. Choose the Pick tool (the top icon in the right column of the Toolbox).

   This activates the Paintbrush Pick tool.

2. Position the mouse cursor outside the area you want to copy.

3. Press and hold the left mouse button.

4. Drag the mouse cursor until the resulting dotted line surrounds the area you want to copy.

   A dotted outline surrounds the area as you drag.

5. Release the left mouse button.

   This "picks" the selected area.

6. Select Edit from the Paintbrush menu bar.

   Paintbrush displays its pull-down Edit menu.

7. Select Copy.

   This places a copy of the selected area in the Windows Clipboard. □

 Tip: You probably will want to increase the size of the Paintbrush window to simplify this operation.

Use this Quick Start to clip a copy the company icon from Paintbrush.

Step 8 selects a rectangular section of your Paintbrush file, called a cutout in the Paintbrush vernacular, that includes the corporate logo created in Chapter 9, "Paintbrush." After a cutout exists, you can copy it.

292

It might look like nothing happened but, trust me, something did. To see what, return to the Write window.

1. Press Ctrl+Esc to display the Task List.
2. Double-click Write—SAVELET.WRI.

This redisplays the Write window containing our letter announcing the impending price reductions from Wonderful Widgets. Now, get ready to be impressed.

Pasting Items from the Clipboard into a Window

Use the **P**aste command to transfer items from the Clipboard into a second window. Add that corporate logo to our sample letter. First, press Ctrl+Home to make sure the cursor is at the beginning of the Write file.

293

 To Paste Items from the Clipboard into a Document

| 1. Choose Edit from the Write menu bar. | The pull-down Edit menu is displayed. |
| 2. Choose Paste. | Windows inserts the contents of Clipboard into the active application. |

Use this Quick Step to paste the logo into your Write document. Voilà! There's your corporate logo, sitting, if you'll forgive the pun, pretty as a picture at the top of our sample letter, as shown in Figure 12.4.

Things still don't look quite right. That corporate logo would look better positioned in the middle of the page. Of course, I wouldn't suggest this if it weren't possible.

Moving Graphic Elements in a Write Document

To move an image in a Write file, you must first select that image. There are, however, no graphic tools in Write. How do you accomplish this?

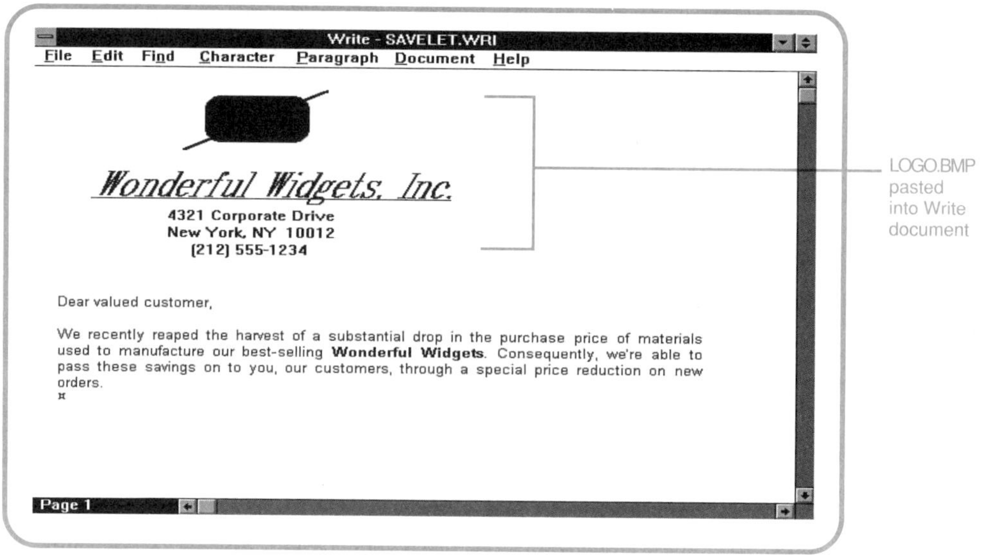

Figure 12.4. Objects in the Clipboard can be pasted into any
Windows accessory.

To Select a Graphic Image in Write

1. Position the mouse cursor anywhere in the general vicinity of the graphic you want to select.
2. Click the left mouse button.   The image you selected can now be manipulated with Write commands.   □

That was simple, wasn't it. Placing the Write cursor within a graphic image selects that image for subsequent operations. After you select an image, you can use the Move Picture command to move that image within your Write document.

✓ To Center the Logo in Your Write Document

▶ Choose Edit from the Write menu bar.

▶ Choose Move Picture.

▶ Slide your mouse to the right until the outline box identifying your Paintbrush image is centered on the Write text.

▶ Click the left mouse button.

▶ Position the mouse cursor before the word Dear in the salutation of the sample letter.

▶ Click the left mouse button.

Your display now resembles Figure 12.5, which shows the Paintbrush image centered on the document text.

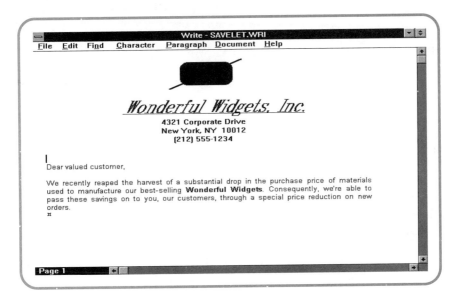

Figure 12.5. Selected images can be moved within a Write document.

The sample letter is beginning to shape up. About the only piece missing now is a mailing address, the specific customer to whom it will be sent. Adding this information gives us another opportunity to examine another way in which data can be exchanged between multiple applications running in a Windows session.

Marking and Copying Text to the Clipboard

Suppose that you want to send this letter to MiniCorp, Inc., one of the customers you entered earlier into the Cardfile database. Again, we use the Task List to call that accessory.

295

1. Press Ctrl+Esc to display the Task List.
2. Double-click Cardfile—PRACTICE.CRD.

This redisplays the Cardfile window containing the customer database records. After this window is displayed, you can use Clipboard to mark and transfer text information from it to your Write document. Mark the address of MiniCorp, Inc.

 To Mark a Portion of a Text File

1. Position the mouse cursor at the beginning of the text you want to mark.	This indicates the beginning of your marked text.
2. Press and hold the left mouse button.	
3. Drag the mouse until all the text you want to mark is highlighted.	This indicates the end of your marked text.
4. Release the mouse button.	This selects the high-lighted text. □

Use this Quick Step to mark the two address lines for MiniCorp, Inc. As was true with Paintbrush, marked text in a Windows application can be copied to the Clipboard.

 To Copy Marked Text to the Clipboard

1. Select Edit from the program's menu bar.	The Edit menu is displayed.
2. Select Copy.	This places a copy of the selected text into the Windows Clipboard. □

Again, the marked item—this time, the specified text from your Cardfile database record—is copied into Clipboard. All that remains now is to transfer this text into the sample letter.

Transferring Text from Clipboard

Before transferring MiniCorp's address, you'll need to return to the Write file and prepare that letter for this information.

1. Position the mouse cursor before the word `Dear` in the saluta-tion of our sample letter, which is visible behind the Cardfile window.
2. Click the left mouse button.
3. Press Enter twice to insert two blank lines in the sample letter.
4. Press the up arrow twice to move the cursor up two lines.
5. Type **MiniCorp, Inc.** and press Enter.
6. Choose **E**dit from the Write menu bar.
7. Choose **P**aste.

Windows automatically inserts MiniCorp's address into the Write file. Before checking one more Windows feature, let's save our polished letter as a new file and then clean up our desktop.

✓ To Save a Letter with a New Filename

▶ Choose **F**ile from the Write menu bar.

▶ Choose Save **A**s.

▶ Press Backspace to remove the current filename when the File Save As dialog box appears.

▶ Type **SAMPLE.DOC** and press Enter.

Now that we have a new file containing the sample letter, close these accessories and return to the Program Manager.

1. Choose **F**ile from the Write menu bar.
2. Choose E**x**it.
3. Choose **F**ile from the Cardfile menu bar.
4. Choose E**x**it.
5. Choose **F**ile from the Paintbrush menu bar.
6. Choose E**x**it.

 Tip: Double-clicking the Control icon is an excellent shortcut for closing a window.

> **Note:** Although unlikely, it's possible that a file within one of these accessories was accidentally modified during the previous exercises. If this happens and Windows displays a caution box as you **E**xit a given accessory, simply respond No to the Save Changes prompt.

When all accessories are closed, your workspace contains only the Program Manager icon minimized earlier. Restore Program Manager to an active window.

✓ To Restore Program Manager to an Active Window

▶ Click the Program Manager icon.

▶ Select Maximize from the subsequent Control menu.

This restores Program Manager to a full-screen window. Next, we're going to go back to a special icon you created in Chapter 5, "Managing a Windows Session," and see why we set it up as we did.

298

Automatically Loading Data Files with an Accessory

If you remember, the Sample Document icon in your Book Exercises is associated with both the Write accessory and a file named SAMPLE.DOC. Specifically, we entered the following Command line into the Program Item Properties dialog box:

```
WRITE.EXE C:\WINDOWS\WINBOOK\SAMPLE.DOC
```

Associating a filename with a Windows program in this manner causes that file to be loaded automatically each time its corresponding icon is selected. Double-click the Sample Document icon in your Book Exercises program group.

A few seconds later and there it is—your polished letter, automatically loaded into Write and ready for further processing, as shown in Figure 12.6. Now we're talking fast, organized PC operations. Now you're getting a glimpse of the real power of Windows, but there's more to come.

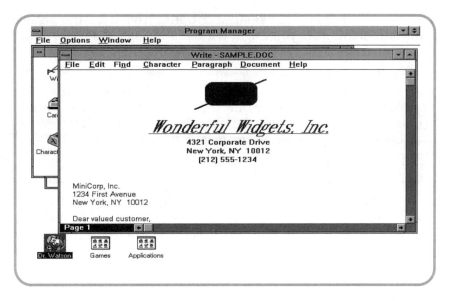

Figure 12.6. Organizing your Windows environment wisely can
greatly improve the efficiency of your PC operations.

299

Say, OLE!

Beginning with Windows 3.1, Microsoft added a powerful new
feature to the Windows environment. That feature is called *OLE*, or
Object Linking and Embedding. That fancy name merely means it's
now possible to take elements created in one Windows application
(called objects) and embed them in a file created by a second
Windows application.

> **Note:** Objects in this context can represent various types
> of data. It is possible to link a picture from Paintbrush,
> spreadsheet data from Excel, or other objects to your Windows
> programs that support OLE.

OLE goes beyond the simple cut-and-paste capabilities of the
Windows Clipboard supported by versions of Windows prior to 3.1.
In those earlier Windows releases, Clipboard took a metaphorical

snapshot of the selected item and transferred it to the second application, much as you might cut out an image and paste it on a second piece of paper (hence the phrase *cut-and-paste*).

With OLE, you actually create a link between the embedded object and the application that created it. In other words, even though the corporate logo in our SAMPLE.DOC looks like a simple picture, with OLE, it actually represents a gateway to Paintbrush, the Windows Accessory used to create it. A simple experiment demonstrates what I mean.

> **Note:** As I mentioned earlier, OLE was not added to Windows until Windows 3.1. If you are using an earlier version of Windows, you cannot perform the following exercise.

 To Access a Linked OLE Object

Double-click anywhere in the linked object.	Windows opens the application that created the linked object for additional processing. □

It might take a few seconds for Windows to perform some pretty impressive technological juggling, but your screen ultimately resembles Figure 12.7, which shows a Paintbrush window containing our corporate logo and identifying it as an embedded object.

What advantages are associated with object linking? To determine this, try another experiment.

1. Click the Line tool in the Paintbrush window.
2. Add a horizontal line running through the middle of the widget portion of this logo.
3. Choose **F**ile from the Paintbrush menu bar.
4. Choose E**x**it and return to SAMPLE.DOC.
5. At the Update Embedded Object prompt, choose Yes.

After the Paintbrush window closes, your screen resembles Figure 12.8. Notice that the logo in the SAMPLE.DOC letter has changed to reflect the modifications made with Paintbrush in the previous exercise. That is the potential power of OLE!

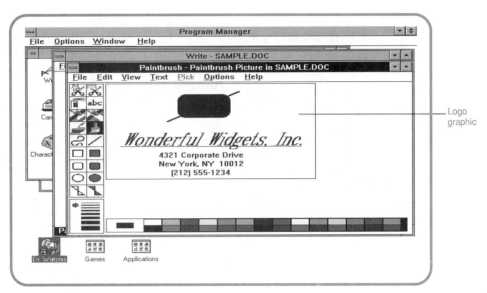

Figure 12.7. Using Windows' new OLE feature, you can embed objects created in one application into a second file created by another application.

301

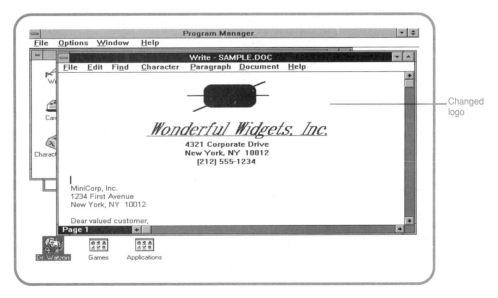

Figure 12.8. With OLE, you can modify dynamically the embedded objects using the application that created them.

In the past, the only way to accomplish this process would have been to delete the older logo from SAMPLE.DOC, open Paintbrush, edit the original LOGO file, and then repaste it into Write, using the Windows Clipboard. Thus, you would have had to repeat completely the complicated steps performed earlier in this chapter.

 Establishing OLE Links

1. Open separate windows containing the various objects you want to link.

2. Click the Window containing the source object—that is, the object you want linked to another file. | This makes the application containing your source object the active window.

3. Using the appropriate steps for the Source application, Cut or Copy the source object to the Windows Clipboard. | This places the source object into the Windows Clipboard.

4. Click the Window containing the target file—that is, the file into which you want the linked object imported. | This makes the target file the active application.

5. Position the cursor in the location at which you want the linked object inserted.

6. Use the Paste option on the Edit menu to create the OLE link between the source object and target file. | The selected item is copied to the target file with an OLE link established to the application that created the file. □

I don't know about you, but I like the OLE approach a whole lot better!

Caution: It's up to individual manufacturers to incorporate this impressive feature into their programs. Not all software, therefore, supports OLE—a fact of which you should be aware as you choose the Windows applications you'll use in your day-to-day PC operations.

302

√ **Close the Sample Document**.

► Choose **F**ile from the Write menu bar.

► Choose E**x**it.

► At the Save Current Changes prompt, choose Yes.

This concludes our tour of Windows. Don't desert me yet, however. So far, we've looked only at Windows itself, the various features and accessories Microsoft includes with each copy of Windows it sells. Other companies also produce programs that are designed to take full advantage of the Windows GUI. Additionally, Windows is capable of helping you organize any standard DOS application programs you use. We look at these topics in Part Four, "Beyond Windows."

What You Have Learned

► Windows includes several special functions designed to enable its various applications to interact with one another. Chief among these is the Task List, used to switch quickly among several Windows programs running in a multitasking session.

► The Windows Clipboard lets you exchange data between different applications. Using the Clipboard, for example, you can incorporate Paintbrush graphics into a Write document. After the image has been imported with Write, you can modify that image's size and location to enhance your printcd documents.

► You can set up special icons in Program Manager that not only run an application program but also automatically load a specified data file each time that icon is selected. You can further automate your Windows-based operations using this feature.

► Using the new (in Windows 3.1) OLE feature, you can create dynamic links between elements that are created with different Windows applications.

Part Four

Beyond Windows

As mentioned several times throughout this book, the primary function of the Windows GUI is to help you coordinate and manage your PC activities. These activities can, and probably will, include working in several application programs other than the various accessories shipped with the basic Windows package. In this, the final part of *The First Book of Windows 3.1,* we examine some of the alternatives available when you begin putting together a comprehensive Windows environment. First, we review several Windows-aware applications—that is, programs designed to take full advantage of the Windows GUI. Finally, I provide information on how to run standard DOS applications—that is, programs that do not directly support the Windows GUI—from within a Windows session.

A Windows Sampler

In This Chapter

> ▶ *A look at software that is designed to run exclusively under Windows*
>
> ▶ *How to install third-party software in your Windows environment*
>
> ▶ *An overview of Windows-aware programs available in several different application areas*

Installing Programs for Windows

There is no universal way to install external programs into the Windows environment. As a rule, each program includes instructions on the procedures required for installing and running it under Windows. Read these instructions carefully. With few exceptions, Windows applications cannot be installed by simply copying the files to a hard disk directory. Quite often, a given program alters the WIN.INI initialization file to inform Windows of its presence and to establish certain operating parameters it needs to run properly within the Windows GUI. After performing the prescribed installation steps, it's a good idea to run Windows Setup (in the Main Program Group) and use the Set Up Applications option to guarantee that your Windows environment recognizes the new program.

> **Note:** If a program is DOS based and not Windows based, there will be an additional step: creating the PIF file (which will be described later in this chapter).

Windows Product Profiles

As we've seen, Windows is a flexible yet friendly operating environment. Furthermore, Microsoft did its best to help you become immediately productive in the Windows GUI by bundling several impressive miniprograms—Write, Cardfile, Calendar, and Terminal—with each copy of Windows it sells. You might find that the basic Windows package, as shipped by Microsoft, is all you ever need to turn your PC into the perfect productivity tool. Then again, you might not.

No PC program can be all things to all people; it's a fact of life. The key word in the phrase personal computer is *personal.* My personal needs differ from your personal needs, and someone else's probably differ from both of ours. Luckily, Windows has generated enough excitement within the PC community that everyone seems to be jumping on its bandwagon. Literally dozens of programs specially designed to take full advantage of the Windows GUI have been released. A partial listing of Windows-aware programs currently on the market is discussed in this section.

Hopefully, the information contained in these product profiles simplify the process of selecting the programs you want to include in your total Windows environment. To simplify matters even more, I've organized these product profiles by application type. If you're looking for a word processor, therefore, a quick look at the section on word processors provides a basic idea of the available options in this application genre.

> **Note:** New programs designed to take advantage of the Windows GUI are announced and released almost weekly. By definition, this chapter represents what's available; it is not a comprehensive compendium of the Windows software market. My goal is to hit the highlights. The basic information provided here, however, helps you know what to look for when you look for the Windows application to meet your personal needs. Also, the views and opinions expressed in this chapter are exclusively mine—and are admittedly subjective in nature.

Word Processors

Two programs, Microsoft Word for Windows and Ami Professional, entered the Windows word processing arena early and energetically. Each sports a list of features that should finally put to rest the debate of whether it's practical to process text in a graphics environment like Windows. Two new word processors for Windows, Word Perfect for Windows and WordStar for Windows, were released just as I was finishing this book. Look for these two new options, both of which are available in standard DOS versions, to heat up the competition among Windows-based word processors.

Both Word and Ami include an on-line spell checker and thesaurus, two items that are customary in today's word processing market. Each also includes a mail-merge module to simplify distributing your documents among a large audience, something lacking in the basic Windows package. Additional features common to both Word and Ami include context-sensitive help, automatic indexing, the capability of creating easily a table of contents based on major document headings, multicolumn formatting, background printing, macro support, and rudimentary math functions.

Ami Professional

Lotus Development
5600 Glenridge Drive
Atlanta, GA 30342
(404) 851-0007
$495

Ami straddles the fence separating word processing from desktop publishing (DTP) a little more comfortably than Word. Ami includes built-in Draw and Charting modules, two features Word lacks. Although both programs import, size, and crop graphics, with Ami, you can rotate any images you import into a document file. In fact, unless your printed pages tend to be complex, you might find that owning Ami eliminates the need to purchase a second dedicated DTP package.

Operationally, Ami also resembles a desktop publishing program. As you enter text, your screen shows precisely how that text will appear as a printed document. Fonts, type styles, justification, line spacing, and margins, among other attributes, are accurately depicted on your display screen for review and adjustment. A second way in which Ami resembles many desktop publishers is that it uses the paragraph as its basic formatting unit. You structure your document by assigning formatting characteristics to all the text in a given paragraph. After your paragraph looks exactly as you want it to, you can assign a tag name to this basic design. After that, any other paragraphs that you tag with this name take on the same appearance. Of course, you always can alter the formatting characteristics of individual words or blocks of text within a given paragraph. For emphasis, you might elect to italicize a single word, for example. All tags for a given document can be saved to disk as a Style Sheet, which then can be used as the basic design for future projects.

If you ever have tried to mix text and graphics on the same page with a traditional, text-based DOS word processor, you will appreciate Ami's reliance on the Windows interface. Being in essence, a graphics program itself, Ami handles graphics from other applications easily. Mark the area in which you want your graphic to appear (called a *frame* in the Ami vernacular), select the Import File option, identify a file type, select a file, and it's done. A Graphics Scaling option makes it easy for you to size, crop, and even adjust the positioning of an image within its frame for greater visual impact. Ami Professional imports files in several graphic formats, including images in PC Paintbrush (PCX) format and scanned TIFF files. You also can use the Windows Clipboard to import graphics into an Ami document from virtually any other Windows application.

Microsoft Word for Windows

Microsoft Corporation
One Microsoft Way
Redmond, WA 98052
(206) 882-8080
$495

Word's text-editing features, on the other hand, are slightly more sophisticated than Ami's. Word, for example, enables redlining and document annotation, two popular editing tools missing from Ami Professional. Outlining is another area in which Word excels. Word for Windows also profits from its own electronic ancestry; Word for Windows is a direct descendent of earlier releases of Microsoft Word. Millions of people who already feel comfortable using Word in the standard DOS environment have little trouble adapting to the Windows version.

Word for Windows adds a second option bar (called *Ribbon*) below the standard Windows menu bar. You can use this option bar to specify quickly such formatting elements as font selection, line spacing, and justification. Below this formatting option bar sits a stylized ruler, which is used to specify a document's margins and tabs. Word for Windows' default display closely resembles Windows Write when that accessory's Ruler is activated.

311

One of Word for Windows' most impressive features is the flexibility of its macro language. A macro is a small program you create that imitates the steps you would take to complete a certain task. You should be aware, however, that some familiarity with programming is helpful, if you expect to take full advantage of Word's macro feature. Using Word's BASIC-like macro language, you can create custom menus and dialog boxes that automate any word processing activities you perform regularly.

JustWrite

Symantec Corp.
10201 Torre Avenue
Cupertino, California 95014
$199

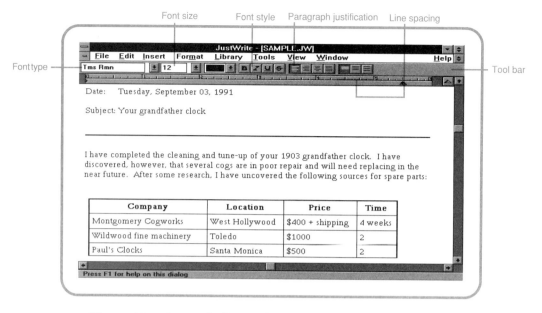

Figure 13.1. A sample JustWrite screen.

Given JustWrite's retail price of $199, it seems fair to assume that Symantec, the company responsible for this Windows-based word processor, has elected to concede the battle of the big rollers to such high-priced alternatives as Ami and Word for Windows.

JustWrite lacks some useful features those two programs have, such as a built-in grammar checker, math functions, *kerning* (the ability to adjust spacing between individual letters when using proportional fonts), and a redlining feature for automatically keeping track of any revisions made to a document during various stages of the editing cycle.

Despite its low cost and lack of certain conveniences, however, there are areas in which JustWrite shines. For example, with JustWrite, you can open as many as eight separate document windows concurrently. This feature is useful especially when you need to cross-reference different sections of a long document. You can use JustWrite to generate automatically a table of contents for a document, based on any section headings it contains. The process of indexing a document also can be automated with JustWrite.

Anyone who works in a multiplatform environment where several different programs are used for text editing will appreciate JustWrite's capability of identifying files created by several popular word processors and automatically reading them into a JustWrite document. Supported programs include WordPerfect, Microsoft Word, and Word For Windows, among others. Left to their own devices, JustWrite's **S**ave and Save **A**s commands store files back on disk in their original format, incorporating any changes you made during the current session. By creatively overriding this default feature, it's possible to use JustWrite as a primitive but functional file-conversion utility. JustWrite fully supports Windows Dynamic Data Exchange (DDE), which enables you to create dynamic links between it and any other DDE-aware Windows-based application. It's possible, for example, to use DDE to incorporate an active Enable spreadsheet in a JustWrite document.

JustWrite displays some interesting characteristics that serve to identify its family heritage. Symantec, in case you don't know, also manufacturers Q&A, a non-Windows integrated word processor/ database manager. Unlike its DOS-based cousin, JustWrite does not include a database module. JustWrite, however, can read files created by Q&A. JustWrite also recognizes data files stored in the ever-popular dBASE format. Records stored in either of these formats can be queried and, at print time, selectively merged with a JustWrite document to generate typeset-quality, formatted mass mailings with relative ease—an area in which Windows-based word processors have tended to lag behind their standard DOS counterparts.

Additional JustWrite features include a 100,000-word spell checker, a thesaurus, automatic page numbering, setting text and decimal tabs, and inserting bookmarks within your document.

JustWrite displays an on-screen Format Bar (similar to the Word for Windows Ribbon) containing individual buttons that can be used to select text attributes, such as italics, boldface, and underline. Use additional options on the Format Bar to modify quickly text alignment (left-justified, centered, right-justified), line spacing, and font size for selected blocks of text. The Format Bar also contains the buttons you use to turn on and off JustWrite's automatic hyphenation feature.

Nothing spruces up the appearance of the printed page quite as nicely as a couple of well-placed pictures. By creating a JustWrite Graphic Frame, you can import files created with several popular DOS and Macintosh graphics programs and then incorporate them into your document. Supported file formats include PCX, TIFF, Macintosh Paint, Lotus PIC files, and Windows Metafiles. As was true of text, you also can cut-and-paste images into a JustWrite frame using the Clipboard or Windows DDE. After a Graphics Frame exists, you use a special Format Bar to crop or scale its contents, as needed. You can even modify the horizontal/vertical ratio of a graphics image, elongating or scrunching it to suit your tastes.

Let's face it, not everyone needs the power of an Ami or Word for Windows. Nor can everyone justify the cost of those programs for relatively simple tasks. JustWrite offers a practical alternative to these high-powered programs at less than half the cost.

Professional Write Plus

Software Publishing Corporation
1901 Landings Drive
P.O. Box 7210
Mountain View, CA 94039
(415) 962-8910
$295

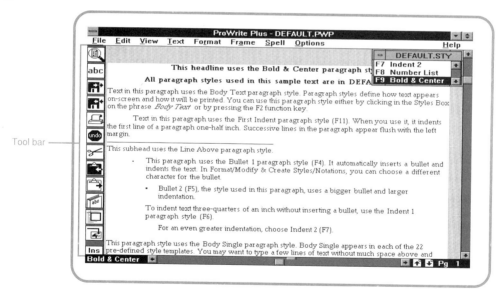

Tool bar

Figure 13.2 A sample Professional Write Plus screen.

Software Publishing Corporation's Professional Write Plus stands in the same middle-ground market as JustWrite. It contains many fundamental features missing from Windows' own Write program, such as a built-in, 130,000-word spell checker, an easy-to-access, on-line thesaurus, and the capability of creating and reusing style guides to simplify text formatting. However, you will also find a couple of surprises in the Professional Write package. Features in this second category include a semi-integrated version of Reference Software's popular Grammatik grammar checker, as well as full implementation of Microsoft's Dynamic Data Exchange (DDE) standard. Perhaps the most pleasant surprise in Professional Write Plus, however, is its inclusion of a front-end electronic messaging system and E-mail (electronic mail) manager. This last feature can't be found in any other Windows word processing program, including Ami and Word for Windows.

Communications software and dedicated E-mail packages often include a primitive text editor. The operative word in that previous sentence, however, is *primitive*. Consequently, those serious about electronic messaging generally spend much time switching back and forth between full-featured word processors and their favorite communications program. Professional Write's extremely flexible E-mail module eliminates this digital dance.

315

Professional Write's E-mail manager is more than a tag-on file exchange module and terminal emulator. For starters, it's fully compatible with other E-mail systems that implement the MHS (Message Handling System) standard. Transmitting a message with Professional Write is a simple matter of selecting the E-mail option, identifying the file or portion of a file you want to transmit, and sending it merrily on its way. At your option, messages can include formatting codes. This means you can use Professional Write to send and receive fully formatted documents over an E-mail channel. (Of course, the person on the other end of the connection must have access to a copy of Professional Write Plus in order to reconstruct any documents you send.) You can even create distribution lists for transmitting the same document to multiple destinations. In truth, the E-mail module of Professional Write would be an adequate stand-alone electronic messaging center. The fact that it is only one component of a full-featured word processor makes Professional Write even more impressive.

Professional Write Plus adds speed to the sometimes sluggish Windows environment by enabling you to view and work with a document in so-called Draft Mode. Selecting Draft Mode changes the screen to a bare-bones display. When running in Draft Mode, Professional Write Plus suffers only the slight, but still noticeable, slowdown that is common to all Windows-based applications. Consequently, Draft Mode is the ideal choice for entering or editing long text passages.

However, Professional Write's full-graphics mode—or Layout Mode, as it's called—also has its advantages. Because it provides a true WYSIWYG display, it's the mode of choice for fine-tuning a document—after you've entered the majority of your text using Draft Mode, of course. Select a new typeface for a section heading while working in Layout mode, for example, and you immediately see how this modification influences the document's overall appearance and layout. The familiar option menus and command icons that make working in the Windows environment so attractive in the first place greatly simplify these formatting operations.

Nothing spruces up words like pictures. Recognizing this, Software Publishing designed Professional Write Plus to import graphics from a number of well-known PC programs. These include Lotus PIC files, PC Paintbrush PIX files, and images created by the company's own popular Harvard Graphics. Other familiar file formats that can be directly imported into a Professional Write Plus document or, alternately, run through the program's impressive graphics-coversion utility, include EPS (Encapsulated PostScript), HP PCL (Hewlett-Packard's laser-printer language) and, from the Macintosh side of the PC fence, MAC and TIFF. Imported graphics can be cropped and rescaled easily—or even inverted, if necessary—to create a truly impressive finished product.

Electronic Spreadsheets

Electronic spreadsheets forever changed how people manipulate numbers. Similar to an accountant's ledger, an electronic spreadsheet enables you to automate complex calculations by entering formulas into individual *cells,* intersections of rows and columns in their simulated ledger design. Several powerful spreadsheets are available for the Windows' GUI.

Microsoft Excel for Windows

Microsoft Corporation
One Microsoft Way
Redmond, WA 98052
(206) 882-8080
$495

Menu

Tool bar

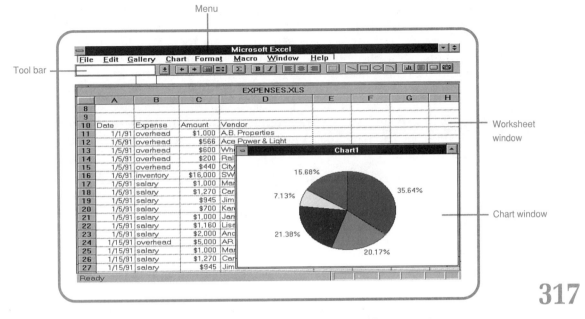

Worksheet
window

Chart window

Figure 13.3. A sample Microsoft Excel for Windows screen.

Excel's mathematical functions are comparable to any other spreadsheet program on the market, including Lotus 1-2-3. The graphics it generates—bar graphs, pie charts, and the like—leave the competition standing in the dust. It's worth installing Windows 3.1 on your PC so that you can use Excel. This program is that impressive.

Excel's graphics-based architecture permits incredible flexibility when specifying the screen appearance of your spreadsheets and charts. You can, for example, tell Excel to display automatically all entries below a certain value as red numbers on a white background, an easy way to identify potential problems in a budget projection. You also can adjust the height of individual rows within your spreadsheet and select from a variety of font styles for ranges, individual cells, or even single letters or numbers. Headers and footers, including automatic page count, can be added to an Excel spreadsheet at print time. Combine these formatting capabilities with a decent printer, and you can use Excel to generate reports of near-typeset quality.

Building spreadsheets in Excel's graphics-based environment is mostly intuitive. Using either a mouse or Excel's alternate keyboard commands, virtually every feature any serious spreadsheet user might ever need sits at your fingertips. Without even opening a manual, you can start using Excel, immediately incorporating some of the program's more advanced features. Enter unfamiliar territory, and context-sensitive help screens are available to provide assistance. Should you get lost, the program includes a comprehensive, on-screen tutorial, which you can run at any time during an Excel session. In an interesting tip-of-the-hat to two successful spreadsheet programs that have preceded it, Excel provides a special Help feature that you can use to enter a 1-2-3 or Multiplan command and then see the Excel command sequence required to perform the same operation.

Excel makes it easy to convert your numbers into graphs—especially when you consider how convoluted this task is with traditional DOS spreadsheets. When you want to create a graph from numbers in an Excel spreadsheet, use the mouse to highlight the appropriate cell range, specify the **C**hart option, and then select one of Excel's 44 available chart types from the program's **G**allery option. Your graph immediately appears in a second window. Excel automatically differentiates between text and numeric values in the specified range and places each in its appropriate place on the requested chart. Fine-tuning this initial chart to precisely the graphic you want is a breeze.

Wingz

Informix Software, Inc.
4100 Bohannon Drive
Menlo Park, CA 94025
(415) 926-6300
$495

Wingz is one of several Windows-aware programs born on the other side of the tracks. Initially designed to run on the Macintosh, this graphics-based spreadsheet recently moved into the DOS community. One advantage inherent in this lineage is that Wingz supports Informix's HyperScript application development language, a script language modeled after Hypercard and its programming language HyperText popularized on Macintosh systems. (Stated simply, Hypertext promotes the free-form association of diverse elements within an operating environment, so you can jump quickly from one task or operation to a second different but related task.) With HyperScript, it's possible to create a wide range of personal applications in Wingz, some of which can transcend the program's fundamental spreadsheet structure.

Lotus 1-2-3 for Windows

Lotus Development Corporation
55 Cambridge Parkway
Cambridge, MA 02142
$595

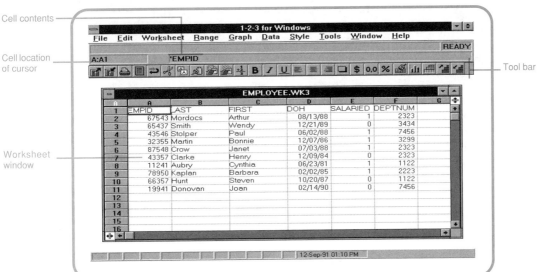

Figure 13.4. A sample Lotus 1-2-3 for Windows screen.

319

Lotus 1-2-3, a program that contributed greatly to the initial success of the IBM PC, is now available for Windows. More than a year in the making, Lotus 1-2-3 for Windows was worth the wait—especially for anyone familiar with the standard DOS version of this best-selling electronic spreadsheet.

One particularly interesting aspect of Lotus 1-2-3 for Windows is its so-called 1-2-3 Classic feature. The original 1-2-3 boasts several million satisfied users. Lotus wisely chose not to alienate these potential purchasers in migrating its premier product over to the Windows environment. Pressing the slash key in Lotus 1-2-3 for Windows calls menus that mirror the command structure of its highly popular predecessors. Consequently, Lotus veterans can begin using the Windows version productively within minutes of installing it on their PCs. They won't even have to sacrifice their existing data. The Windows version of 1-2-3 reads files created with any of its DOS counterparts. New users can disable the 1-2-3 Classic feature if they feel more comfortable with the standard Windows interface.

Representing more than a facelift of 1-2-3's DOS ancestors, 1-2-3 for Windows is a legitimate Windows application. The program fully supports all major Windows' features, including using the Windows Clipboard and DDE to exchange data with other Windows applications. (The initial release of 1-2-3 for Windows does not support OLE, but Lotus has promised support for this feature in future upgrades.)

Perhaps the most startling difference between 1-2-3 for Windows and standard DOS releases of 1-2-3 is its stunning charting capabilities. This shouldn't surprise you, considering the graphics nature of Windows itself. Anyone who's ever struggled to create a professional looking chart or graph with other releases of 1-2-3, however, will fall in love immediately with the Windows version.

If nothing else, 1-2-3 for Windows should add excitement to the wonderful world of Windows. Until now, Microsoft Excel has all but dominated the Windows spreadsheet market. The introduction of 1-2-3 for Windows has irreversibly altered that situation.

I Hate Algebra

T/Maker Research Company
812 Pollard Road, Suite 8
Los Gatos, CA 95030
$79.95

How can you not like a program called I Hate Algebra? Oh, you could find it disappointing if your spreadsheet demands exceed the program's 5000-cell maximum. You also might be frustrated if you're one of those people who enjoys impressing others with attractive but often perplexing three-dimensional graphs, which I Hate Algebra doesn't offer. You might even be confused initially while learning the unique method this program uses to build mathematical formulas. It's difficult not to fall in love with I Hate Algebra, however, for several reasons.

First, there's its price. At $79.95, I Hate Algebra is one of the lowest priced Windows spreadsheets currently on the market. Even more attractive, however, is the program's unique approach to data entry. As anyone who's ever used an electronic spreadsheet knows, most programs in this software category perform calculations based

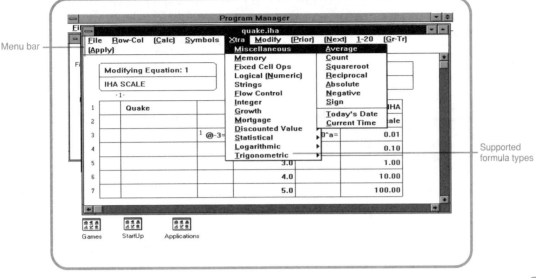

Menu bar ——

Supported
formula types

Figure 13.5. A sample I Hate Algebra screen.

on formulas that contain precise and potentially confusing cell references. Not I Hate Algebra. Instead, it works much like a traditional calculator. Building even complex equations in I Hate Algebra is a simple matter of selecting a mathematical operator from the program's pull-down Symbols menu and then entering the value you want applied to it. To multiply one number by another, for example, you simply type the first value, click Symbols, select Times (*), and enter the second value. I Hate Algebra takes care of the rest. Individual equations are assigned numbers, which can be referenced for future calculations.

As I admitted earlier in this book, math has never been my forte. When it comes to number crunching, I'm a lot like the class nerd trying to crush a beer can. I might despise math, but I could grow to like I Hate Algebra.

Telecommunications

While utilitarian, and certainly convenient for making quick-and-dirty connections, Terminal lacks some of the more advanced features traditionally found in stand-alone communications programs. Three companies, Digital Communications, Software Ventures, and Future Soft Engineering Inc., however, have released Windows-based products that bring a wealth of telecommunications features to the Windows environment.

CrossTalk for Windows

DCA
1000 Alderman Drive
Alpharetta, GA 30201
(800) 241-4762
$195

Communication
parameters

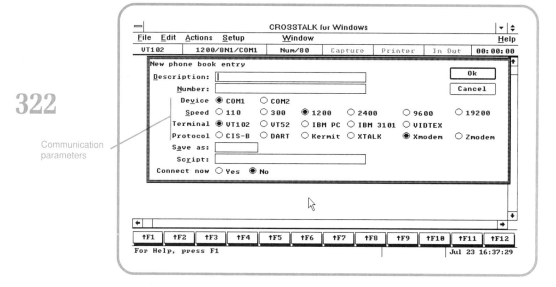

Figure 13.6. A sample CrossTalk for Windows screen.

CrossTalk for Windows is another application adapted from a successful DOS program to take advantage of the Windows GUI. Like its DOS ancestor, CrossTalk Mk.4, Crosstalk for Windows includes a powerful script language that you can use to automate your on-line activities.

Like most Windows applications, CrossTalk's workspace is topped by the Windows menu bar. Top-level menu options in CrossTalk for Windows include **File**, **Edit**, **Actions**, **Setup**, **User**, and **Help**. Just below this menu bar is a status bar—not a universal Windows display element but rather a feature unique to CrossTalk for Windows. Using the status bar, you can discern at a glance important information about your current CrossTalk session: the type of terminal emulation in effect, your communication parameters (baud rate, parity, data bits, stop bits, and the COM port your modem is using), whether you have opened a log file to capture this session, a stopwatch used to time on-line connections, and the like. In short, almost any information you might desire about the current status of your telecommunications session is readily available on the CrossTalk for Windows display.

You initiate on-line sessions by calling phone book entries. Before you can call a phone entry, you must create that entry with the New phone book entry... command, which you access from the Files option of the Windows menu bar. Selecting this command calls a series of dialog boxes requesting the information CrossTalk needs to dial a specific remote system—access number, line settings, the terminal emulation it requires, and so on. After supplying all the required information, you can place your call immediately or save this new phone entry for later use. With other File options, you can open a previous phone entry, send terminal output to a system printer or file, initiate file transfers during an on-line session, and exit CrossTalk for Windows.

323

The Actions menu is where you initiate and coordinate most of your on-line activities. It includes the Connect option (used to call the current phone entry) and Dial, which displays a list of all phone entries you have created. Then you can replace the currently active entry with a different one. The Actions menu also includes the Script option, which you use to automate your on-line activities by executing a series of preprogrammed commands from a CrossTalk for Windows script.

Use options in the Setup menu to temporarily change the current program settings without having to load a new phone entry. This is where you specify items like communication parameters and line settings, terminal emulation, file-transfer protocol, modem type, and so on. CrossTalk for Windows supports transmission rates of 110 to 19,200 baud. Emulation options include VT52, VT102, IBM 3101, and standard ASCII terminals. You also can specify terminal width and how line feeds and carriage returns should be handled during an on-line session. With CrossTalk for Windows, you can choose from a wide range of file-transfer protocols, including XMODEM, YMODEM, CompuServe B, Kermit, and two protocols popularized by previous CrossTalk versions: DART and the proprietary CrossTalk protocol.

In short, CrossTalk for Windows packs telecommunications power into your Windows environment.

MicroPhone II
Software Ventures Corporation
2907 Claremont Avenue, Suite 220
Berkeley, CA 94705
$295

324

Communication parameters

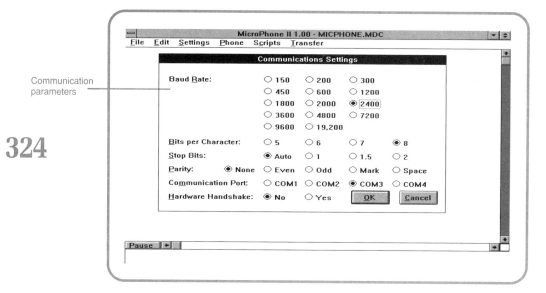

Figure 13.7 A sample MicroPhone II screen.

Given my interest in telecommunications, I tend to test communications software more harshly than I do programs in other application areas. MicroPhone II passed all my tests, which included connecting with several on-line services I use and transferring files under a variety of conditions, without a hitch. It also simplified each of these activities so that within twenty minutes or so of installing MicroPhone II on my system, I felt totally at ease using it. The credit for this, it seems to me, must be divided equally between the Windows environment, which reduces most procedures to simple point-and-click operations, and MicroPhone II itself, which takes full advantage of Windows and then throws in a few additional conveniences of its own.

One of the most convenient—and, I must admit, impressive—features of MicroPhone II is its script language. *Scripts* are preprogrammed sequences of commands you can use to automate many on-line activities, a real time-saver given the potentially high cost of telecommunications. Most communications programs include a script feature, but MicroPhone II's has to rank among the most elegant I've seen.

Creating scripts with MicroPhone II is an almost totally automated procedure. For one thing, MicroPhone II includes a learn feature, which you can use to have the program automatically record all the keystrokes and commands you enter during a given on-line session to a script for subsequent replay. Creating scripts from scratch in MicroPhone II also is a breeze. Whereas most communication programs force you to create and edit scripts with a script editor—a procedure not unlike using a programming language such as BASIC—MicroPhone II includes a special script construction module so that you can pick and choose interactively the operations you want performed during the execution of a given script.

325

When you select the MicroPhone II **C**reate Script option, a special dialog box appears in your Windows workspace. You can use this window to name your script, assign that script to a function key for automatic execution, and the like. This function also contains a text editing window into which you can begin entering the commands you want executed each time this script is run. What if, however, you don't know the specific commands MicroPhone II uses for a certain procedure? No problem. You see, a second window in the **C**reate Script dialog box contains a listing of all available MicroPhone II script options—dial a service, set parameters, send file, receive file, hangup a line, and the like. Clicking one of these options inserts it into your script, using the appropriate command. Furthermore, MicroPhone II automatically prompts you for any additional parameters a given command might require to execute properly.

After a script exists, a special **C**heck option analyzes it for any potential syntax errors that might render it unusable. There's also a **T**est option so that you can interactively run a script, viewing both the script contents themselves and the results of any commands it contains. Finally, MicroPhone II ships with over 65 preprogrammed scripts to simplify everything from calling a specific on-line service to initiating a file transfer. As I said, the process is fully automated, intuitive, and easily accessible even to neophyte scripters. All in all, I give MicroPhone II an A+ for ease of use, especially where its script language is concerned.

MicroPhone II ships with preprogrammed scripts for several popular commercial on-line information systems, including CompuServe, BIX, Dow Jones, MCI Mail, and GEnie. When you first load a script for one of these services, clicking a special Profile button causes MicroPhone II to display a series of prompts requesting the information it needs to connect you to that service—access number, your user ID, your password, and so on. The Profile button also can be used to change any of these items, which would be required, for example, if you moved and had to use a different access number to contact a given service. Again, ease of use seems to be the primary aspiration of MicroPhone II, a goal it achieves with ease.

Like many communications programs, MicroPhone II includes a Host mode feature. Put simply, setting MicroPhone II to Host mode causes it to answer automatically incoming calls and establish an on-line connection with any authorized callers. After this connection is made, the remote caller can use MicroPhone II to transfer files to and from the host system, leave messages for other callers, or page and communicate with a user at the system running MicroPhone II—an individual called a system operator, or sysop, in the often arcane language of telecommunications.

If you're worried about security when MicroPhone II is operating in Host mode, don't be. Each caller must enter an assigned name and his or her personal password before MicroPhone II completes the connection and grants that person access to the system. With MicroPhone II, you also can assign different security levels to different callers, a useful tool for limiting the operations a given caller can perform after he or she is connected to your PC.

For all its pluses, MicroPhone II does have a few limitations. For one thing, it supports fewer file-transfer protocols than many other communication programs. Your options are limited to several XMODEM and YMODEM protocols, ASCII file transfers, and a standard binary protocol. (As partial compensation, however, MicroPhone II automatically determines the appropriate protocol for the host system to which it is connected. Consequently, you don't need to know and specify this information prior to initiating a file transfer.) Terminal emulation is similarly limited. MicroPhone II also does not currently support Dynamic Data Exchange (DDE), a special Windows feature with which you can create dynamic links between multiple programs running in a Windows session.

Despite these minor shortcomings, MicroPhone II is a powerful and impressively easy to use communications program—a rarity in the PC marketplace. If you need to open your Windows environment to the rest of the world, MicroPhone II is the logical choice for doing so.

DynaComm

> Future Soft Engineering, Inc.
> 1001 S. Dairy Ashford, Suite 101
> Houston, TX 77077
> (713) 496-9400
> $295

If you like Terminal, you'll love DynaComm, because Terminal is actually a stripped-down version of DynaComm, which Microsoft licensed from Future Soft. DynaComm adds several impressive features to Terminal, including support for more file-transfer protocols and expanded terminal emulation options. DynaComm also includes a powerful script language that you can use to automate the majority of your on-line activities.

DynaComm employs the Windows 3 Help engine (a series of standard routines programmed into Windows that simplifies linking Windows-aware applications with their external Help files) to provide comprehensive information on virtually all aspects of its use.

327

Desktop Publishing

When Johann Gutenberg invented movable type in the 15th century, documents could be produced more quickly, cheaply, and in greater quantities than ever before. As a result, information was more accessible. Although the masses became a welcome market for the printed word, its actual production remained in the hands of a relative few—professional printers and major publishing houses like the one that produced this book.

The emergence of desktop publishing (DTP) in the late 1980s changed all this. Suddenly, anyone who knew how to use a DTP program had the potential to produce a professional-looking document, providing access to the right PC and printer. The Windows graphics-based interface is suited ideally to DTP, which relies as much on coordinating the visual elements of a page as the creative writing that page contains. Two programs are currently duking it out for dominance in the high-end Windows desktop publishing arena: Aldus PageMaker and Ventura Publisher.

Aldus PageMaker

Aldus Corporation
411 First Avenue South
Seattle, WA 98104
(800) 333-2538
$795

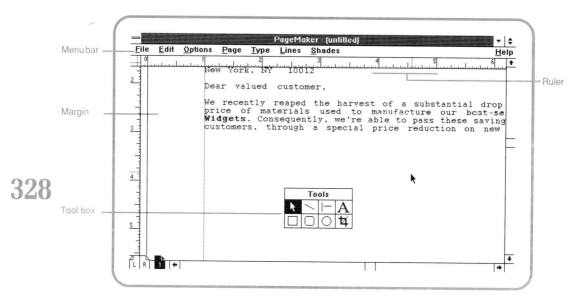

Figure 13.8. A sample Aldus PageMaker screen.

In many ways, PageMaker is the glue that held Windows together during the early years, back when the latter program was still struggling for acceptance. Desktop publishing in the Windows environment—even more specifically, desktop publishing with PageMaker in the Windows environment—lent validity to Microsoft's claim that the potential existed for a graphics-based user-interface to succeed within the DOS marketplace. That folks were willing to put up with earlier and admittedly clumsy versions of Windows simply to use PageMaker in many cases speaks highly of that program's popularity.

Basically, you start a PageMaker document by using text and graphics elements that have been imported from your favorite programs. PageMaker can read files created by a wide range of Windows-aware and standard DOS applications. After PageMaker converts these various elements, you can use that program to organize and arrange those elements into a fully formatted, professional-looking final printout.

Because PageMaker emulates an artist's paste-up board in your Windows workspace, it's ideal for creating and formatting short, graphics-intensive documents. If on the other hand, you find yourself regularly creating longer documents with a greater emphasis on text—a book like this one being a prime example—then you might want to look at PageMaker's closest competitor, Ventura Publisher.

Ventura Publisher 3.0

Xerox Desktop Software
15175 Innovation Drive
San Diego, CA 92128
(619) 695-6416
$895

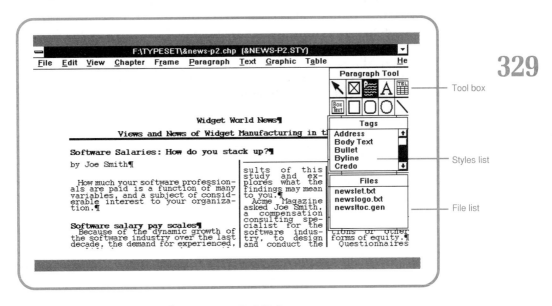

Figure 13.9. A sample Ventura Publisher screen.

I've been a big fan of Ventura Publisher for years. Admittedly, this is more a consequence of the type of writing I do than any objective analysis of how much more impressive Ventura might be than other DTP programs currently on the market.

Like PageMaker, Ventura works best when it's working with document elements created in other programs. (No DTP program is particularly adroit at creating text or images; this particular software genre's forte is organizing and formatting what exists.) Also like

PageMaker, Ventura can import data from several popular DOS and Windows-aware programs. One advantage Ventura does have over PageMaker, which actually converts any data it uses into its own format, is that it preserves external files in their native format. If you need to revise the text of a Ventura document, therefore, you can return to your favorite word processor and perform these revisions. The next time you read that file into Ventura, the modifications you made are reflected in your DTP-formatted document. Because of the lackadaisical word processing and graphics features built into most DTP programs—Ventura included—this feature can be a real godsend.

Judge desktop publishing programs wisely. The investment required for a truly useful DTP setup can be steep. In addition to the mandatory software (which doesn't come cheap), you want a printer capable of producing quality output. Also, a high-resolution display and a mouse are essential for DTP. When you're shelling out the kinds of bucks desktop publishing requires, you want to be extra careful in the DTP program you pick. Make sure the program you pick is suited well to your needs. Two other desktop publishing programs to look at are Microsoft Publisher and Legacy.

Database Management

Many database managers designed to run under Windows are programs that, like PageMaker and Wingz, initially were introduced in the Macintosh market. This isn't necessarily bad, however, because it means the folks over there have had time to refine their programs and eliminate shortcomings (in some cases, also correct operational bugs that usually infest early versions of any application) prior to porting them over to the Windows environment.

Another phenomenon surfacing in Windows database programs is widespread support for Structured Query Language (SQL), an advanced technique for finding specific information in a data file developed for mainframe database applications. This might seem surprising until you understand that numerous experts consider the Windows GUI to be a preliminary step in establishing a universal interface across all computer platforms—PC, minicomputers, and mainframes. Building SQL capabilities into Windows database managers now, it is believed, will simplify matters later if such a universal interface standard emerges.

Several Windows-aware database programs have emerged recently as more and more companies realize that managing information in a visual environment like Windows represents a major advance over more traditional, text-based DOS database applications. Consequently, I'm not going to profile any individual packages. Rather, I'll list alternatives, including the address and phone number for each program so that you can obtain more information.

Omnis 5
Blyth Software Inc.
1065 E. Hillsdale Blvd., Suite 300
Foster City, CA 94404
(415) 571-0222
$795

Superbase 4
Precision Software, Inc.
844 Sterling
Irving, TX 75063
(800) 562-9909
$695

331

SQL Windows
Gupta Technologies
1040 Marsh Road
Menlo Park, CA 94025
(415) 321-9500
$1,295

Access SQL
Software Products International
10240 Sorrento Valley Road
San Diego, CA 92121
(800) 937-4774
$695

Thinx
Bell Atlantic Corp.
13100 Columbia Pike, Suite D37
Silver Spring, MD 20904
(800) 388-4465
$495

Ace File
Ace Software Corp.
1740 Technology Drive, Suite 680
San Jose, CA 95110
(408) 437-3456
$295

WindowBase
Software Products, International
9920 Pacific Heights Blvd.
San Diego, CA 92121
(800) 937-4774
$495

Utilities

Utility programs flourish in the DOS environment. To be honest, the roots of this phenomenon lie in the many weaknesses exhibited by early versions of the MS-DOS operating system. Over time, however, DOS utilities have carved their own unique niche within the marketplace.

It's no surprise, therefore, that the recent emergence of Windows has invigorated the utilities market. A whole slew of new utility programs has emerged, utility programs designed to build on the foundation laid by Windows 3.1. Several dozen such programs exist. Two of these deserve special attention, primarily because of the great success the companies responsible for them have previously enjoyed within the DOS marketplace.

PC Tools 7

Central Point Software, Inc.
15220 N.W. Greenbrier Parkway
Beaverton, OR 97006
(503) 690-8090
$179

PC Tools 7 is the Swiss Army Knife of PC software. It contains everything from a simplified DOS Shell to a so-called Desktop package that includes a text editor, a dBASE-compatible database manager, a telecommunications module, and a workgroup scheduler. Many of the individual modules in PC Tools are standard DOS applications. Beginning with PC Tools 7, however, Central Point bent over backward to make its premier product Windows compatible.

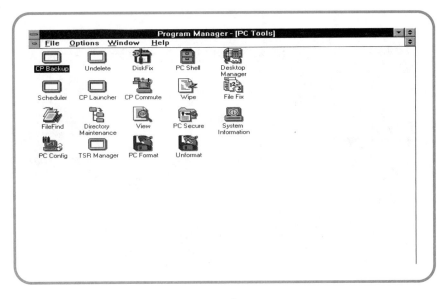

Figure 13.10. A sample PC Tools 7 screen.

During installation, PC Tools creates a new program group to provide easy access to its most used modules. Additionally, this program group contains three Windows-specific applications: a hard-disk Backup utility, a file Undelete utility, and a Program Launcher. The Program Launcher is a utility that runs behind Windows so that you can run any program whenever and from anywhere within a Windows session.

It's hard to imagine a package that gives you more "bang for the buck," as the cliche goes, than PC Tools 7. This always impressive program now supports Windows 3.1, which only adds to its previous appeal.

Norton Desktop for Windows

Symantec Corporation
10201 Torre Avenue
Cupertino, CA 95014
(408) 253-9600
$149

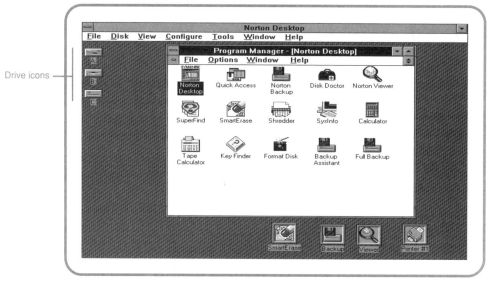

Drive icons

Figure 13.11. A sample Norton Desktop for Windows screen.

334

Here's another program that successfully transplants several previously popular utilities to the Windows environment. Peter Norton has long been recognized as the true guru of DOS file and disk management. As its name implies, however, Desktop for Windows goes far beyond simple utilities. Norton's Desktop actually serves as a replacement for the two primary elements of Windows' own metaphorical desktop: Program Manager and File Manager.

Many people are comfortable with the more "Macintosh feel" of Norton's Desktop. It includes several more icons than the default Windows display, including a SmartErase icon so that you can preserve recently deleted files for easy restoration. Desktop also includes a File Viewer utility, which can recognize and display files stored in a variety of popular file formats.

Unlike Windows sans Desktop, with Norton's package you can nest program groups—that is, an icon in a program group can actually represent a second program group, which contains multiple program and data files. This certainly comes in handy when you need to organize complex projects visually.

For all the changes it brings to Windows, Norton Desktop doesn't interfere with that GUI's normal operations. Menu options and mouse commands accomplish the same things as they do under native Windows. Consequently, you don't have to learn any new procedures to continue using Windows after installing this impressive arsenal of useful utilities.

Windows 3 is a giant step in the right direction to making MS-DOS computers accessible to the "average Joe (and Josephine)." Still, it's not perfect. Norton Desktop for Windows advances this cause several large paces. Other utility programs include

Ater Dark
BeckerTools
Distinct Backup
hDC File Apps
hDC First Apps
hDC Windows Express
Microsoft Project for Windows
WinConnect
WinSleuth

Miscellaneous Software

We have looked at profiles of several Windows-aware programs in five major software categories. Space considerations prohibit my covering every available program in all application categories. It would require an entire book to present a comprehensive compendium of all the Windows programs out there or planned for release in the near future. Therefore, I conclude this chapter by listing a few of the more intriguing Windows programs with which I am personally familiar. After each program's listing, I've included a brief description on the type of program it is.

This represents only a few of the various third-party applications you can incorporate into your Windows environment. New names continue to be added to the list. Somewhere in this list—or perhaps among the scores of other Windows-aware programs out there—an application almost certainly exists that's perfect for your personal situation.

Graphics and Draw Programs

Aldus Persuasion
Corel DRAW!
IBM Hollywood
Micrographx Charisma

Publishers Paintbrush
Microsoft PowerPoint for Windows
Micrografx Designer
CA-Cricket Presents

Grammar Checkers

RightWriter 5.0 for Windows
Correct Grammar for Windows
Grammatik

Personal Information Managers

IBM Current
PackRat
Your Way

Programming Environments

Asymetrix's Toolbook
Borland's Turbo Pascal for Windows
deskMinder
Microsft Visual Basic
Borland's Object Vision
Spinnaker Plus

I might not have included your favorite program either through oversight or worse still, because it was one of the many Windows applications I didn't receive in time to meet this book's deadline.

We're almost but not quite done. One topic will bring us back full-circle to where we started—how Windows 3.1 handles standard DOS applications—and that subject is discussed in the next chapter.

What You Have Learned

▶ Windows has generated much excitement within the PC community. Consequently, dozens of programs are available that are specially designed to take full advantage of the Windows GUI.

▶ Installing a Windows-aware application generally includes several special steps, the main purpose of which is to inform Windows of what that program is and how it operates. As a rule, any Windows applications you buy will include specific instructions on how best to install that program to run properly in your Windows environment.

▶ The variety of Windows-aware applications entering the market is impressive. Specific programs are now available in all major software categories and more are appearing all the time. Consequently, it's possible to set up a comprehensive PC environment that runs exclusively under the Windows GUI.

337

The Windows/DOS Connection

In This Chapter

▶ *How to access the DOS command prompt from within Windows*

▶ *How to run standard DOS applications from within Windows*

▶ *How Windows uses PIFs*

▶ *How to modify a PIF*

Windows Does DOS

At the end of this chapter, we conclude our discussion of DOS—the operating system under which Windows runs. Although it's possible to manage all your PC activities from within the Windows GUI, there might be times when you find it advantageous to initiate an operation directly from the DOS prompt. For someone familiar with DOS, issuing a command from the standard DOS prompt can often be an easier and more efficient way to accomplish something than choosing the corresponding Windows menu options.

Instead of forcing you to terminate the current Windows session, Windows 3.1 includes a DOS icon that, when selected, suspends all Windows operations and accesses a special DOS shell—a temporary "opening" in Windows through which you can issue and execute standard DOS commands.

Accessing the DOS Command Prompt

During installation, the Windows Setup program automatically added an MS-DOS prompt icon to your Main program group. Accessing the DOS command shell is a matter of displaying the Main program group and then double-clicking the DOS icon.

 To Display the DOS Command Prompt

1. Position the mouse cursor in any visible portion of the Main program group.

2. Click the left mouse button.

   This makes the Main group the active window.

3. Double-click the MS-DOS Prompt icon.

   Windows displays the standard DOS system prompt.

Selecting the MS-DOS Prompt icon temporarily suspends Windows and displays the DOS system prompt, as shown in Figure 14.1. (Notice that the DOS shell also reveals information about which version of DOS you are using prior to displaying the system prompt.) After this prompt is displayed, you may issue DOS commands and even execute DOS applications, just as you would if Windows were not running on your system.

340

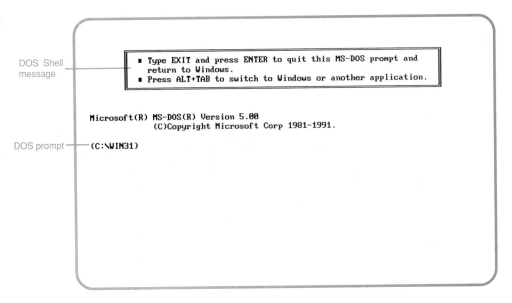

DOS Shell
message

DOS prompt

Figure 14.1. Selecting the DOS Prompt icon suspends Windows
and displays the DOS system prompt.

 Caution: Whenever you are working in the Windows
DOS shell, do not issue commands or run programs that
modify file allocation tables. For example, if you issue a
CHKDSK command from the Windows DOS shell, don't include that command's /F parameter, which causes DOS to
convert any unallocated file clusters CHKDSK discovers to
temporary files. Other examples of the types of programs that
you should not run from within the DOS shell include so-called
undelete programs and utilities that compress or optimize disk
files. If you need to use such programs, exit Windows completely before running them.

Exiting the DOS Shell and Returning to Windows

After you're finished working in the DOS shell, use an exit command
to reactivate the interrupted Windows session.

Q **To Exit the DOS Shell and Return to Windows**

Type EXIT and press
Enter.

Windows closes its DOS
shell and returns you to
whatever you were doing before
you accessed the DOS system
prompt. □

> **Tip:** If you want to keep the DOS shell active while
> working in Windows, use an Alt+Esc key sequence to
> return to the interrupted Windows session. This places a
> minimized DOS Shell icon at the bottom of your Windows
> workspace. Double-clicking this icon reactivates the DOS shell
> without forcing you to access the Main program group again.

Running DOS Programs from Within Windows

Certainly, the ability to execute DOS commands and run programs
from the DOS shell is a welcome convenience. In truth, however, it
would be more convenient to include standard DOS programs in
your total Windows environment—that is, without first having to
suspend your current Windows activities and switch to the DOS
system prompt.

The Applications Icon

Chances are you already have some non-Windows applications
installed on your Windows workspace. One of the options steps we
performed in Chapter 2, "Installing Windows," was to have **S**etup
scan all your disk drives and add any programs to your Windows
environment. Any standard DOS applications that **S**etup recognized
were automatically installed in an Applications program group, and
each was assigned its own icon on your Windows workspace.

To Display the Non-Windows Program Group

Double-click the
Applications icon.

This opens an Applications
window in your workspace. □

Selecting the Applications icon opens a window containing individual icons for any standard DOS programs **S**etup discovered during installation. (See Figure 14.2.)

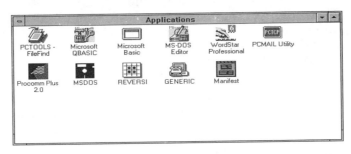

Figure 14.2. Setup automatically established a special program group for any non-Windows applications it discovered during installation.

343

> **Note:** Your display will differ from Figure 14.2 in that it will contain icons for the specific DOS applications **S**etup found on your disks.

Usually, **S**etup knows enough about a DOS application to assign it the appropriate icon, as was the case with my system, where **S**etup assigned a stylized telephone icon to Procomm Plus, a standard DOS telecommunications program Setup located on my system. WordStar, my word processor of choice, is another example of a standard DOS application with which **S**etup associated a suitable icon.

Starting a Non-Windows Application

You start a non-Windows application as you would any other program or accessory within your Windows environment, by double-clicking the application's corresponding icon.

Q To Start a Non-Windows Application

Double-click the
application's icon.

Windows opens its DOS shell
and starts the requested
program.   □

I have Procomm Plus on my system, which is a DOS application, not a Windows application. I use this Quick Step to run my Procomm Plus program, and a few seconds after double-clicking its icon, I see the initial Procomm Plus screen shown in Figure 14.3. I'm now running Procomm Plus from within Windows. Furthermore, when I'm done using Procomm Plus, the usual exit from that program returns me to the Windows GUI.

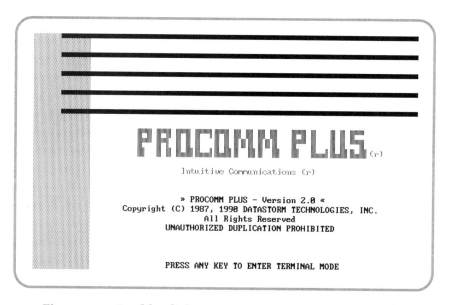

*Figure 14.3. Double-clicking a Non-Windows Application icon
runs the corresponding program from within Windows.*

Windows' Strengths and Weaknesses

Windows is capable of doing some nifty things while running standard DOS applications. Not all these things can be accomplished in all PC environments. How many of Windows' advanced features you can take advantage of depends on what type of PC system you own and how you've configured Windows to run on that system. Specifically

▶ When operating in Standard mode, Windows runs standard DOS applications in a full-screen display, similar to the one shown in Figure 14.3.

▶ When operating in Standard mode, with Windows you can switch among any non-Windows applications running in a full-screen display. Windows suspends operations of all but the currently displayed non-Windows application, however, with this configuration.

▶ When operating in 386 Enhanced mode, Windows can run most standard DOS applications in their own window—a small window displayed as part of the Windows workspace.

▶ Depending on the DOS programs being run, Windows also might be able to multitask non-Windows applications when operating in 386 Enhanced mode.

▶ Running Windows in 386 Enhanced mode on an 80386- or i486-based PC also might enable you to cut and paste data from a non-Windows application into the Windows clipboard, depending on how you configure that application's PIF file.

345

How Windows Uses PIFs

Most non-Windows applications installed in your Windows environment have their own *Program Information File,* or PIF. A PIF is a special file that contains information Windows needs to run a standard DOS program successfully within the Windows GUI. The basic Windows package includes PIF files for several popular DOS programs. When you use the Setup Applications option in the Windows Setup accessory, **S**etup automatically installs in your Windows environment any non-Windows applications for which it finds a PIF file. (That's how Procomm Plus, WordStar, and Microsoft Bookshelf made it into my Applications program group.)

If you try to start a standard DOS application for which no program information file exists, Windows attempts to run that program using its default PIF. Usually, DOS applications work fine when loaded with this default PIF. There might be times, however, when a specific program requires customized PIF settings to peacefully coexist with the Windows GUI. Should this happen, you need to modify the current PIF settings or create a new PIF for the troublesome program, using the Windows PIF Editor accessory.

Working with PIFs

Windows needs to know certain information about every program it runs. For one thing, Windows has to be able to find that program, which means Windows needs to know the directory in which the program is stored, called the Start-Up Directory in Windows parlance. If Windows isn't told that your WordStar files are in a subdirectory called \WS, for example, how is it going to know where to look for the WS.EXE file to load that program's opening menu. The additional information that Windows needs includes a program's memory requirements, how that program handles writing to the screen, whether the program can display graphics, what serial ports the program uses (if any), and whether the program should be given access to expanded memory. Beyond these critical items, there is additional information that can help Windows control how well a program runs within your Windows environment. Where does Windows look for this information? In the PIF.

As mentioned earlier, Windows knows this information about several popular programs. Consequently, all you need to do when you add one of these programs is to have Windows discover where that program is stored on your system. (This is basically what happens when you choose the **S**etup Applications option in Windows **S**etup.) Windows then appends the program's location with additional information in its PIF and assigns that PIF a program code associated with the appropriate program. On my disk, for example, is a file called WS.PIF, the program information file associated with WordStar.

Each time you start a DOS application program, Windows reads the corresponding PIF to determine how that program should be configured, as well as where it will be found on your system.

How do you configure a program you regularly use, a program that is not automatically recognized by Windows? What if you need to change the default information about a program to make it more compatible with your Windows environment? To accomplish either of these tasks, use the Windows PIF Editor accessory, which automatically was placed in the Main program group during installation.

> **Tip:** Windows' default PIF file sets up a bare-bones environment. For example, the default only allocates 128K of RAM and supports none of Windows more advanced features, such as screen exchange, expanded memory, and so on. It's a good idea, therefore, to create a dedicated PIF file for any DOS applications you regularly use.

The PIF Editor

347

Use the PIF Editor to edit the information contained in an application program's PIF. To study the information stored in a PIF, let's examine the contents of the PIF for WordStar on my system, WS.PIF.

 To Access the PIF Editor

1. Position the mouse cursor in any visible area of the Main program group.
2. Click the left mouse button.

This makes Main the active program group.

3. Double-click the PIF Editor icon.

This runs PIF Editor.

□

If you are running Windows in Standard mode, selecting the PIF Editor icon displays the PIF Editor dialog box shown in Figure 14.4.

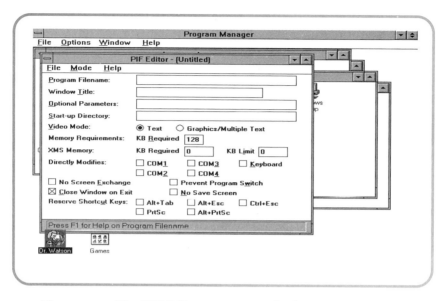

348

Figure 14.4. The PIF Editor screen used when Windows is operating in Standard mode.

If you are running Windows in 386 Enhanced mode, you see a different opening PIF Editor dialog box, the one shown in Figure 14.5.

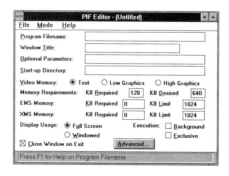

Figure 14.5. The PIF Editor screen used when Windows is operating in 386 Enhanced mode.

> **Note:** When Windows is configured in 386 Enhanced mode on an 80386- or i486-based system, it can use the advanced memory management features built into those microprocessors to set up a virtual 8086 system in RAM for each application being run in a multitasking session. To accomplish this, Windows needs and therefore requests more information about non-Windows applications when it is running in 386 Enhanced mode.

Regardless of the type of system you own and how you have configured Windows to run on that system, certain basic program information is stored in every PIF. We examine that information in the next section.

The Contents of a PIF

349

The information stored in a PIF can be broken into five major categories.

1. Information that identifies the program in a Windows program group.
2. Information pertaining to how this program is usually accessed at the DOS level.
3. Information about how Windows should allocate system memory for the program.
4. Information about how the program should be configured within the Windows environment.
5. Information about how Windows should handle this program during a multitasking session.

Some information contained in a PIF is self-explanatory. The Windows Title field, for example, contains the descriptive name you want displayed below its icon and in the Windows Title bar. Other obvious fields include Program Filename (the program's name—for example, WS.EXE for the WordStar executable program) and Memory Requirements (the program's published memory requirements). Other PIF information, however, is more technical and might require further explanation. To avoid confusion, let's start with the Real/Standard PIF dialog box.

350

Program Filename	This is the name of the executable program used to start this application. Usually, this is a file with an .EXE or .COM extension in its filename. You also can open an application window using a DOS batch file, which would have a .BAT extension.
Window Title	This is the name assigned to this program as it will be displayed below the corresponding icon. This name also appears in the title bar of any window into which you load this program.
Optional Parameters	This field contains any program parameters you usually would enter after the program name were you typing this information on the DOS command line. For example, this could be a data file you want the program to load at startup if the program usually enables entry of such an item when it is loaded from the DOS prompt. It also could be a DOS switch or command parameter (vis-à-vis, the B: in the DOS command FORMAT B:) used to clarify or refine a program command.
Start-Up Directory	This is the drive and directory you want Windows to make the current directory whenever this program is started.
Video Mode	Check Graphics/Multiple Text if a program ever uses graphics (a bit-mapped display) during execution. This instructs Windows to set aside the extra memory required to manage such a

display. Specifying Text for DOS programs that use a character-based display makes more memory available for your total Windows environment.

Memory Requirements

This field specifies how many kilobytes of conventional memory must be available to start this application. As a rule, you should leave this value set to the 128 default value. (This is not the total amount of memory that is allocated to an application. Windows itself determines that amount when a program is run. Rather this is the amount of memory that must be free for Windows to even attempt to run this application.)

351

XMS Memory

The values in these fields represent the minimum (KB Required) and maximum (KB Limit) amounts of expanded memory, EEMS or EMS 4.0, in kilobytes, that should be made available to this program. Leaving the latter field blank instructs Windows to place no limit on the amount of expanded memory this program can use.

Tip: Some programs immediately grab all available expanded memory if they are configured to do so when installed on your system. (Microsoft Excel is one such program.) To guarantee that some expanded memory remains available for your other Windows applications, enter a workable value in this field when configuring programs like Excel to run in the Windows environment.

Directly Modifies	Information in this field helps Windows eliminate conflicts resulting from multiple programs trying to access the same serial (COM) port concurrently. You should mark the box for any port this application uses. A communications program, for example, might use the second serial port for its modem connection. In this case, you would click the COM2 box. You also should tell Windows when an application takes over the keyboard—bypasses the standard keyboard I/O BIOS routines—during execution (like some remote access programs do).
=No Screen Exchange	Checking this box tells Windows to deactivate the Windows Clipboard while this application is running. Doing so makes more memory available for the application.
Prevent Program Switch	Checking this box tells Windows to deactivate its Program Switch feature while this application is running. Doing so makes more memory available for the application. It also means, however, that you need to quit this application completely to return to Windows or switch to another application running in a multitasking session.
Close Window on Exit	If an X appears in this box, whenever you exit this program to DOS (use the program's **Q**uit or E**x**it command, for example), Windows automatically performs a Close Window operation. If no X appears in the Close Window on Exit box, quitting the program

returns you to a DOS system prompt and leaves the application window open. You could then close the window manually by typing exit at the system prompt.

Reserve Shortcut Keys As you've already seen, Windows uses several keystrokes to initiate special procedures during a multitasking session. Pressing Ctrl+Esc, for example, displays the Task List. What if you run a DOS application that also uses the Ctrl+Esc key combination to access for one of its functions? Usually, that application would never see this command, because Windows would intercept the Ctrl+Esc sequence for its own purposes. Checking the Ctrl+Esc box in the Reserve Shortcut Keys section of the PIF Editor dialog box tells Windows to pass that key combination onto the application. You should check all key combinations listed here that might conflict with a particular application.

353

Next, we'll describe the fields that appear on the 386 Enhanced PIF Editor dialog box. (See Figure 14.5.) Six of these fields should be familiar.

► Program Filename
► Window Title
► Optional Parameters
► Start-Up Directory
► Memory Requirements
► Close Window on Exit

The values you enter into these fields are identical to those when you are running Windows in Standard mode.

There are, however, two additional fields in the 386 Enhanced dialog box. These fields are used to enable features available only when Windows is running on a 386 or 486 system.

Display Usage	Checking the Full Screen option forces Windows to run this application in a full-screen display only. You might find it necessary to do this if a particular program misbehaves—that is, it bypasses the normal BIOS routines used to display information to your system monitor. If a program freezes (ceases to operate) or garbles your Windows display, try setting the Display Usage option to Full Screen in that program's PIF.
Execution	Checking the Background option tells Windows to enable full multitasking when this application is running. Thus, this application continues to run in the background whenever you switch to another window. If a particular program causes problems whenever it is running in the background of a multitasking session, you might want to try setting the Execution option to Exclusive in that program's PIF.

354

Advanced 386 Enhanced Options

There are additional, advanced options that you can specify in the PIF of an application you expect to run under Windows in 386 Enhanced mode. To see the advanced PIF options, you would choose **A**dvanced in the 386 Enhanced PIF Editor dialog box.

Clicking the Advanced button displays the Advanced Options dialog box shown in Figure 14.6. Options in this dialog box specify precisely how Windows should set up and manage the virtual machines it creates during a 386 multitasking session. Several of

these options are exactly what their name implies: advanced. Therefore, do not adjust them unless you know exactly what you are doing.
Given the beginners nature of this book—and recognizing the
wisdom of an adage that proclaims a little knowledge to be a
dangerous thing—I'll leave them unexplained. As you learn more
about your system and more about Windows, you'll begin to understand how these advanced options are used.

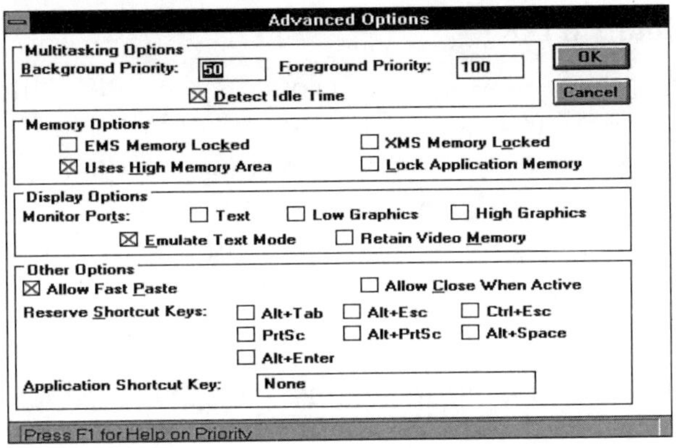

Figure 14.6. Advanced PIF options.

To return to the initial PIF Editor Options Box, double-click the
control box in the top-left corner of the Advanced Options window.

Now that you have a basic idea of what the various PIF settings
represent, let's outline the basic steps required to modify them.

Modifying a PIF

To demonstrate the basic steps involved in modifying a program
information file, I'm going to alter one setting in my WordStar PIF.
Specifically, I'm going to tell Windows that I still use an earlier
version of that venerable word processor, one that does not employ
graphic screens.

> **Note:** Of course, unless you also own WordStar, you cannot perform the following exercise. Still, this exercise gives you an idea of how to modify your PIFs, should the occasion arise.

To Modify a PIF

1. Choose **File** from the PIF Editor menu bar.	This displays PIF Editor's pull-down **F**ile menu.
2. Choose **O**pen.	This displays the Open dialog box.
3. Double-click WS.PIF (the program information file for WordStar).	PIF Editor reads in the selected file and displays the Edit screen. □

Use this Quick Step to modify your PIF files for any DOS programs. The PIF file in Figure 14.7 for example, contains the appropriate information for WordStar releases 5 or higher, which employ a graphic display for their Page Preview feature.

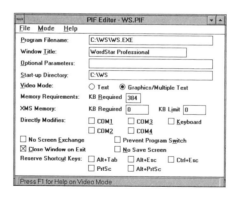

Figure 14.7. Windows default WordStar PIF.

I use WordStar 4, an earlier version of WordStar that does not support Page Preview. In my case, therefore, changing the Video Mode setting to Text would free additional memory on my system whenever WordStar is running. To change the Video mode setting to Text mode

1. Position the mouse cursor in the circle to the left of the **Text** setting in the Video Mode field.
2. Click the left mouse button.

That's really all there is to it. All that remains is to save the modified PIF back to disk, so its settings can be used the next time I load WordStar.

 To Save the Modified PIF to Disk

1. Choose File from the PIF Editor menu bar.	PIF Editor displays its pull-down **File** menu.
2. Choose Save.	Editor saves the modified file to disk. ☐

 To Exit the PIF Editor

357

Double-click the control box in the upper-left corner of the PIF Editor window.	The PIF editor closes and returns you to the Main Program group. ☐

From now on, whenever I run WordStar within the Windows GUI, its windows will be configured for a character-based display.

We've covered much technical ground in this chapter. Still, knowing how Windows runs DOS programs and understanding the information a PIF contains is critical to getting the most out of your Windows environment. Luckily, it also is the last chapter in our tour of the Windows GUI. You can rest now, knowing that you know more about Windows than when you first started down this path. I hope the trip was fun, and I hope you have fun using Windows. It really does—both literally and figuratively—put a new face on your PC.

What You Have Learned

▶ The Windows DOS Prompt icon lets you temporarily suspend a Windows session and issue commands from the DOS system prompt.

▶ You can install standard DOS programs—that is, non-Windows applications—within your Windows environment. The easiest way to accomplish this installation is with the **S**etup Applications option in the Windows Setup accessory.

▶ Windows uses program information files, or PIFs, to record critical information about how non-Windows applications should be handled within the Windows GUI. **S**etup automatically creates a PIF for any programs it recognizes. Windows also includes a default PIF that will run most DOS applications successfully. If you encounter problems running a specific non-Windows application, you can create a new PIF—or alternately, modify a currently existing PIF—to eliminate them.

358

Maximizing Windows

In This Chapter

▶ *Using DOS 5 memory management to improve Windows performance*

▶ *Shortcuts to common Windows procedures*

Windows and DOS 5

As I explained in Chapter 1, "Welcome to Windows," Windows, like thousands of other PC programs, runs under MS-DOS. By extension, therefore, Windows 3.1 inherits all the strengths and weaknesses of that popular operating system, which currently controls an estimated 60 million IBM-compatible PCs.

Until recently, one of DOS's most obvious weaknesses was a dearth of advanced memory-management capabilities. For one thing, DOS limited to a mere 640K the total amount of random-access memory, or RAM, available to applications such as Windows. Worse still, DOS insisted on reserving a large chunk of this meager (640k) memory pool, referred to as *conventional RAM,* for its own uses. Until DOS 5, merely loading DOS during system startup effectively reduced the amount of memory available for running application programs to less than 600K on most systems.

That figure dropped even lower for anyone who relied on *terminate-and-stay-resident* (TSR) utilities to enhance the performance of their PC. Terminate-and-stay-resident utilities stay in memory once loaded and are accessed from within any program by the touch of certain keys. By forcing these utilities also to be installed in conventional RAM, DOS further exacerbated the memory shortages brought on by its incapability of breaking the 640K barrier—a situation made all the more frustrating by the fact that additional RAM was available on almost all IBM-compatible PCs; DOS simply wasn't able to use it.

Beginning in June, 1991, all this changed. That's when Microsoft started shipping MS-DOS 5, the first version of DOS that could actually load portions of itself, as well as many TSR programs, into the so-called *high memory area,* or HMA.

What Is HMA?

Stated simply, HMA, sometimes referred to as *expanded memory,* is a 384K block of RAM located between 640K and the 1-megabyte address at which extended memory begins. Technically, this area of RAM consists of several discrete *Upper Memory Blocks,* or UMBs, unused sections of RAM between the 640K and 1-megabyte memory addresses. Nevertheless, High RAM has become its popular sobriquet, so High RAM is how I'll refer to it.

All versions of DOS set aside portions of High RAM for specific operations: controlling your PC's display comes immediately to mind. Even on the most feature-laden system, however, some UMBs inevitably remain unallocated and therefore potentially available for other operations.

Recapturing the High Ground

On an 80286, 80386, or 80486 system, it's possible now to load portions of MS-DOS 5 into HMA. To do so, use the SYSEDIT.EXE program described later in this chapter to place the following two lines at the beginning of your CONFIG.SYS file:

```
DEVICE=HIMEM.SYS
DOS=HIGH
```

> **Caution:** All examples in this chapter assume that any files DOS relies on for memory management are stored in the root directory of your boot drive. If this is not the case on your system, be sure to include the appropriate path information so that DOS can find the various programs and device drivers referred to in the following exercises.

As an added attraction, loading DOS high automatically also causes it to place any buffers you create with CONFIG.SYS into HMA. At first, this might not seem like such a big deal. Because each DOS buffer consumes slightly more than 500 bytes of memory, however, loading 30 buffers into HMA releases almost 16K of conventional RAM for other uses. Inserting the following three lines at the beginning of your CONFIG.SYS file accomplishes this task:

```
DEVICE=HIMEM.SYS
DOS=HIGH
BUFFERS=30
```

361

How much memory have you reclaimed? A quick check, using the DOS 5 MEM utility, shows that this increases to approximately 620K the amount of conventional RAM available to your DOS application programs, including Windows. By contrast, using DOS 3.3 under similar conditions—assuming DOS 3.3 and 30 buffers were all you loaded into memory at start-up—this figure would have been around 570K. A quick calculation reveals that simply relocating DOS and your buffers into HMA increases by approximately 50K your available reserves of conventional RAM.

We're not finished yet, however. For some lucky folks, the news from the RAM front gets even better. That's because, on 386 and 486 systems, DOS 5's new EMM386.EXE utility can be used to transfer additional programs—specifically, device drivers and TSRs—out of conventional RAM and into HMA. To prepare your system for doing so, begin your CONFIG.SYS program with the following four lines:

```
DEVICE=HIMEM.SYS
DEVICE=EMM386.EXE RAM
DOS=HIGH,UMB
BUFFERS=30
```

The primary purpose of DOS's EMM386.EXE memory manager is to convert extended memory to expanded memory. Including the RAM parameter in line 2 of this listing also causes EMM386.EXE to configure HMA to accept device drivers and TSRs. We look at the specific steps required to accomplish this in the next section.

> **Note:** In case you're curious, the UMB parameter I added to line 3 of this new listing (DOS=HIGH,UMB) tells DOS 5 to load any drivers and utilities it can into HMA as well.

Avoiding RAM Cram

Now that we've prepared HMA to accept device drivers and TSRs, let's see how it does so. The process involves two powerful new commands Microsoft added to DOS 5:

DEVICEHIGH
LOADHIGH

> **Note:** Remember, the following procedures only work with 386 and 486 systems on which EMM386.EXE has been loaded from CONFIG.SYS, using that utility's RAM parameter.

Use DEVICEHIGH to take device drivers and TSRs usually placed in conventional RAM from a CONFIG.SYS file and relocate them to HMA. Many people, for example, use the DOS ANSI.SYS driver to modify the display colors of DOS on their system. Without the DEVICEHIGH command, using ANSI.SYS forced you to reduce the amount of conventional RAM available to your application programs. The DEVICEHIGH command can be used only in your CONFIG.SYS file. Structuring our previous CONFIG.SYS file as follows tells DOS to relocate as much of the ANSI.SYS code as possible to HMA:

```
DEVICE=HIMEM.SYS
DEVICE=EMM386.EXE RAM
DOS=HIGH,UMB
BUFFERS=30
DEVICEHIGH=ANSI.SYS
```

> **Note:** As this example illustrates, you must place all DEVICEHIGH statements after the line used to load EMM386.EXE. The DEVICEHIGH command can be used with almost any device driver or TSR you usually would load from your CONFIG.SYS file.

LOADHIGH is similar to DEVICEHIGH. Instead of being limited to inclusion in the CONFIG.SYS file, however, by using LOADHIGH, you can relocate into HMA executable programs and utilities that would usually be run from the DOS system prompt. DOS 5's new LOADHIGH command provides one obvious advantage for almost anyone who uses Windows: the ability to load an executable mouse driver into HMA—that is, a MOUSE.COM program—into HMA.

Why use LOADHIGH? Well, mouse users are forced to sacrifice anywhere from 10K to 15K of valuable memory to a mouse driver. Without LOADHIGH, the memory required for a mouse driver gets gobbled from conventional RAM. By activating the RAM option of EMM386.EXE and then using LOADHIGH to force DOS to relocate a mouse driver into HMA, however, you can reclaim a sizable chunk of conventional RAM for your Windows environment. To accomplish this, use the following command to load your mouse driver prior to running Windows:

```
LOADHIGH MOUSE
```

Of course, you need to modify this command to reflect the correct location and name of your mouse driver, but you get the point. One convenient place to use LOADHIGH is in your AUTOEXEC.BAT file. LOADHIGH can, however, be run anytime you're at the DOS system prompt.

Given the number of third-party utilities and exotic device drivers people rely on to enhance the standard DOS environment—mice, scanners, network drivers, CD-ROM devices, and the like—taking full advantage of DOS 5's capability to utilize HMA can increase greatly the amount of conventional RAM available on your system and, by extension, for your Windows-related activities. Incorporating the appropriate statements (HIMEM, EMM386, DEVICEHIGH and LOADHIGH) into your CONFIG.SYS and AUTOEXEC.BAT files guarantees that you set up the most efficient Windows environment possible each time you start your PC.

363

Quick Tips for Using Windows

Over the course of the past several months, I've discovered a number of shortcuts so that you can perform certain Windows-related activities more quickly or in some cases, more conveniently. To close out this final chapter, I thought I'd share a few of them with you.

Some of these "quick tips" are buried so deeply in the Windows documentation that you'd never find them unless you know what you're looking for. Others are tricks Microsoft neglects to reveal. None of them would be classified by the government; the security of the civilized world doesn't depend on whether you know about them or not. They are nifty, little procedures that can simplify working with Windows. Check 'em out and then feel free to ignore any you don't find useful.

Bypassing the Opening Windows Screen

No one ever accused Microsoft of modesty. The company flaunts its name whenever and wherever possible. Hey, why not? It's only marketing. One example of this is the opening screen displayed by Windows before you get to the Program Manager. There's Microsoft's name—big, blue, and hard to ignore.

If you want to suppress this Microsoft miniadvertisement, simply place a colon (:) at the end of the command you usually use to run Windows. To bypass the opening display and run Windows in standard mode, for example, use the following command:

```
WIN /S :
```

The colon tells WIN.COM, the program that loads Windows, to bypass the copyright message and move directly to the Program Manager screen.

Automatically Loading Applications at Startup

Windows' WIN.INI file (located in the \WINDOWS directory) contains a special parameter, LOAD, that lets you specify the applications you want loaded as icons whenever you start a Windows session. This provides a convenient way to start Windows and set up your normal work space in one step.

Suppose, for example, you want to start each Windows session with clock, calculator, and notepad running within your Windows environment. To accomplish this, use Windows Notepad (or SYSEDIT, as explained in the next section) to edit the line containing the LOAD parameter in WIN.INI to the following:

```
LOAD = CLOCK CALC NOTEPAD
```

The next time you start Windows, the icons associated with each of these accessories are displayed across the bottom of your workspace. The programs are running, but they are reduced to an icon. Simply double-click one of these icons to access the program.

> **Tip:** Place a copy of your program icons in the Startup group to have them automatically start when you start Windows. If you also use the **M**inimize On Use on the Program Manager's **O**ptions menu, the startup programs will load and be placed neatly at the bottom of your desktop. If you load Clock with this procedure, you will always know what time it is whenever you switch back to Program Manager.

365

Quickly Accessing the Editing Tools

Speaking of modifying your Windows environment, the Windows package includes a special System Configuration Editor utility that lets you quickly access four files that influence how Windows runs on your system. These files are

```
SYSTEM.INI
WIN.INI
CONFIG.SYS
AUTOEXEC.BAT
```

Immediately after you install Windows, however, the only way to run the System Configuration Editor is either by manually entering its program name, SYSEDIT, in the File Run dialog box or double-clicking the SYSEDIT.EXE file-folder icon in the File

Manager directory listing. To simplify the process of modifying your Windows environment, use the following Quick Step to add the System Configuration Editor to your Accessories program group:

 To Add the SYSEDIT Editor to the Accessories Group

1. Set up your Windows display so that it contains partial windows for both the Accessories program group and File Manager.

2. From within the File Manager window, click the System subdirectory running off your default Windows directory.
   This makes \WINDOWS\ SYSTEM the active directory.

3. Position the mouse pointer over the file called SYSEDIT.EXE.

4. Hold down the left mouse button.
   This selects SYSEDIT.EXE.

5. Drag the mouse pointer to anywhere within the Accessories program group window.

6. Release the left mouse button.
   Windows places an icon representing SYSEDIT.EXE in the Accessories program group.   □

This creates a new icon in the Accessories program group called SYSEDIT. Double-clicking this icon opens an on-screen window containing a basic text editor and the four files listed previously. SYSEDIT is actually a Write application. See Chapter 6, "Windows Write," for information on how to edit files with Write.

Caution: Be careful when working in the Windows INI files. Any incorrect modifications you make can have adverse effects on the behavior of Windows itself or Windows applications. Be certain also to save any files you modify back to disk to preserve your edits.

> **Tip**: While your setting up this new icon, why not go ahead and use the File Preferences option to change its name to something less cryptic than SYSEDIT.

Spacing Icons

In its default mode, Windows 3.1 places icons so close together the text descriptions accompanying these icons can overlap one another. You can use the Desktop option of the Windows Control Panel to eliminate this problem. Use the following Quick Step to manually increase icon spacing:

To Manually Increase Icon Spacing

1. Start Windows 3.1.
2. Double-click the Main icon. This makes the Main program group the active window.
3. Double-click the Control Panel icon. This starts the Windows Control Panel utility.
4. Double-click the Desktop icon. This displays the Desktop options box.
5. When the Desktop dialog box appears, click the up arrow next to the Icon spacing prompt to increase the default spacing Windows uses to separate icons. (I find a value of 100 to be sufficient for most situations.)
6. Click the OK button. Windows stores your new icon spacing and returns you to the Control Panel. □

367

When you exit the Control Panel, Windows begins positioning icons using the new, larger default setting. Consequently, full-text descriptions should now fit easily below each one. (Be aware, however, that the new settings are not applied to current screens until either a previously existing icon is selected or you end the current session and restart Windows.

Placing an Icon in Multiple Groups

Are you looking for a simple way to duplicate an icon in a second program group? With your mouse and the Ctrl key, it's easy—just use the following Quick Step:

 To Duplicate an Icon in a Second Program Group

1. Open two windows, the first should contain the icon you want to replicate and the second should contain the program group you want to add this icon to.

2. Position the mouse cursor on the icon to be replicated in the first window.

3. Hold down the Ctrl key.

4. Click and hold down the left mouse button as you drag the mouse cursor to any visible part of the second window.

   An image of the original icon follows the mouse cursor.

5. Release the Ctrl key and the left mouse button.

   A copy of the icon is placed in the new group. □

The icon in either program group can now be used to run its associated application.

Changing Disk Drives Within File Manager

The Ctrl key also provides a convenient method for changing the active disk drive from within the Windows File Manager. Holding down the Ctrl key while pressing the appropriate drive letter activates the specified drive. For example, pressing Ctrl-D from within a File Manager window changes the active drive to D.

Saving Disk Space

After installation, Windows 3.1 can use over 6 megabytes of disk space. If you expect to use only the default Windows background screen (you do not plan to install a special "wallpaper" background for your Windows display), you can recapture some of this storage space by deleting the .BMP bitmap files Windows uses to create fancy backgrounds. You find these files, which all use the file extension .BMP, in the directory you specified during Windows installation.

Keeping TEMP Files in Check

During installation, Windows creates a special TEMP directory that Windows applications use to store any temporary files they create during a Windows session. Although rare, it's possible that some files can remain in this directory when you exit Windows, taking valuable disk space. It's a good idea, therefore, to check and if necessary clear out the TEMP directory from time to time.

369

To clean the TEMP directory, simply use the DOS DEL command to delete any files it contains when Windows is not running. (You should never erase files in the TEMP directory during a Windows session, because Windows might be using those files for current operations, so do not use the File Manager for this operation.) Other extra baggage you can safely eliminate from outside Windows includes Windows swap file (WIN386.SWP) and any application swap files (files that begin with the characters ~WOA). Under normal conditions, Windows deletes these files as part of its own housekeeping chores. Should an application or Windows terminate unexpectedly, however, some swap files might need to be manually erased, using the procedures outlined here.

 Caution: Do not delete the TEMP directory. Windows uses this directory to store its temporary files.

Easy DOS Program Switching

With Windows, you can easily switch between standard DOS and Windows applications during a multitasking session. When working in a DOS program loaded from Windows, pressing Ctrl-Esc temporarily exits that program and displays the Windows Task List, from which you can select the application you want to use. (If your system has enough free RAM, the DOS application continues running in the background of the current session.) When it comes time to switch back to your DOS application, click the DOS icon Windows automatically created for that program when you initially pressed Ctrl-Esc.

 To Switch Between Running Programs

1. In the program you are running, press Ctrl-Esc.

   The Task Window appears.

2. Double-click on the name of the program you want to switch to, or use the arrow keys to highlight it, and press Enter.

   Windows switches you to that program.

□

Improving the Performance of DOS Applications

DOS programs tend to suffer somewhat when forced to rely on Windows as a "go-between." One way to improve the performance of a DOS application running in Windows' Enhanced 386 mode is to disable any unnecessary compatibility options activated in its PIF file, using the Windows' PIF Editor. Most DOS applications, for example, run perfectly well if you turn off all the Monitor Ports options, which are located in the Advanced Options dialog box. Other areas worth investigating are the various Memory Options and the Allow Fast Paste option, also Advanced features.

Speeding Up Program Swaps

Left to its own devices, Windows uses your hard disk for program swapping. Given that RAM is faster than a disk, using expanded memory for some of your program-swapping activities can speed this process considerably. To accomplish this, add /e to the swapdisk variable in your WIN.INI file.

For example, specifying `swapdisk=C:\ /e` in WIN.INI tells Windows to delay placing its temporary swap files in the root directory of drive C (C:\) until after there is no more room in expanded memory. (See my previous tip on SYSEDIT for a quick and easy way to edit your WIN.INI file.)

Modifying the Size of an Application Window

Here's a shortcut for modifying the size of an application window. Rather than depending exclusively on the Maximize and Minimize buttons, try double-clicking the window's title bar, a much larger target. Doing so toggles the application between a full-screen size and a regular-size window.

What You Have Learned   371

- ▶ MS-DOS 5 provides a number of memory-management features that can be used to free additional memory for your Windows environment. By placing portions of the basic DOS code, device drivers, and TSR utilities into your machine's High Memory Area, or HMA, DOS 5 can increase to approximately 620K the amount of conventional RAM available for Windows.

- ▶ Windows SYSEDIT.EXE utility is a primitive text editor that can be used to access your SYSTEM.INI, WIN.INI, CONFIG.SYS, and AUTOEXEC.BAT files. By creating a SYSEDIT icon in your Accessories program group, you can modify quickly these files, each of which influences your Windows environment.

- ▶ Windows provides shortcuts for a wide range of common procedures. In some cases, this involves bypassing Windows pull-down menus in favor of easily entered keyboard commands. Other shortcuts require that you press specific keys while performing mouse operations.

Pen Windows

As popular as personal computers are, not everyone likes them. Theories abound as to why certain individuals still are scared to death of using a PC. One prominent reason, according to some experts, is the fact that the majority of PC applications still rely on a keyboard for data entry.

There has been a movement within the PC industry to endow personal computers with a quality called "user-friendliness." Windows itself is a product of this movement. Windows' reliance on graphical displays, interactive dialog boxes, and point-and-click procedures, rather than convoluted commands entered at a noninformative system prompt, reflect a concerted effort on Microsoft's part to make the process of using a PC more familiar and less intimidating than under standard DOS. Even with Windows, however, the predominant input device—ignoring, for a moment, your mouse—is a keyboard. Soon, however, this might change, thanks to *pen-based computing*.

Exactly what does pen-based computing entail? Stated simply, it means interacting with a computer through the use of electronic "pens"—input devices that you can use to enter text much as you would with a traditional pen or pencil.

Impressive Technology

This is no small feat. I don't know about you, but I have trouble reading my own handwriting sometimes. No two people write or print exactly the same way.

That's a problem, you see, for pen-based computing to be practical, a PC has to be able to recognize the printed or script characters entered by hand and to convert them into the electronic data it relies on to work properly—a fairly advanced process called *character recognition.*

With a keyboard, this recognition process is easy. You press the A key, and a PC knows exactly what you mean. I doubt if any PC could recognize my signature, however.

Still, the appeal of pen-based computing is undeniable. Beyond ultimately replacing the keyboard, and long before character recognition is fully developed—an accomplishment that even the proponents of this advanced technology admit is still quite a ways off—a pen device can simplify a number of current applications, including

- ▶ Inventory control
- ▶ Forms registration
- ▶ Free-form drawing
- ▶ Engineering and drafting

Consider, for example, the advantages of using a pen device with a notebook computer running a custom designed inventory program. On the screen, you might see a display that looks exactly like a paper-based inventory control form. To record current inventory for a specific product, all you'd have to do is use the pen device to enter the appropriate number in a series of boxes next to that product's name. (It's much easier for a computer to recognize a hand-printed number than someone's handwriting.) All of this may sound futuristic, but it's happening right now. Windows 3.1 is designed to support pen-based computing.

Consider the following scenario: Your notebook computer comes with Windows set to use a pen device with a Windows-based word processor like Lotus Ami Professional. (Ami doesn't recognize pen devices yet, but you can almost bet your last dollar it will someday.) As you've seen, this program makes it easy for you to mix

374

text and graphics within the same file. When you get right to it, writing—that is, the actual process of placing words on paper—is not that different from drawing. Imagine, then, that a coworker sends you a draft of a report written in Ami, asking for your reactions. With the right software, a pen device could be used to enter your comments directly on the screen, then you could save back to the original file itself. This is analogous to writing your comments in the margins of a printed report with a pen or pencil.

Microsoft's Contribution

All the specifics are not decided as I'm writing this book, but don't be surprised to see Windows play a major role in the future of the pen-based operating environment.

375

Figure A.1, for example, shows an input screen from a demonstration program Microsoft shipped with my copy of Windows 3.1. It certainly looks like a typical paper form, doesn't it? Like that inventory control program I mentioned earlier, it recognizes hand-entered input.

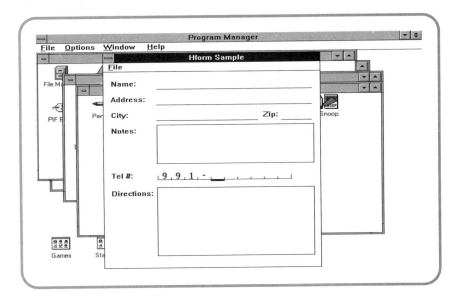

Figure A.1. Windows for Pen Computing converts printed input into more familiar data.

> **Note:** I stress the word *demonstration* in the previous paragraph. Pen Windows, the Windows interface for pen-based computing, is evolving constantly and probably will be customized by individual manufacturers for their specific systems. The various screen shots in this appendix, therefore, are strictly representative. You might never see the specific application shown in any Pen Windows environment. Pen-based computing is a nifty enough phenomenon, however, that I wanted to introduce it here.

For example, I didn't use the keyboard to enter information in the Tel # field. Rather, I "wrote" it on my desk, using an electronic stylus. As I "wrote," Pen Windows converted my input into the printed numbers you see in Figure A.1.

How flexible is Windows for Pen Computing? Take a look at Figure A.2, which shows the Control Panel for a Windows environment in which the Windows for Pen Computing utilities have been installed.

376

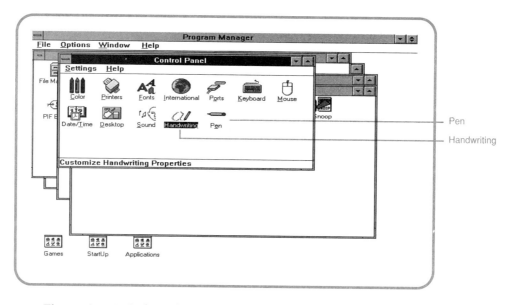

Figure A.2. Windows for Pen Computing adds additional items to your Control Panel.

Notice that there are two icons in this Control Panel you've not seen before:

Handwriting
Pen

Each of these relate to using Windows for Pen Computing. With Handwriting, for example, you can personalize the pen environment to match the way you write. As Figure A.3 illustrates, you can use this utility to specify, among other things, whether you're right- or left-handed, a factor that greatly influences the appearance of your handwriting.

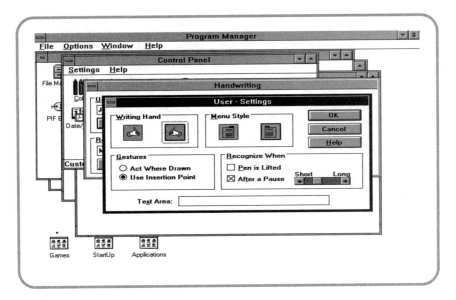

377

Figure A.3. The Windows for Pen Computing environment can be modified to reflect your writing habits.

Windows for Pen Computing represents a major change in how people and PCs interact with one another. In truth, the potential uses for an interface like Windows for Pen Computing are limited only by technology and our own imaginations. Technology is moving forward rapidly; we might take a little while to catch up. Personally, I can't wait to see what happens when we do.

Index

381

383

384

385

386

388

395

Sams' First Books Get You Started Fast!

"The First Book Series ... is intended to get the novice off to a good start, whether with computers in general or with particular programs ...."

The New York Times

The First Book of WordPerfect 5.1
Kate Miller Barnes
275 pages, 73/8 x 91/4, $16.95 USA
0-672-27307-1

Look For These Books In Sams' First Book Series

SAMS

See your local retailer or call 1-800-428-5331.

Sams Guarantees Your Success In 10 Minutes!

The *10 Minute Guides* provide a new approach to learning computer programs. Each book teaches you the most often used features of a particular program in 15 to 20 short lessons—all of which can be completed in 10 minutes or less. What's more, the *10 Minute Guides* are simple to use. You won't find any "computer-ese" or technical jargon— just plain English explanations. With straightforward instructions, easy-to-follow steps, and special margin icons to call attention to important tips and definitions, the *10 Minute Guides* make learning a new software program easy and fun!

10 Minute Guide to WordPerfect 5.1
Katherine Murray & Doug Sabotin
160 pages, 51/2 x 81/2, $9.95 USA
0-672-22808-4

10 Minute Guide to MS-DOS 5
Jack Nimersheim
160 pages, 5 1/2 x 81/2, $9.95 USA
0-672-22807-6

10 Minute Guide to Windows 3
Katherine Murray & Doug Sabotin
160 pages, 5 1/2 x 81/2, $9.95 USA
0-672-22812-2

10 Minute Guide to PC Tools 7
Joe Kraynak
160 pages, 5 1/2 x 81/2, $9.95 USA
0-672-30021-4

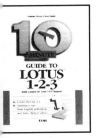

10 Minute Guide to Lotus 1-2-3
Katherine Murray & Doug Sabotin
160 pages, 51/2 x 8 1/2, $9.95 USA
0-672-22809-2

10 Minute Guide to Q&A 4, Revised Edition
Arlene Azzarello
160 pages, 51/2 x 81/2, $9.95 USA
0-672-30035-4

10 Minute Guide to Harvard Graphics 2.3
Lisa Bucki
160 pages, 51/2 x 81/2, $9.95 USA
0-672-22837-8

SAMS

See your local retailer or call 1-800-428-5331.

Wp' 92

Look to Sams for THE BEST
in Computer Information!

The Best Book of MS-DOS 5
Alan Simpson
650 pages, 73/8 X 91/4, $24.95 USA
0-672-48499-4

The Best Book of Harvard Graphics
John Mueller
400 pages, 73/8 X 91/4, $24.95 USA
0-672-22740-1

Look For These Books In Sams' Best Book Series

SAMS

See your local retailer or call 1-800-428-5331.